THE [illegible]SHUA JAMES [illegible]ROJECT

44 [illegible]alty-free short plays

J[illegible]HUA JAMES

Defiant Press

The Joshua James Project

New York playwright and screenwriter Joshua James (SPOOGE - The Sex & Love Monologues) has made forty-four of his popular short plays royalty-free for independent and amateur production in THE JOSHUA JAMES PROJECT.

That's right, you can produce these plays, royalty-free, if the right circumstances are met.

Included in this collection are the favorites ALL THE RAGE, A GAY THING, AMBIVALENT, SOMETHING SITUATION, THE BEAUTIFUL ONE and the Off-Broadway premiering EXTREME EUGENE, among many others.

Cover by Bosa Grgurevic www.buddhacandy.com

Foreword by Ato Essandoh

Created with Vellum

P[illegible]e for Joshua James

"Joshua James' work is [illegible] *intelligent and subversive. Read it. Then find a way to make it happen o*[illegible]*e."* – Award-winning playwright Naomi Wallace.

Introduction

WHAT IS T [illegible] JOSHUA JAMES PROJECT?

Simply put, I'm offeri [illegible] p nearly ninety percent of my short and one act plays to the [illegible] lic free of royalty for theatrical performances, under certai [illegible] nditions. It's true; you can produce any play in this book, FO [illegible] REE, under the right circumstances. You don't have to pay a ro [illegible] or even write to ask my permission, you can simply just produ [illegible] e play, as long the production meets the following conditions:

1. It's a student o [illegible] ege production of less than 30 performances.
2. It's an indepen [illegible] showcase where no one else gets paid and a run of le [illegible] an 30 performances.
3. Bottom line, if [illegible] short run and no one else gets paid, I don't need to [illegible] aid. If it's a longer run at a professional th [illegible] and the actors, stage managers and stagehands are [illegible] ng paid, then I expect to get paid, too.

There are requirements, which are as follows:

1. Any program or publicity that features the title of the produced play must also feature my name as the author. More on that below.
2. Don't rewrite it or change the text. You want to improvise, join an improv group. You want to do my play, then you must do it as it's written (there are some exceptions, which are noted in the individual play notes following each.)
3. Less than 30 performances by the same company in a single calendar year.

Why 30?

Because that's enough performances for an independent showcase or college run, and because when I was younger I was convinced that I'd never live to see the age of thirty.

I did make it that far (and then some), and have had a lot of fun with independent productions of my work over the years and so now I'm paying the universe back.

And that's it, that's The Joshua James Project. I'm putting nearly all my work out there for you, the independent artist. You want to produce a play in this collection for a few nights at your theatre? Go ahead, with my blessing.

The free royalty appli)NLY to amateur and educational stage
productions, not profe ıal ones. And this is for live performance
stage productions onl ıese plays are under my copyright and I
reserve all other rigl including professional, motion pictures,
radio broadcasting, t ;ion, and the rights of translation into
foreign languages, all t rights are strictly reserved. Copying from
this book in whole or ɔart is strictly forbidden by law, and the
right of performance i transferable.

If it's a professional tl e for a longer run, then that's a different
story and you should ıtact me via my website to secure the
professional performa ights. www.writerjoshuajames.com

But you CAN produc hort theatrical run of any or all of these
plays without even a g. Whenever the play is produced the
following notice must ar on all programs:

"Produced by s al arrangement with The Joshua ımes Project."

Due authorship cr ıust be given on all programs and advertising for the play.

And that's all you to do. If it goes well, all I ask is that you
purchase a **paperba version** of this collection of plays for
yourself or to give to a ıd and spread the word.

Pay it forward, please.

Foreword

I've known Joshua fo r ten years. He's been my mentor and confidant and most i tantly, my friend. I wrote my first play because he dared me He liked it and The Defiant Ones, our production company, born. It was a wild time. We did theatre with no money, no con and nothing to lose.

We did it because th vas a space, or because we had a crazy idea, or because we kn bunch of great actors who were wasting away waiting tables. N y though, we did it for the fuck of it. We did it because it was This is the kind of theatre I was introduced to by Joshua Jar nd I am eternally grateful.

What follows is not jus hology of short plays, it's a snapshot of a fervent time in und und NYC theater: An open, scrappy, wantonly iconoclastic free collaborative effort amongst artists. We discovered our v during these years. We discovered our passion for storytellin ring these years. We also discovered the often overlooked -and vned upon- rule that a well placed fart joke will bring the house down every time. No matter what the frumpy theater mavens say. Every time.

Enjoy these wonderfully vivid pieces. I did. Most of all, have fun. For the fuck of it.

Peace.

Ato Essandoh is an actor, playwright and human being. He's been seen in the films GARDEN STATE, BLOOD DIAMOND, DJANGO UNCHAINED, JASON BOURNE and on television in ELEMENTARY, BLUE BLOODS, Netflix's ALTERED CARBON and many others, in addition to two years as a series regular on BBC America's COPPER. He also plays a mean guitar. www.atoessandoh.com

T ſen Minute Plays

In the 90s and early 2(all I did was write plays.

I moved to New York after grad school to be an actor, couldn't afford new headshots instead joined a writing group. I had my first plays produced le: ın a year after I arrived, and they kept on being produced. I sto] being an actor, which was fine with me because I hated aud: ;, and discovered that I loved being a playwright.

What follows is nearly y ten-minute play that I've written during that time.

There are four missin ur which are already published by Original Works Publishing collection called **The THE Plays**. They are The Itch, The Daı The Pap and The Race. If you like what you read here, please c : those out. Here are the rest.

Whenever possible, I'll list in the notes the original creators involved. Regrettably I don't have all the programs any longer, so some names are lost in time, but I will do the best that I can. Some show notes are expansive, some others, it's only what I can remember.

I've worked with some really great people over the years. The great ones will be named whenever possible. The not-so-great ones will not be named.

This book is dedicated to all the great ones.

My Tc [illegible] ive Ten Minute Plays

I stand by and am pro[illegible] f all the work in this collection, but these five ten-minute plays [illegible] specific favorites of mine for profoundly personal reasons.

I'll do my best to share [illegible] in the notes after each.

1

A he Rage (1m, 1f)

CHARACTERS:

MARCUS – A very ha me, charming man in his 30s.

LISA – An equally att ve woman in her late 20s who is also an edgy, raw wound on th side.

SETTING: A bar.

TIME: Present.

(EVENING at a dark se wded singles bar.

MARCUS, a slick h ne dude in his thirties, sits by himself at a table.

He holds his drink up and gestures to someone across the room. He is signaling a bartender that he wants to buy a drink for someone. After a moment …

LISA, an attractive woman in her twenties with a drink in her hand, joins him.)

LISA: Thank you for the drink.

MARCUS: Hey, it was my pleasure. My name's Marcus.

LISA: Lisa.

MARCUS: Hey Lisa. Lisa, I have a confession to make.

LISA: You do?

MARCUS: Yeah, see I've never done anything like this before.

LISA: Like what?

MARCUS: Bought a drink for a woman I didn't know.

LISA: Really?

MARCUS: It's true, all true, this is my first time. I was sitting here thinking to myself, Marcus, it's time to do something different in your life, do something out of character for a change. Smile to someone you don't know, order a vodka martini with a twist instead of a Jack and Coke, and buy a pretty lady a drink. Do something new with your life. Do one thing, ONE thing that you've never done before, Marcus, and if you get nothing else out of it, at least you get that. You know what I'm saying?

LISA: Um. I think so.

MARCUS: You do?

LISA: I think. Trying something new.

MARCUS: That's what I'm saying. Take a chance, buy a pretty lady a drink.

LISA: You think I'm pretty?

MARCUS: I think you're very attractive. You are a very attractive woman.

(Short pause.)

LISA: Okay. Thank you.

MARCUS: You're welcome. *(Short pause.)* So.

LISA: So.

MARCUS: So tell me about yourself.

LISA: I'd rather not.

MARCUS: Excuse me?

LISA: I'd really rat not.

MARCUS: Oh. O

(Short pause. LISA ta sip of her drink.)

MARCUS: So wh uld you like to talk about?

LISA: Anything yo e.

MARCUS: Anythi .

LISA: Except me.

MARCUS: Except . Okay.

LISA: We can talk ut you, if you want.

MARCUS: Hey, I do that—

LISA: Only if you t to—

MARCUS: Talkin out myself—

LISA: You don't h o.

MARCUS: Not a lem, one of my favorite subjects.

LISA: Okay.

MARCUS: Okay. *rt pause.)* Well, like I said, my name's Marcus, and I—

LISA: Are you hap

MARCUS: I'm so

LISA: Are you hap

MARCUS: Happy what?

LISA: Happy with know, your life.

MARCUS: Happy my life?

LISA: Yes.

MARCUS: Pretty h, I think, yeah. I'd say yeah.

LISA: You would.

MARCUS: I woul mean, there are some things I could have that would make thi etter, I mean, the promotion I've been waiting for, I want a car, those things. More money is always welcome, but for the m part, I'm pretty satisfied. With my life.

LISA: You are.

MARCUS: Yeah, retty satisfied, yeah.

LISA: Oh. Okay.

(Short pause.)

MARCUS: So. Un ike I was—

LISA: What about ple?

MARCUS: I'm sorry?

LISA: How do you feel about people?

MARCUS: How do I feel about people?

LISA: Yes.

MARCUS: Which people, where?

LISA: All people, do you like people? In general.

MARCUS: Am I a people person, is that—

LISA: Yes, that's it.

MARCUS: I would say yes, I like people. I'm pretty social, I like most people. Not all people, but—

LISA: Who don't you like?

(Very brief pause.)

MARCUS: I don't like Barbara Walters, no reason, really, she just annoys me, and this guy in accounting at work because he's a snide bastard, but for the most part …

LISA: As for most people …

MARCUS: I like them, yeah. I like people.

LISA: Okay.

MARCUS: People like you.

LISA: Oh. Okay.

(Short pause.)

MARCUS: So …

LISA: I don't think I like people.

MARCUS: You don't?

LISA: I don't. I don't like people.

MARCUS: Most people?

LISA: Just about all people.

MARCUS: Almost all people, you don't like?

LISA: Pretty much, yeah. Just about every person out there, I don't like.

MARCUS: Oh. Well …

LISA: Can I ask you a question?

MARCUS: Sure you can ask me a question.

LISA: It's kind of personal.

MARCUS: I can take a personal question.

LISA: Okay. *(Ver[illegible]f pause.)* Have you ever felt like killing somebody, I mean RE[illegible]Y felt like actually killing somebody?

MARCUS: Uh …

LISA: It doesn't h[illegible] to be anyone you know, it could be just Joe-Schmoe on the st[illegible] you know? You ever just see somebody and get the urge to hi[illegible]m, you know, over the head with something hard and heavy?

MARCUS: Well ..

LISA: Or have yo[illegible]r been standing in line behind somebody at the grocery store, st[illegible] behind a very loud person with nowhere to run and she's con[illegible]ning to the check-out person and she's usually complaining a[illegible] something completely beyond the power of the clerk to do anyt[illegible] about, say she's mad because macaroni's not on sale this week, [illegible]s on sale last week why can't it be on sale this week too and you[illegible]k at this person standing in line bitching about NOTHING an[illegible] just want to rip her arm off and beat her to death with it. Just h[illegible]ner her over her head with her own arm, screaming over and o[illegible]SHUT UP SHUT UP SHUT UP! IT'S JUST A COUPON S[illegible]IUT UP!" That ever happen to you?

MARCUS: Actual[illegible]

LISA: And the w[illegible]me people get off the bus or train, run into you and not have[illegible] common fucking decency to say "excuse me," and sometimes t[illegible]won't even look at you, like they couldn't be bothered, and it m[illegible] you just want to take out your apartment keys, go up to them an[illegible]b them right in the eyes!

MARCUS: As a m[illegible] of fact …

LISA: And especi[illegible]eople with cell phones, I am to the point now where anytime I s[illegible]meone with a cell phone I want to take it away from them and [illegible] them EAT IT whole, it's like you can't go anywhere without [illegible]ng someone else's boring fucking private conversation forced d[illegible] your throat! I was standing in line at the movie theater and I w[illegible]rced to listen to some asshole discuss the results of his proctolo[illegible]am with his doctor! I wanted to take the phone away from him [illegible] shove it straight up his ass! I was even on a date last week, we w[illegible] out at dinner and he took a call right in the middle of the appetizer that lasted halfway through our main course! And it wasn't even anything important, he was setting up a squash match with one of his buddies! And I had to sit there and listen to him josh around with his pal, like I had nothing better to do! You know what I did, you wanna know what I did?

MARCUS: What?

LISA: I waited until we were finished eating, because it was a wonderful filet mignon and I didn't want to waste it, excused myself, went to the ladies room, called him from there on his cell phone and screamed "HEY ASSHOLE! DON'T EVER CALL ME AGAIN YOU SELF-IMPORTANT CONDESCENDING PRICK WITH TOO MUCH MONEY AND NOT ENOUGH HAIR! ASSHOLE ASSHOLE ASSHOLE! And then I left.

(MARCUS reaches into his pocket with no small amount of stealth, takes out his cell phone and turns it off. Tucks it back in his pocket.)

LISA: I wanted to do more, I did, I wanted to really hurt him. But I had to settle for just screaming at him. People, people just drive me crazy sometimes, sometimes I want to crush them all, they're so stupid.

MARCUS: Well. Wow.

LISA: I think I'm kind of angry. Do you think I'm kind of angry?

MARCUS: I think you might be a little angry.

LISA: You do?

MARCUS: Just a little bit, a little bit angry.

LISA: Don't you ever get angry?

MARCUS: Sure I do.

LISA: When was the last time you got really angry?

MARCUS: Well. I'm not sure. Ah, I know. At work, every time I get on the elevator to go home, this guy, this guy from accounting I don't like, he gets on usually right after me, from the floor below. And I've already pressed the button for the first floor, the button is lit up so you know it's been pressed and we're already going to the first floor but it never fails, it never fails, when he gets on the elevator, he presses the button for the first floor as well, even though it's already lit, it's like he doesn't trust me, a guy from marketing, to push the right elevator button, he always has to push it again himself, always. And I always, ways feel a little … peeved … when he does that.

LISA: Peeved?

MARCUS: Peeved

(Very short pause.)

LISA: Haven't you r thought about just grabbing him by his tie, twisting it around eck until he turned purple, then banging his head against the el or doors, again and again and again until he learned his lesson, ver thought about doing that?

MARCUS: I have ght about that, yes. Once or twice.

LISA: Don't you ju ant to kill him? Don't you just want to kill him and everybody lik m? Just find all the assholes of the world and just kill kill kill?

(Short pause.)

MARCUS: Well I I'm going to be utterly honest with you. Much as I think that ing rid of the genius that invented car alarms, long-distanc elephone commercial pitchmen and members of the Repu n National party would be a step in the direction toward gre good, much as I believe that there are people, annoying peop ke Pat Robertson, Bill O'Reilly and Jenny McCarthy who well a ruly deserve a fate such as the one you describe, no, I do not to kill people. Not them or anyone. Not that I haven't thought ut it, not that I don't get homicidal urges whenever someone cal e on my home phone and tries to sell me something I don't ne do. But I don't act on it. I don't and I won't.

LISA: Why not?

MARCUS: Well, ess it's because … you know, I could sit here and bitch about gym teacher I had in junior high, I could hunt down the sadistic k and really make him pay for being such a mean, scheming as all throughout my puberty, I could do that, but ultimately … nately I think it's better to forgive and let it go. Almost sounds k of like some retro-sixties bullshit, I know, but it's what I believe. ive them. Forgive all the petty assholes of the world, forgive the ies, the plastic people, the fruitcakes, the pre-packaged teen boy bands, the telemarketers, the born-again Christians and the Scientologists. Forgive the bullies that have beaten you up. Forgive the psychotic ex-girlfriend who's still obsessing and stalking you despite the fact it's been five years and there's a restraining order. Forgive the relatives that keep forgetting what it is you do for a living. Forgive the woman that refuses to wear a bra and yet gives you shit about looking at her chest. Forgive the men in charge everywhere that feel free to look you right in your face and lie their ass off. Forgive the slick guy in the suit who's pretending he's never bought a woman a drink before just so he can get into her pants. Forgive all the bullshit and let it go. Let all the anger and rage go. You have to do that in order to get to the good stuff. That's what I believe, I believe … ultimately I believe in love. Not love in the Jesus-freak kind of way, but love in the sense of all the great things that can sometimes happen between people. I believe in love. And what I think is that you can either kill all the people in the world that deserve it, or you can love all the people that deserve it. But you can't do both. You can only do one. And I choose love. That's what I believe.

(Short pause. LISA finishes her drink. Looks away.)

LISA: Huh. Well.

MARCUS: Yeah. Yeah.

(LISA stands, prepares to leave.)

LISA: Thanks for the drink and for … everything.

MARCUS: No. Thank you.

LISA: Okay. Good-bye.

MARCUS: Good-bye.

(LISA walks away.)

MARCUS: Lisa?

LISA: Yes?

MARCUS: Take care of yourself, all right?

(She looks at him a full moment.)

LISA: I'll try.

MARCUS: Okay. Good.

(LISA exits. MARCUS finishes his drink.)

THE END

ALL THE RAGE NOTE[illegible]

First produced in [illegible] at Manhattan Theatre Source by The Defiant Ones as part [illegible] the evening CLOSE ENCOUNTERS, directed by the auth[illegible]nd featuring Ato Essandoh and Carrie Keranen. Subsequent[illegible]roduced by All You Can Eat Theatre Company, Common [illegible]r, The Barrow Group, and many, many others.

ALL THE RAGE [illegible] inspired by a real life incident wherein I once bought a drink f[illegible]beautiful woman in a bar and discovered, during the conversatio[illegible]at she was actually emotionally disturbed and on the verge of a [illegible]kdown.

I wrote this piece [illegible]cifically for my buddy Ato for CLOSE ENCOUNTERS. Ato [illegible]umber one on the list of great ones that I'm fortunate enough [illegible]ave worked with and he's also one of my very best friends.

We didn't have an [illegible]ess for the part, and neither of us liked to audition actors. Anot[illegible] actress in the show recommended her roommate Carrie for t[illegible]art. Ato said that he'd seen her in a show earlier that summer a[illegible]he was brilliant. So we cast her without even meeting her, just [illegible]d her up and offered her the part.

We later discovere[illegible]at Ato had been mistaken, the actress he thought she was actua[illegible]urned out to be someone else. Neither of us had set eyes on Ca[illegible]until she showed up but she was also brilliant. She rolled in a[illegible] immediately killed it on the first read-through. She is a phen[illegible]nal actress and a good friend to this day.

In the show, Carri[illegible] Lisa) built it up beautifully, unrolled it bit by bit until she was fu[illegible]ottle by the time the anger starts and, by the end, was at an em[illegible]nal point where, when Marcus lays it out for her in the end, o[illegible]oped, she was actually going to try and change. It was an incr[illegible]y complex and nuanced performance.

And Ato also naile[illegible]th his, he let the audience in so that they understood that the [illegible]ience may have also changed him, too, that perhaps he'd ne[illegible]personally considered what he (Marcus) stood for until the very[illegible]ment that he was asked by Lisa.

Both actors were perfect.

This play has been done numerous times since, in New York and across the country. I have to note that, far too often in the later productions that I saw, a director would cast a balding geeky guy as Marcus. So that the play becomes a joke about THIS dweeb trying to buy this beautiful woman a drink, and that she is simply torturing him for that.

That particular approach has never seemed to work. It gets a couple laughs, but the emotional reality gets lost. It becomes too absurd and, in the end, fails the piece.

It got so bad that I actually changed the stage directions to underline the fact that Marcus is a charming and very handsome man who could believably buy a pretty girl a drink and score. When Marcus says, "forgive the slick guy in the suit who's pretending he's never bought a woman a drink before just to get into her pants," he's finally being honest about his intentions and who he is. And that's important. That's his epiphany.

Likewise, Lisa is well and truly damaged and, while we don't know exactly what happened to her and why, it's necessary to make her rage REAL. It's not a joke. She's not one-note crazy, she's emotionally damaged, and that's a very important distinction.

When Marcus tells her that you can either kill all the people who deserve it or love all the people who deserve it, but you can't do both … that's her epiphany, and we are left with the impression that she's going to think long and hard about that choice after this.

That was my intent when I wrote this piece. It's why it's one of my favorites. You can either honor that or not. It's in your hands from this point onward.

2

Marks (1m, 1f)

CHARACTERS:

ALEX – A man in his

MELISSA – A woman er 30s.

SETTING: A bar.

TIME: Present.

(MELISSA SITS at a tal a bar, nursing her drink. ALEX walks in.)

ALEX: Hi. Are yo lissa?

MELISSA: Are yo x?

ALEX: I am.

MELISSA: I'm Melissa. Nice to meet you.

(They shake hands and ALEX sits down with her.)

MELISSA: Would you like a drink?

ALEX: No thank you, I don't drink.

MELISSA: Not at all?

ALEX: Not at all.

MELISSA: Oh. I do.

ALEX: That's okay.

MELISSA: I'm not an alcoholic or anything, but I definitely drink. Were you an alcoholic, or …

ALEX: No. I just don't drink.

MELISSA: Wendi never told me that you didn't drink.

ALEX: That's all right, I'm not rabid about it.

MELISSA: Oh.

(MELISSA takes a big drink.)

ALEX: So. So you know Todd, right?

MELISSA: Only indirectly. Since he's been dating Wendi.

ALEX: Todd and I are good friends.

MELISSA: I've known Wendi for a long time. *(Long pause.)* So. I guess that they thought we would … hit it off. Or something.

ALEX: Yeah. Yeah. I guess. *(Another long pause.)* So. Todd tells me that you're an editor, an assistant editor at Parcells.

MELISSA: Yes. Yes. In Young Adult books. Yes.

ALEX: Hey. That must be fun.

MELISSA: No. Not really. No. I hate my job.

ALEX: Oh. I'm sorry.

MELISSA: Me too. *(Pause.)* But you're a doctor, Wendi said you're a doctor.

ALEX: Yes, I am.

MELISSA: Wow. That's something. So do you do surgery and all that …

ALEX: No, I'm not a surgeon, I don't do any cutting. I specialize in internal medicine.

MELISSA: That must be pretty fascinating.

ALEX: It's not, really. It should be, but it's not.

MELISSA: Oh.

ALEX: I work nin ive, I see patients with generally the same problems and complai nd prescribe the same medications, over and over again. Day af lay. It's actually kind of dull.

MELISSA: Oh. W 'm sorry.

ALEX: Me too. M).

(Pause.)

MELISSA: This bl date really isn't working out, is it?

ALEX: No, I'm af not. I'm sorry.

MELISSA: Me to u seem like a really nice man—

ALEX: And you, y eem really wonderful.

MELISSA: It's jus s not the right time for me to see other people.

ALEX: Me too. Le ll it a night, shall we?

MELISSA: Yes. I' glad we understand each other.

(They each stand up a ach for their coats.)

MELISSA: I mea new I wasn't ready, I only agreed to get Wendi off my back.

ALEX: Me too. W odd, I mean. He's always hounding me, trying to get me out of house.

MELISSA: She's a s trying to get me to meet people.

ALEX: And I love guy and all that, but sometimes—

MELISSA: Some s you just want to scream at them, scream—

ALEX: Leave me !

MELISSA: Leave lone and stop bothering me!

ALEX: Exactly. I n, blind dates? Who goes on blind dates anymore?

MELISSA: No on

ALEX: No real pe go on blind dates, do they? As if dating ITSELF isn't hard e gh, talking to someone you've already MET—

MELISSA: To go igh it with a complete stranger?

ALEX: No way! E se in futility.

MELISSA: Exactl actly. Yes.

(Brief pause.)

ALEX: Well. It wa e to meet you.

MELISSA: It was nice to meet you, too.

(Short pause.)

ALEX: A blind date. I can't believe I went on a blind date!

MELISSA: I was just thinking the same exact thing!

ALEX: I can't believe it!

MELISSA: Who would have thought that I could sink this low?

ALEX: I know! What a joke I have turned into.

MELISSA: I know. I mean, I'm bad enough at regular dating.

(Short pause. ALEX sits down.)

ALEX: I haven't been on a date since 2001.

MELISSA: Really?

ALEX: Really. I just did the numbers in my head. It was February 9, 2001. Last real date.

MELISSA: Wow. What have you been doing all that time?

ALEX: Married, I was married.

MELISSA: Oh. Divorced?

ALEX: Just. Just last year. Married seven years, together nine. Then BANG! All over.

(Short pause. MELISSA sits down.)

MELISSA: I wasn't married, but I do consider myself divorced.

ALEX: Really?

MELISSA: My uh … my EX-boyfriend, or what have you, we were together for six years. Lived together for five.

ALEX: Five years. That's longer than the average marriage.

MELISSA: I know. And then … BANG! It was all over. *(Short pause.)* So what happened? With yours?

ALEX: Another man.

MELISSA: Ahh. That must've hurt. How'd it happen?

ALEX: Actually, they met at the hospital. He's a nurse. She worked in Administration.

MELISSA: Wait. Your wife left you for a nurse?

ALEX: Yep.

MELISSA: That's kind of ironic, isn't it?

ALEX: My wife and he seem to think so. I have yet to find the irony in the situation.

MELISSA: I'm sorry.

ALEX: Me, too. *(S* [illegible] *pause.)* What happened with you?

MELISSA: You m [illegible] why did he leave?

ALEX: Yes. Anoth [illegible] oman?

MELISSA: Other [illegible] en. Woman plural. He wanted his sexual freedom. He loved m [illegible] he wanted to have sex with a variety of long-stemmed beautif [illegible] omen. As that he's a fashion photographer, he has ready acc [illegible] a large supply.

ALEX: Ouch.

MELISSA: He sti [illegible] ls. Every other day. He still says he loves me. He just wants to [illegible] rm deviant sexual gymnastics on lovely but stupid women. Hi [illegible] ds. But he says he misses me. He says so, anyway. *(Very brief paus* [illegible] niss him.

ALEX: I miss her. [illegible] s her terribly.

MELISSA: I told [illegible] not to call me anymore and I know that was the right thing to [illegible] ut I really miss the sound of his voice.

ALEX: I called m [illegible] e ten times a week, for a year or so, after it was over. At all h [illegible] And she would talk to me, she would. Sometimes we would [illegible] h and I could almost forget we weren't together anymore.

MELISSA: Me to [illegible] was almost like it never happened. Right until we had to hang u [illegible]

ALEX: Right until [illegible] . It was torture. I finally forced myself to stop calling her. I stop [illegible] but I still miss her. I miss her more than anything.

(Short pause.)

MELISSA: You k [illegible] what I miss the most? The little things, the little silly things th [illegible] would do to drive me crazy. Like, like his big feet. He had these [illegible] e big feet, and he just loved to park them up on a table or wher [illegible] he liked, and I would slap at the feet and knock them down, an [illegible] d grin and put them right back up there. I miss doing that. I miss [illegible] noises he would make, he like, made the most horrible noise w [illegible] e ate, big disgusting chewing noises that horrified me and I mi [illegible] em, every one of them. He would talk to me while I was in the [illegible] room. I would be in the bathroom, and he would knock on th [illegible] r and say "MELISSA!" And I would go "What?" "What are y [illegible] oing in there?" "What do you think I'm doing in here, leave me alone!" I'd say, and he'd go "Are you doing something nasty in there, you are, aren't you? You nasty, nasty girl." And I would get so mad at him for that, so mad. He was such a goof, a big goofy kid. I miss his goofiness.

ALEX: My wife loved tofu.

MELISSA: Tofu?

ALEX: Yeah tofu, you know? Which in itself isn't that unusual, but see, she wasn't a vegetarian. She wasn't a vegetarian yet she loved tofu. I've never met anyone who wasn't a vegetarian that loved tofu. Of course, vegetarians always say they love tofu, but what the hell else can they say? There's nothing else for them to eat, they have to love tofu. But she just loved it even though she also ate meat, I never understood that about her. It was one of those inexplicable things about her that always fascinated me. She loved tofu.

MELISSA: I can't stand tofu.

ALEX: Me neither.

(Short pause as they look at each other.)

MELISSA: I miss the sex too. I will admit that, since you're a doctor I can say that to you, right?

ALEX: You can.

MELISSA: I can and I will. I miss the sex. I had been having sex with him on a regular basis for five years. Good sex, good and plentiful. Then it stopped and I miss it. I haven't had sex with anyone since he left. I don't even know if I can.

ALEX: Yeah. Me neither.

MELISSA: It's so sad. But what can we do?

ALEX: I've been playing a lot of video games.

MELISSA: Really?

ALEX: The bloodier the better. HALO is a personal favorite, you get a really big gun, all sorts of weapons of destruction and do your utmost to annihilate and destroy your opponents.

MELISSA: Has that helped?

ALEX: It's not a good as sex, but it's not that bad either. What about you, what have you been doing to cope?

MELISSA: Drinking.

ALEX: Ah.

MELISSA: Drink ınd staring at my cat. We have staring contests, we stare at e other for hours, and then he pretends to ignore me for awhile, he stares at me again until I freak him out and he goes into t her room. This whole break-up has been very hard on my cat.

ALEX: Yeah. I bet

(Short pause.)

MELISSA: You kn vhat I miss the most?

ALEX: What?

MELISSA: His se of humor. I know that sounds weird, but he had the strangest, g est sense of humor I'd ever seen in a man over thirty and I miss u know what he would do? He would do things like … he'd co ut of the bathroom in the morning after his shower wearing h derwear on his head and nothing else. "I'm a bit turned ar today," he'd say. Sometimes when we ordered food over the ıe, he would do it in a Scottish accent, or Indian or Jamaican ıt, depending on his mood. Just to be weird. He would pass he would do this in front of me, crack a good one and then g Melissa quick, there's a duck loose in the apartment, quick we a get it, it's over here, no, no, it's over there" running aroun r apartment breaking wind and I would want to get mad at hi t I just couldn't, I would be laughing too hard. I miss that. I mis t the most. You know what I mean?

ALEX: Yeah.

(Short pause.)

MELISSA: What u miss the most?

(Pause.)

ALEX: I miss mill lifferent things, all at once. Her blue eyes, red hair and the freck n her shoulders. Her pale, pale skin. Her pigeon-toed feet and she loved to wear different colored socks on each foot, just to b ıny. The naughty little giggle that she did only around me and n e else. The secret spot in the small of her back that always excit r. The secret smile, the secret touch. The secret language that l have only with each other. Our secret world. Sometimes I'd up in the middle of the night, open my eyes and her face wou only an inch from mine, eyes open and smiling. I loved touching her, running my fingers up and down her skin in all places, not just sexually, but in every way. Holding hands, she could hold hands with me in a way that … that was special, sexual and sacred without being dirty. I loved making love with her, but even more than that I loved, loved touching her, I loved it. And sometimes I dream I'm still touching her. I wake up and I'm surprised she's not in bed next to me. Almost two years and I'm still surprised she's not lying next to me. More than her giggle, her socks and pigeon-toed feet, I miss her touch more than anything else. I miss that. You know what I'm saying?

(Short pause as MELISSA looks at ALEX. Then she takes his hand in hers.)

MELISSA: It's going to be quite sometime before we're over all of this, isn't it?

ALEX: I'm afraid so.

END OF PLAY

BURN MARKS NOTES:

First produced by The Defiant Ones as part of the evening CLOSE ENCOUNTERS, directed by the author, featuring Adam Rothenberg and Luisa Battista.

This was paired with ALL THE RAGE in the evening, and the actors knocked it out of the park. They made it funny and also brought the pain, which is necessary for this piece.

It's since been produced many times in other venues, but notably by Common Factor at the D2 Theatre featuring Carrie Keranen and the Jeff Bender, another great production, and at Under The Volcano featuring Luisa Battista and Lou Carbonneau.

Note, if you need to change the date of Alex's last real date to make the numbers add up to the present day production, you have my express permission to do so. But only that, nothing else.

Clearly this work comes from the idea of trying to date when one still bears the emotional scars from a previous relationship. It's a simple, concise idea a [illegible] works best when it's kept that way. Pain sometimes separates us [illegible] netimes binds us.

Personal confessio [illegible] y wife is the one who loves tofu and is not a vegetarian.

I confess, I still don [illegible] t it.

And I love that ab [illegible] er.

3

Ambivalent (2m, 2f)

CHARACTERS:

SAM: A man in his late 40s, very dry and fatalistic.

GINNY: An actress in her 20s, prone to outbursts.

MOOG: A hipster musician.

BEVERLY: A woman in her late 40s, early 50s, a voice of reason.

SETTING: Gate 13 at JFK.

TIME: Present.

GATE THIRTEEN AT [illegible]

(Scores of people sit [illegible] g to board. One man, SAM, clad in a suit and tie and carrying a briefcas[illegible] ds and catches people's attention.)

SAM: Excuse me, [illegible] orry, but excuse me, everyone, can I have your attention? Please [illegible] ore they allow us to board, there is something very important [illegible] d to share with all of you. My name is Sam Hunnicut, I'm f[illegible] our years old, I'm an account associate with Bristol-Meyer, I [illegible] a wife, two children, three cats and a large mortgage. I'm a [illegible] dinary man living an ordinary life and I just want to say, befor[illegible] all get on this airplane, that I have been suddenly overcome w[illegible] n overwhelming sense of doom and I'm absolutely convinced t[illegible] e're all going to die. Thank you.

(SAM sits down. GI[illegible] a young woman, jumps up.)

GINNY: What the [illegible] L is wrong with you?

SAM: I just thoug[illegible] ryone should know.

(MOOG, a hip youn[illegible] chimes in.)

MOOG: You're sa[illegible] this plane is going to crash?

SAM: This plane [illegible] rash and we're all going to die.

GINNY: Are you c[illegible] Stop trying to scare us!

SAM: I'm not de[illegible] ately trying to scare you or anyone. I simply thought you'd [illegible] to be informed.

GINNY: If you're [illegible] T trying to scare anyone, you're doing a piss-poor job of it, you [illegible] ing psycho.

(A middle-aged woma[illegible] EVERLY, stands.)

BEVERLY: Listen [illegible] yone, let's all just calm down, please. It's quite natural to feel n[illegible] s. We're going to be fine, you're going to be fine, sir. You're just [illegible] d of flying.

SAM: I'm not afra[illegible] flying. I fly all the time.

MOOG: So what's [illegible] big deal, man?

SAM: This time i[illegible] ferent, this time I have a premonition, a vision or what-have-y[illegible] hat this plane we are about to board is destined to go down s[illegible] ming in a twisted fiery ball of death and destruction.

GINNY: Oh my G[illegible]

BEVERLY: Please, this isn't helping any of us—

SAM: Of course, I could be wrong, I've been wrong about other things.

MOOG: Like what?

SAM: Reagan, I was really wrong about Reagan and Reaganomics, a huge miscalculation.

BEVERLY: See? None of us is omnipotent, I myself never thought rollerblading would be as popular as it turned out to be.

SAM: Enron, really wrong about Enron. Beanie babies. The euro-dollar, took me by surprise. Rap music, never thought that would cross over. The DeLorean. The XFL. My marriage, big mistake. So I've been wrong about a lot of things.

GINNY: Why is it every time I leave my apartment all I run into are lunatics?

SAM: I should add, however, that those were mistakes in judgment, I never had the premonition I have now about any of those things. I've had a premonition like this only ONCE before.

GINNY: Oh really. You've had this "psychic email" before? When?

SAM: 2004 American League championship, Sox down three games to none to the Yanks. That's when it hit me for the first time, the premonition, I somehow knew the Sox would pull it out and win it all in spite of the odds. I almost called my bookie and put down a thousand dollars on Boston at twenty to one. But I didn't, damn it. I should have bet ten or twenty grand but I didn't, I was afraid of getting my legs broken if they lost. I didn't know at that time how right my premonition was.

MOOG: Fuck me, man, this is freaking me out.

BEVERLY: Listen to me, please. Everyone. THERE IS NOTHING TO BE AFRAID OF. We are all going to be fine. My cousin was a stewardess for fifteen years and was never in a crash. You are safer on an airplane than you are in a car on the freeway.

GINNY: Which is why I DON'T DRIVE! Oh God, oh God oh God. Oh good God, why does this happen? Why oh why did I agree to an audition in LA, I should have just sent a tape, it's not even a real show, it's on the fucking food network! I'm an actress, why should I have to tion for something on the FOOD NETWORK? Why sh any self-respecting actress have to audi- tion to be a CO-HO for a FUCKING COOKING SHOW? This is insane, I'm not g to DIE FOR A COOKING SHOW!

BEVERLY: It's ok oney, I swear to you, there is nothing to be afraid of. Thousan planes crisscross this country every hour of the day with no inci -

MOOG: Some pla DO crash, though, right?

GINNY: Planes cr don't try and tell us they don't crash, we see it on the news! Pla rash or they're hijacked, engines fail, the toilets don't work and etimes passengers get food poisoning, shit like that happens, don' and tell us it doesn't happen because WE KNOW IT HAPPEN

BEVERLY: Pleas m down, there are incidents, yes, but statistically-

GINNY: Oh God, freaking out, I'm going to have a break- down, I swear I'm hav heart attack right now!

SAM: I knew this broker during the crash of eighty-seven, he jumped out of a t y-story window and the autopsy revealed he died not from th l but from a heart attack he evidently suffered prior to impac

GINNY: That's it, it, I'm not doing this. I'm outta here.

BEVERLY: Wait cond, please wait. I will admit that bad things do happen fro me to time. Plane crashes, tidal waves, preemptive wars and f elections, unfortunate events do happen. They can happen on ne, in a cab or in a bathtub. Bad things can happen to us any e at anytime. It's important for us to take precautions and be sa t neither can we run from the possibility of unfortunate events. e hide, if we cower in fear, afraid to take two steps from our ca well, that may not be dying, but it's not what I call living, eithe

(Pause.)

GINNY: Fuck yo m outta here. Who else is going? *(to MOOG)* Are you comi

MOOG: Fuck ma an't. I can't. I gotta get on the plane.

GINNY: You don't k looney-tunes here could be right?

MOOG: I hope to God he ain't, but even if he is, I still gotta get on the plane, man.

GINNY: Are you nuts?

MOOG: I gotta go, it's my band man, they're waiting for me in L.A. We have a private audition with a major label, it's tonight and if I don't show … this is our big break, this is what we've been working for, for ten years, me and my band have grinded it out, pinching pennies for demos and headshots, playing shithole dives at four in the morning for no money in front of a few drunks and our girlfriends, we ate shit and paid our dues until we finally got a manager and now we got a chance, a chance to do this for the Big Time. If I don't show they'll kill me. I hope he ain't right, but even if he is I still gotta go. This is my dream, I let this go, I let it slip through my fingers and have to go back to waiting tables, no health insurance, sponging off my folks and girlfriends, I don't know if I even want to live anyway. I'm getting on this motherfucker no matter what happens.

(Brief pause.)

GINNY: You're a MUSICIAN? A MUSICIAN? I am definitely not getting on this fucking plane NOW!

SAM: She's right, you know, a lot of musicians have died on airplanes.

(Many other passengers, silently watching, get up and immediately leave.)

MOOG: Fuck me. Dude, I'm telling you, if this is some kind of sick reality TV show prank, I want you to know I'm not signing any release and you won't be able to use ANY of this footage, for real.

(Very brief pause.)

GINNY: Wait a minute, I'll sign a release, is it a network show?

SAM: This isn't a reality show, I'm not messing with you, I'm totally serious, I really did have a premonition and you should use this chance to change flights if you can.

BEVERLY: If what you're saying is true, then why are you still here?

SAM: What?

BEVERLY: Why are you still here, why haven't you changed flights?

SAM: Well, I coulc wrong—

GINNY: But you c think you're wrong, do you? You believe this plane is going to c

(Very brief pause.)

SAM: I don't real ive much to live for, anyway. That's why I'm not afraid.

BEVERLY: You're ng that you're suicidal?

SAM: Not suicida n not nearly that ambitious. I guess you could say I'm just am ent on living or dying. It wouldn't really matter to me, either w

BEVERLY: Why n

SAM: Well, I've d pretty much everything I can do, up to this point. I got my co degree, got married and bought a house. I've worked for the sa company for twenty years as an account associate, which is fan alk for salesman. A man of twenty-eight was promoted over m ist recently, he has no experience in the job, he's just younger a prettier and now I report to him. I'm basically being put to pas in no uncertain terms, even though I'm twenty years from re nent I've been deemed unnecessary to management and pret on I'll be forced out. With the mortgage I'm carrying, that's ba lly a quick trip to extreme poverty. So it doesn't matter what ha ns, not really.

MOOG: Shit on ck, I don't believe this. I hope to Christ you're not seated next e for the whole flight.

BEVERLY: What t your family?

SAM: What about n?

BEVERLY: Don't u think they'll need you, that they'd miss you?

SAM: My wife de s me, she won't admit it but it's true. I know because I read i her journal last week. It takes all her will power just to look at m the morning without screaming. Twenty-one years of marriage l she's hated me since year two. She was just too afraid to lea e. In her eyes I am good for only two things, paying the bill l impregnation. Paying the bills will soon be out and impregnat s now past us. She'd been badgering for children for years and ally gave in. We have two.

(SAM stands up and stretches.)

SAM: My son, Brandon, he's five and a homosexual. My five-year old son is homosexual. I know because he told me, he said, "Daddy, I think I'm a homosexual." Not only does HE know he's a homosexual and I know he's a homosexual, anyone that's ever MET him knows he's a homosexual. He came out of the womb a homosexual and knew it when he opened his eyes. I love my son, but I thought I'd have years to prepare for the possibility of a homosexual teen-aged son, not a homosexual five year-old son, it's too much to even rationally consider, and one thing I know is that there is nothing I can say or do that will in any way help him with the truly shitty adolescence he's about to embark on. I've got nothing and as a result, if he lives, he'll be sure to hate me for not being able to at least give him one decent piece of advice on anything. Add to that, I'm about to be unemployed so the dance lessons he wants will be out of the question and he'll never forgive me for that.

(SAM loosens his tie and undoes the buttons of his shirt collar.)

SAM: Christine is the youngest, she's three and a monster. I mean really, she's a monster. She's not human. She's a serial killer in progress. She enjoys causing pain. She once drove a corkscrew into my foot and giggled when blood came out. I'm totally serious, she kills things, we have to keep the cats separate from her, she tried to put one in the microwave. She tried to cook one of my cats. My wife insists it's just a phase, but she also said that about our lack of sexual intimacy and that phase has lasted eighteen years. Short of electroshock therapy, Christine is certain to end up on a federal watch list some day. She's my wife's favorite, of course. She hates me. I know because she told me, she said, "I hate you, Daddy." Someday she'll grow up and kill me and you'll be able to see the whole sordid tale on cable late at night.

(An announcer rings out over an intercom, can also be done live by a person.)

ANNOUNCER: Ladies and Gentlemen, sorry for the delay but the problem has been fixed and we are now prepared to board Northwest Airlines Flight 113 from JFK non-stop to Los Angeles. Please have your boarding passes ready.

(Nobody moves for a moment. SAM picks up his bag and looks at everyone.)

SAM: The one thi [illegible] did have was baseball. Now that the Red Sox have beaten the [illegible] s and went on to win the World Series, now that the curse of [illegible] ambino has been lifted, I am for certain sure that I've seen ev [illegible] ing life has to offer and so, even if this plane does crash, it wi [illegible] t be saving me from a dismal existence of poverty, anger, embar [illegible] nent and extreme boredom. So I'm not afraid of dying, I'm pr [illegible] much ambivalent about the whole thing.

(BEVERLY stands a [illegible] ks up her bag.)

BEVERLY: I'm g [illegible] on this plane to visit my sister in Los Angeles. She's in the [illegible] tal with breast cancer. She never smoked, drank or ate bad food [illegible] still she got cancer. She taught yoga and ran marathons and s [illegible] ill got cancer. She's been fighting it for three years, she's ha [illegible] mastectomies and countless rounds of chemo and radiation [illegible] ments. She's lost all her hair, half of her body weight and quit [illegible] ew of her teeth. In spite of all that, she smiles every time I se [illegible] Every time I see her, she smiles because she's happy just to be [illegible]

(BEVERLY takes he [illegible] and walks to the boarding gate.)

BEVERLY: She's [illegible] things that are much worse than a dead-end job, an unhappy [illegible] nd two problematic children. She's faced pain and agony far wo [illegible] han any of us here can imagine and she's smiled through it all. [illegible] s currently in the last stage. She's dying soon, and if I don't ge [illegible] this plane, I won't see her, hold her or get to share that smile of [illegible] ever again. I'm more afraid of that than dying myself.

(Very calm and coll [illegible] BEVERLY stops right before she enters the boarding gate. She looks ri [illegible] SAM.)

BEVERLY: So I'm [illegible] ing on this plane, and shame on you, sir, for airing your fears [illegible] irresponsibly as you have and scaring everyone here, sham [illegible] you for making a scene here because you're too scared to g [illegible] parent counseling or couples therapy or make a career chang [illegible] st of all, shame on you for being afraid and acting ambivalent [illegible] t it. You may not fear death, but you are certainly scared of lif [illegible] tell you this much. There are things in the world much wors [illegible] n getting on an airplane. One of those things is being as AFR [illegible] of life as you are.

(BEVERLY boards the plane. MOOG glances at SAM and then picks his bag up and enters the gate, boarding the plane.

GINNY, torn, finally picks her bag up and follows. She boards the plane.

SAM sets his bag down and slowly sits, unable to move.

Lights fade.)

END OF PLAY.

AMBIVALENT NOTES:

This play was developed as part of a playwrights group with The Barrow Group. It was later produced as a showcase there in 2005 as part of THE FEAR PROJECT, but ultimately this work was left out that show's move to Off-Broadway.

It later received its professional premiere at Miami's City Theatre in 2007 to good reviews, though I wasn't able to attend that performance.

There is much I'm proud of in this play, not the least with what Beverly finally says at the end and how it sums up. It reflects what took me decades to learn for myself. And in the readings leading up to the workshop and showcase, it was electric.

The first production at The Barrow Group, however, was problematic. We had a first-time director. The actors playing Ginny and Moog were great, but the actors playing Sam and Beverly decided, once the play was on its feet, to just do their own thing and interpret things how they saw fit, regardless of what the director or I thought.

"Sam" had already told me that he didn't believe in memorizing lines or doing the same thing the same way twice, and so he was all over the place with no consistency. I had no idea what "Beverly" was doing when she was onstage, perhaps because she didn't either. She was in her own world and wanted to do things the way she wanted to do them.

The performance of the play suffered greatly, as a result. There were times I wanted to slit my own wrists, all the more maddening because the next night might be good.

That's the thing, as a playwright, you give someone a play of yours to do and it is li ly out of your hands from that point on. Once you give it to th it's theirs and out of your control. They either do right by it or don't.

That's the theatre man. But the play remains one of my favorites.

4

Something Situation (2f)

CHARACTERS:

BERDENE – A grandmother in her late 50s.

RITA – a 13 year-old math prodigy.

SETTING: A hospital room.

TIME: Present.

LIGHTS UP.

(A hospital room. BERDENE, 58, sits upright in her bed. She wipes tears from her eyes with a handkerchief. RITA, 13, enters the room with a book in hand.)

BERDENE: Rita. t are you doing up here all by yourself?

RITA: Mom sent r cheer you up.

BERDENE: Oh. All right.

(BERDENE shifts in bed. A quiet uncomfortable moment.)

BERDENE: So. W 'd your mother get to?

RITA: She's hiding n Aunt Arlene.

BERDENE: Arlen ere? Oh my Lord, here we go.

RITA: She's on vay. Mom and Aunt Arlene have been fighting.

BERDENE: I'm urprised, they've fought ever since they were your age, so don rry about it. Come here and have a seat. What are you reading ?

(RITA sits in a chair o the bed.)

RITA: The Mecha l Theory of Heat by Rudolf Clausius.

BERDENE: Oh. A ou reading that for a class or something?

RITA: No. Just for

BERDENE: Oh. (.

RITA: Are you fee ll right, Grandma?

BERDENE: Not r no.

RITA: Do you wa to get a nurse?

BERDENE: No, d it's just ... It's just, having to be here, in this situation . . . goin ough this, having all this stuff happen to me and all that. Doesn m right.

(Brief quiet moment.)

RITA: Look at the ht side. It's not a pickle.

BERDENE: What t a pickle?

RITA: This is not kle.

BERDENE: Wher you get pickle, how do you get PICKLE out of all this?

RITA: I'm just say –

BERDENE: Wher his PICKLE THING coming out of?

RITA: I'm just say t's not the pickle that you think it is.

BERDENE: What

RITA: The situatic

BERDENE: My si on?

RITA: The situatic 's not the pickle that you think it is.

(BERDENE looks at her granddaughter for a moment.)

BERDENE: You know, I know that you're supposed to some sort of genius and all that, but would it be TOO much to ask if you could just make a LITTLE bit of sense every now and then instead of throwing pickles at me?

RITA: It's a saying, you know, a folk saying, when something happens to someone and they find themselves in a tight situation, sometimes people say, "She's found herself in a pickle" or "I'm in a heck of a pickle." And all I'm saying is that the something situation that you have currently found yourself in is not the pickle that you think it is.

(Brief pause.)

BERDENE: You READ entirely TOO much!

RITA: Of course I do. That's all I do.

BERDENE: And the OTHER THING, HOW can you say this situation is not a pickle?! This situation is mostly CERTAINLY a pickle, it's nothing BUT a pickle! This is the biggest goddamn dill pickle that I've ever seen, that's for sure!

RITA: I can see how it may be perceived that way.

BERDENE: What other way can it be perceived?

RITA: The other way it can be perceived is as something that happens. It's just something that happens to everyone. All of us. You. Me. Everyone.

(Brief quiet moment.)

BERDENE: And why is it described as "being in a pickle?" Certain situations, I mean. Why would someone say that, where does that come from anyway?

RITA: Because pickles traditionally taste very sour. Actually being INSIDE of one is thought to be sour beyond all recall.

BERDENE: If that's the case, then this situation is definitely a pickle. In fact, pickle is the nicest thing you can say about it. THIS IS A PICKLE!

RITA: It's not the pickle that you think it is.

BERDENE: Well honey, it sure as hell ain't a TWINKIE, either!

(Brief pause.)

RITA: You're right. It's not a Twinkie situation either.

BERDENE: I thoı the reason you were sent in here was to cheer me up?

RITA: It was.

BERDENE: Well] ·y, you're doing a HELL of a job!

RITA: I'm sorry. ocial skills are somewhat stunted. I don't interact with real pe very well, especially during something situations.

(Brief quiet moment.)

BERDENE: Don' ı interact with other people up there at that school of yours?

RITA: I do, but ı of them are more socially handicapped than I am.

BERDENE: You'r handicapped, Honey, don't ever say that you're handicapped a lon't ever let anyone TELL you you're handicapped.

RITA: It's all righ a natural result of my intellectual being growing so much faste n my emotional being. It's just something that happens. I'm on ırteen and I'm going to graduate from MIT this spring. Tha ›mething, and as a result of that, something else happens. I ow things work. The price of being a prodigy.

(Brief moment. BER E sighs.)

BERDENE: I use know this fella named Pickle. He used to come into my Daddy' all the time, almost every day, we'd say "Hey Pickle."

RITA: His name w ickle?

BERDENE: I don nk his real name was Pickle, it's just what everyone called him. er knew what his real name was. We all just called him Pickle. exactly sure why.

RITA: I imagine t here was some sort of sexual connotation attached.

BERDENE: Som s not nearly as socially stunted as she's been pretending to b s, I'm pretty sure he got the nickname because of something that, but he was always real polite and decent to me. I was of sweet on him, even though I was nothing but sixteen a ıe was almost my father's age, I always batted my eyes at him. He always smiled at me. I was always hoping something would happen between us, though it never did. Nothing ever happened. He liked me, though. I could tell. He was always real sweet to me. Real sweet fella.

RITA: So he was more of a Twinkie than a Pickle.

(They look at each other quickly. They both giggle.)

BERDENE: Yes, Pickle was definitely a Twinkie. A big sweet Twinkie. I liked him. I was always sad nothing ever happened between us.

RITA: Where is he now?

BERDENE: I imagine he's passed on. Like my father and mother and brother and sister. Like I'm probably going to do.

RITA: Like all of us.

BERDENE: I shouldn't be telling you this, Rita, but I'm pretty scared right now.

RITA: You haven't even gotten the test results back yet. You could be fine, it could turn out to be benign.

BERDENE: This time, but what about next time or the time after that? I'm old enough that I'm feeling my mortality. I'm feeling it down deep in my bones. I'm feeling the crush of time.

(Brief pause.)

RITA: Have you heard of Stephen Hawking?

BERDENE: Fella in the wheelchair, right?

RITA: Yes. He has some interesting theories on the perception of time. I've been toying with some of his theorems as of late. Can I give you an example?

BERDENE: Keep it simple, Sweetie, remember that I'm a civilian.

RITA: Simple is best anyway. You ever notice a bicycle tire, how when it spins, the spokes of the tire seem to go in the opposite direction of the tire?

BERDENE: Like a wagon wheel.

RITA: Exactly. The tire is going one direction but we perceive it as going the other. Perception is key. Long and short of it, life to us appears as though we are born, we live and then we die.

BERDENE: And that isn't what happens?

RITA: That's wha PERCEIVE happens. The reality, like the spokes of the wagon l, could be and probably is the opposite. Instead of birth as the inning and death as the end of the cycle, birth could be the en d death could be the beginning. That's what it could be and n of us simply aren't in a position to see it.

(Brief pause.)

BERDENE: Are y urrently in that position?

RITA: I think I co e.

BERDENE: And y an see … something?

RITA: I've alway en something. The big difficulty is in describing it.

BERDENE: So it l be?

RITA: It could be. eep working on it.

BERDENE: I just I knew for sure. What happens, I mean, when we … when I I never bought into any of that other jumbo, the bible and at silliness, it just never seemed right or even fair to women. B e only alternative I can see is that nothing happens, and that doe eem right either.

RITA: And that's you're scared?

BERDENE: Yes. use I don't know what's going to happen when I die, if anythin at's what I'm frightened of most. Maybe nothing happens. I hope … I really, really hope … that something …

RITA: Grandma?

BERDENE: Yes d

RITA: I don't kno erything. I know quite a lot about a lot of things, but I don't k everything. But one thing I definitely do know.

BERDENE: What t?

RITA: When you

BERDENE: Yes?

RITA: Something ens. Something definitely happens.

(BERDENE looks a a for a moment. BERDENE opens her arms. RITA goes to her. They h a long moment.)

Lights fade.

THE END.

SOMETHING SITUATION NOTES:

FIRST PRODUCED in 2002 as part of Manhattan Theatre Source's SPONTANEOUS COMBUSTION, featuring Holland Hamilton as Rita and Carla Hayes as Berdene.

SPONTANEOUS COMBUSTION SHOWS were like those 24 hour plays. You showed up on a Friday night and were assigned actors, a first line and something that had to be mentioned in the play at some point (in this case, it was pickle). The writers took those ideas home, wrote a play THAT NIGHT, brought it back Saturday morning and gave to the actors, who memorized it and staged it, and opened to an audience on Sunday night.

It was a lot of fun, and I did four of them, which resulted in the plays THE PAP, THE ITCH, SOMETHING SITUATION and PRETEND IT IS.

Holland, who was 13 or 14 at the time, was someone I'd known already for quite some time. Her father, R. Paul Hamilton, had acted in several of my plays and her mother, Anita Hollander, directed my play QUITTING.

I met Carla Hayes through this play and she'd go on to act in much more of my work. It was one of those instances where everything came together perfectly. They elevated it to a level beyond anything I could have imagined. It really moves me, even to this day.

I actually expanded this play to one act length and added the aunt character, and it also did well. That version is featured in the one act play section of this book.

Personal note, I named the characters after my mom (Rita) and her mother (Berdene). My mom's sister is also named Arlene, but she was nothing like that character, of course. I only borrowed the names, nothing more.

5

E me Eugene (1m)

CHARACTERS:

EUGENE – An affable rming man in his 30s.

SETTING: His apartm

TIME: Present.

(STAGE IS empty except desk and a chair. A computer sits upon the desk.

Eugene, dressed in a ess suit and carrying a briefcase, steps into the room and sets his briefcase n. He sits in front the computer and takes a deep breath. Eugene smiles. Th a camera attached to the computer. Eugene begins his podcast.)

EUGENE: Hello a u happy people. Welcome to the podcast. I know what you're thi g. You think I'm crazy, don't you? No, it's all right, let's be honest with each other, you're sitting there thinking, this guy's a couple cans short of a full sixer, aren't you?

It's all right, really. Seriously. People have always thought that I was little bit nuts.

(EUGENE removes his suit jacket and his tie.)

There's really a perfectly reasonable explanation.

I was the kid, you know, growing up, wore a baseball cap turned around backwards, the kid that climbed the tree that couldn't be climbed, jumped his bike over the ditch that couldn't be jumped, I was the kid that if you dared me to do something, I would do it. Eat a grasshopper? Did it. Throw a rock through the window of the church? That was me. Ride my Huffy bike all the way along the gutter on the roof of my house? Not a problem for Eugene the machine. I was known as the ballsiest kid on the block, hell, the whole neighborhood.

When we were kids, us guys would sometimes all light firecrackers at the same time, together and then hold them out, seeing who could hang on to it the longest before pussing out and throwing it.

I always won that game.

Singed my eyebrows, made my ears ring for a couple days, but I fucking won.

Winning was good, but the bang, the BANG, that was even better.

I spent a large part of my adolescence in plaster, but it was worth it. I was the balls-to-the-wall legend of the neighborhood. It was fun. It was something.

I was something.

(EUGENE takes a pistol from out of a hip holster and sets it in his briefcase.)

Of course, I never figured I would end up an accountant.

(He takes off his shirt and pants.)

It wasn't my plan, being a bookkeeper. Originally I was going in the Marines. First choice was to be a pilot, a Marine-Pilot, and if that didn't work out then I'd join the Special Forces or something. But being a pilot was the number one priority, it's the reason I got such good grades in m ıt school, because Pops told me pilots had to be good at math. St ıt A's, algebra and calculus.

But there was not ɔe. Slight problem with my eyesight, I'd banged up my head p good once, jumping like a stuntman off of a moving freight t when I was eleven. Crossed my eyes a little bit and fucked u peripheral vision. Being a pilot was out. So I figured, Special F , hell, I'd even settle for infantry, but I got shit-canned during th uction physical. I got this thing, nothing really, but it kept me o the service.

It's called a heart r ıur, instead going ba-bump, ba-bump, my heart goes ba-gloop, b ɔop, like it's a little leaky or something. A murmur. It's such l ıit, I'm in perfect shape, I can run marathons, in fact I c n marathons, I can do anything anyone else can. It's a minor t really, but unless they re-instate the draft I won't ever get to serv

So I went to colleg tead. UCLA. Got the math degree, had a lot of fun. Still the c kid addicted to extreme behavior, there wasn't anything I wou do, especially in college. I was the regurgitation champion of teen eighty-nine in my fraternity. It was totally awesome. I als the record for goldfish shots, you know how that works, right? a string to a gold-fish, do a shot, swallow the gold-fish all the w own, then pull it all the way back again. Goldfish shots. There l a plaque in Delta's hall with my name on it. Eighty-eight gol down and back again. That was me.

I just like doing th everybody else is afraid to do, you know? It's a high, it's a thrill, ike a stamp with your name on it. When you're twenty-one yea d, hanging from your feet off the Golden Gate Bridge over the S Francisco Bay, it's like saying, hey, Eugene was here.

(EUGENE folds his t and pants very carefully and places them on the chair.)

When I was in coll I would have sex with the ugliest women. I would be in a bar, s he fattest, ugliest woman you could ever imagine, and I would ɔ and romance the pants right off of her, take the hairy beast e and give her the loving of her life. I would! I would, and I good-looking guy, I could and would get hot babes. But I would fuck the fat hairy ones, too, and you know why? Because no one else would.

Eugene was here.

(EUGENE takes a towel out of the briefcase.)

In case you're wondering, there is a difference, between fucking a hot babe and fucking an ugly woman. Big difference. Ugly woman APPRECIATE it.

What can I say, I'm OUT THERE, I'm Mr. Adrenaline, I'm EXTREME EUGENE, I love skating on the edge. Skydiving? Did it. Motocross? No problem. Bungee jumping? Bungee jumping is for pussies. Free falling from a helicopter into an air bag is what real men do.

Of course, being in California, I learned how to surf. I LOVED surfing, there is something so Zen and surreal about running a tube, tons of water all around you, it's like being transported to another universe. Surfing is one of the all-time great sexual highs.

It was great until I broke my back in Australia.

Wasn't even my fault, I'd caught a high salty one, was hanging some serious ten when some amateur Gumby-head tried to hork my wave, wiped and his board snapped free and BAP! Right between my eyes. That's not what broke my back, of course, the monster wave and the reef did that when I hit the water. Before that, though, whatta rush, I saw all the colors water is and can be, all at once. It was fucking beautiful.

Also, my eyes uncrossed when the board hit me in the head and now I could see better. So except for the broken back, it was a profitable experience.

(EUGENE picks up the pistol and begins cleaning it.)

My medical bills were piling up, so I took this accounting job, originally I was just going to stay while I was in traction and rehabilitation. Ended up staying past that. Been with it eleven years. It pretty much sucks, but what can you do? I've spent weekends spelunking and scuba diving, the occasional radical vacation whitewater rafting down a river. Lately, I've been training in extreme fighting, you know, the no-holds-barred cage match stuff? But I haven't been able to g o a match yet as that none of these pussy doctors will sign off on back.

But I did get a c e to test what I learned, you know, the fighting stuff. I went to Texas, walked into a big shit-kicking bar wearing nothing ather chaps and a pink T-shit that said, "Kiss me, I'm GAY" ed back and waited for the fun to start. Now that was a party. know that jiu-jitsu stuff, that shit really works. No kidding. I ed up something like ten, eleven homophobic cowboys befor y arrested me, only getting a black eye, busted nose and a bro and in return.

Broken hand cam m the cops, AFTER I was arrested and handcuffed. Pigs. My suit's still pending. It was fun, though, lotta fun.

I'm not gay, but so mes I wish I was. Just for the fights.

I had been thinkin out it lately. Not about being gay, I mean, thinking about what I nd why and all that. Couldn't quite figure it out.

Then something h ned.

(EUGENE finishes u e pistol, sets it aside and closes his briefcase.)

I had a sort of ep ny, something like that, on my last vacation. I was on a mou n in Tibet, the Himalayas, actually, and we'd just got caught in hiteout. A whiteout is a blizzard that hits so hard and so fast you 't see anything but white.

We dug a hole in ide of mountain in the snow, me and the Sherpas, and buried lves in the snow. We were tied together, and staked to the side e mountain so we wouldn't get blown off.

The Sherpas were red, both of them. I've been on a lot of expeditions and I did ver remember ever seeing a Sherpa get scared, but these two . I know they were because they told me, they said, "Bwana, I'm ed."

They always call e "Bwana", I don't know why, it not Tibetan. I think it's jus nething they saw in a movie once.

(EUGENE wraps th l around his head.)

Anyway, we're bu in a hole in the snow, and we take our clothes off, it's the on nance we have to stay warm, so we get naked, grab each othe ver up and wait for the mountain to stop screaming at us. It was something, let me tell you. We're entwined together naked, it's forty below, the mountain's shaking and howling, the Sherpa's were praying and shitting, convinced they were gonna die, I know because they told me, they said "Bwana, we die now, we die now!"

The wind screams and all of a sudden, all the snow covering us blows away in a puff, the wind picks us up and yanks us out and away from the side of the mountain.

We're still staked and cabled to the wall, but the storm has pulled us straight out into the air.

We're weaving and bobbing in the wind like a cork on a fishing line, half-naked and pissing ourselves like live bait, the canyon two thousand feet below us, this is happening to us, and the whole time I'm thinking, "Oh my God. This is SO COOL! This is what LIFE is all ABOUT! YEEHAWWW!"

The Sherpas thought I'd lost my mind. We eventually made it off the mountain. I only lost three toes. It was totally fucking awesome.

I had figured it out, I finally got what it all meant!

When I'm at work, crunching numbers, having lunch, home watching television or doing my laundry, I'm not LIVING, I'm not ALIVE. There's no life then.

Maybe what we have here now, with our hearts going ba-gloop ba-gloop together, maybe that's not life or living.

I've been clinically dead three times so far on various adventures.

I'm now of the thinking that THAT'S the only time I've truly, truly lived.

Not while holding the firecracker, not while lighting it, not while watching the fuse burn. That's not life.

I know it. I'm convinced of it.

Life only happens, it only shows its face, at those moments that have the BANG.

That's life.

BANG!

Eugene was here!

(EUGENE grins and [illegible] s the gun to his head.
Lights fade.
Gunshot in black.)
End of play.

EXTREME EUGENE N[illegible]ES:

Featuring Taylor [illegible] el as Eugene, it received its premiere as part of THE FEAR P[illegible]JECT in 2005 and moved Off-Broadway in 2006 for a limited ru[illegible]

Taylor is a friend a[illegible] wrote this with him in mind. He gave an amazing performance[illegible]d got we got some very good reviews. Clearly, it's a dark pi[illegible] given the ending) but I also feel that it captures something un[illegible] about the struggles of life, too.

One other note, ev[illegible]hough this was my Off-Broadway debut, I never received the con[illegible] for it or got paid for the show. Nada, zip, nothing.

There were, I [illegible]ve, six playwrights on THE FEAR PROJECT and the ot[illegible] (save the one playwright who was ALSO the director of the sho[illegible]ND the managing director of the theatre) had the same issues, [illegible]s told, some of them not receiving their money until well after [illegible]un ended (it's supposed to be on opening night) and were frustra[illegible]

I got tired of wai[illegible] for it after the run ended and, since it wasn't much money a[illegible]ly (and there were other issues, too, with that organization), eve[illegible]lly told my then-agent to forget about it and let it go. I haven't [illegible]y had much to do with the theatre since.

As I said before, th[illegible]he theatre biz, man. You're going to hear me say that later, too.

But I'm happy, be[illegible]e as a result of never getting a contract, this piece, a personal [illegible]ite, is officially mine to publish and now to offer to you. Have fu[illegible]

BANG!

[illegible]he Rawness

I got my start as a wri[illegible] eating sketches for No Shame Theatre in grad school, which wa[illegible] last. A lot of those sketches were of the exact type you'd expec[illegible] m a young guy in his early twenties, jokes about sex organs and f[illegible] and so on.

I eventually evolved i[illegible] xplorations regarding love, human sexuality and all the raw b[illegible] ge those things entail. It's a theme prevalent in a lot of my [illegible] as a playwright (I am the author of SPOOGE – THE SE[illegible] LOVE MONOLOGUES, after all).

As a result, what's fea[illegible] d over the next dozen short plays is my own personal evolut[illegible] from silly sex sketches to the harsh emotional rawness of [illegible] love can do to us.

So buckle up.

6

Gay Thing (2m)

CHARACTERS:

CARL – an attractive a uff gay man.

RYAN – an attractive a ouff straight man.

TIME: Present

SETTING: A Bar.

(*RYAN AND CARL, t ry attractive men, sit at a table in a bar, having drinks.*)

RYAN: Speaking o —

CARL: Who was talking about sex?

RYAN: We were talking about sex.

CARL: No, YOU were talking about sex, not me.

RYAN: No wait, this is serious, I gotta ask you something, we've been friends for like, what?

CARL: Years.

RYAN: Friends for years and you've been gay that whole time, right?

CARL: Oh God, here we go.

RYAN: No really, you've been gay the whole time I've known you, right?

CARL: Not another one of THESE talks.

RYAN: What talks, another one of what kind of talks are you talking about?

CARL: We're at that talk, this is the inevitable talk every gay man eventually has with every straight boy he calls friend, the point where you sit me down for a serious talk to find out how I could ever avoid being straight, how in the world could I not possibly be excited by a woman's vagina, aren't women beautiful, did I ever even give it a shot there might still be hope for me, blah blah blah and excuse me, but no thank you, all right? Let's just nip this in the bud right here and now. NO!

RYAN: That really happens?

CARL: Absolutely, you straight boys cannot seem to fathom why we gay boys don't stand up and cheer at the thought of a naked vagina, it's such a mystery to you. Usually you think we just haven't examined it closely enough, that if we take a really good look and eyeball that twat and we'll go "oh my God, it's beautiful! I can't believe I thought I was gay and missed all this beautiful pussy!" and then we'll dive face-first right into your scary straight world.

RYAN: Wow. So the vagina is not beautiful to you, really?

CARL: Eek, that's all I have to say about the vagina. Eek eek, ick ick. So if that's the talk you wanted to have with me—

RYAN: That's not the talk I was gonna have with you.

CARL: It's not?

RYAN: No, but that was very informative, thank you.

CARL: What kind alk were you talking about?

RYAN: I just want o ask you, you are gay, right? I mean, as long as I've known you u've been gay, but that is indeed what you are, right? A gay man?

CARL: I am a gay n, yes.

RYAN: And that's good for you, being gay, right?

CARL: Being gay been extremely good for me.

RYAN: And you've wn you were gay, since how long?

CARL: Since forev

RYAN: Really?

CARL: Really. Wh e—

RYAN: Was there a point where the gay thing just kicked in, you know, or—

CARL: Ryan, wha hell are you talking about?

RYAN: I'm just wo ing, you know, about ...

CARL: Wondering ut ...

RYAN: Wondering ut myself. Lately.

(Short pause, then CA tarts to laugh.)

CARL: No. No wa o fucking way.

RYAN: What?

CARL: No fucking . You are the straightest man I know.

RYAN: But what if

CARL: No way. N AY you are gay.

RYAN: Hey. I coul gay.

CARL: No way. N king way are you gay.

RYAN: Why could be gay?

CARL: Trust me is Ryan, I know things gay, and gay you are not.

RYAN: But what am gay and just don't know it, what about that?

CARL: You dumb . You would know it!

RYAN: How would now? If I've never done a gay thing, how would I know?

CARL: I don't beli his.

RYAN: What abou at guy, that guy in that book I read last

month for that reading circle thing you hooked me up with, what about him?

CARL: What guy, what book, what the hell are you babbling about?

RYAN: You know, that guy I told you I read about, married, three kids, great job, loved his wife and all of a sudden he finds out he's gay, boom, just like that, never knew he was gay until the plumber kissed him, it was a revelation and he found out he was gay. He found out he was living a lie until he did a gay thing and discovered, hey, I'm gay!

CARL: Okay, I remember you going on about this stupid fucking story, and do you remember what I said about it at the time, I said what a fucking joke. He didn't know he was gay, YET he let the plumber kiss him? Bullshit.

RYAN: But you hear about lots of guys, go out with girls, get married, have kids and then the next thing you know, they're gay.

CARL: So they're confused!

RYAN: Well maybe I'm confused!

CARL: Anybody can be confused but not everybody can be gay, it just doesn't work that way.

RYAN: I don't know. I just don't know.

CARL: What the hell's the matter with you, anyway?

RYAN: I don't know, I just haven't been happy these days.

CARL: Oh, and you think BEING GAY will solve all your problems?

RYAN: I don't know, smart-ass! I'm just wondering about myself, would you give me a fucking break and stop busting my balls?

CARL: I'm sorry man, it's just, you're the last person I expected to hear this from.

RYAN: You know, I'm not always happy with women, you know that, right? In fact, I am quite often very miserable with the women that are in my life.

CARL: I have observed this, yes.

RYAN: And to tell the honest truth. I don't particularly find the naked vagina to be all that appealing, in fact, I will even go so far to say that to me, the vagina is oftentimes quite frightening.

CARL: Of course [illegible], I mean, Goddamn, I don't know how you straight boys do it [illegible] se big red lips and that bushy untrimmed hair, looks too much li[illegible]y alcoholic Uncle Raymond the morning after a Memorial week[illegible] bender. Yeeegggh.

(Short pause.)

CARL: But I've di[illegible]ed.

RYAN: And to be [illegible] more brutally, brutally honest, I sometimes find men to be .. [illegible]newhat attractive.

CARL: Really?

RYAN: Really. So[illegible]nen, not all of them, not the fat hairy ones, but …

CARL: You want t[illegible]k men, you think?

RYAN: I don't kno[illegible]mean, that's the thing, I have never in my life done a gay thing, s[illegible]ave no idea if it's the thing for me or not. I mean, maybe I am, [illegible]be I have all the problems with women because I was meant t[illegible] with men, I mean, I understand men. I am one. I am a man.

CARL: You are de[illegible]ly a man.

RYAN: Do you thi[illegible]n attractive?

CARL: Okay, hold[illegible]op right there, we're not going there.

RYAN: Why not?

CARL: I am very [illegible]erable right now, since Chuck left, you know that, I'm not in [illegible]ition to be toyed with.

RYAN: Carl, I'm r[illegible]ying with you, I'm just curious, that's all, I mean, we're just talki[illegible]ere, right?

CARL: So far, we'[illegible]t talking.

RYAN: I mean, I'[illegible]t curious, that's all, I'm just asking questions. I don't know any[illegible]g about gay taste—

CARL: Gay taste [illegible]tentimes a contradiction in terms, especially when it comes t[illegible]t pain in the ass gay tradition of dressing up in drag. Don't try [illegible] figure out if you're in the "gay taste", you'll make yourself c[illegible]

RYAN: I'm just cu[illegible], I was just wondering if I was considered attractive in the gay se[illegible]f things, just in case. That's it. That's all.

CARL: You are att[illegible]ve.

RYAN: Really?

CARL: Trust me.

RYAN: What in particular about me is attractive in the gay way?

CARL: What are you doing?

RYAN: I'm just talking, we're talking here, right?

CARL: How do I get into these conversations?

RYAN: This is how a person finds out about themselves, isn't it? Asking questions, considering new things and ideas, thoughts, emotions—

CARL: Your ass.

RYAN: My ass?

CARL: Much about you is attractive, but in particular I find that ass of yours to be spectacular.

RYAN: This ass?

CARL: That ass of yours, I could eat that ass of yours all day. Breakfast, lunch and dinner, I could eat that ass until the cows came home, I could.

RYAN: Really?

CARL: Really.

RYAN: Wow. No one's ever said anything like that to me before.

CARL: Hey. You asked, I answered.

RYAN: You know, a woman would never say that kind of thing to me.

CARL: Women don't appreciate the ass, they THINK they do, but they don't. Not like us. When I die, I want to be BURIED in ass, that's how much I love the ass.

RYAN: So. If I were gay, do you think you and me would … you know. Go out?

CARL: You're not gay.

RYAN: What if I was?

CARL: But you're not.

RYAN: What if I am and I just don't know it?

CARL: What if you think you are but really aren't?

RYAN: I guess I won't ever know for sure until …

CARL: Until?

RYAN: Until I try a gay thing, once and for all.

CARL: One gay thing?

RYAN: Just one ga ng, just to find out.

CARL: Just one.

(RYAN leans in slow softly kisses CARL on the mouth. CARL kisses him back passionately. Th ak off the kiss and sit quiet for a moment.

They look at each othe

RYAN: I'm not ga

CARL: You are de ly not gay.

(Short pause.)

CARL: Goddamn straight boys, you do it to me every time. Every fucking time!

THE END

A GAY THING NOTES

ORIGINALLY PROD in 2001 by The Defiant Ones at Manhattan Theatre S as part of the evening entitled CLOSE ENCOUNTERS, feat :

CARL – Yuri Lowenth

RYAN - Chuck M ney

DIRECTED by Joshua s

A couple of great s who nailed this piece.

PRODUCED in 2007 Merely Players as part of OPEN 24 HOURS, featuring:

CARL – Alan Velotta

RYAN – Kevin Roach

DIRECTED by Alan Velotta

Also produced by the All You Can Eat Theatre Company, among many others. I keep seeing productions of it, digital video of performances, on youtube. I could ask that it be taken down, but... eh, let those kids have their fun.

AT LEAST FOR NOW.

7

I end It Is (1m, 1f)

CHARACTERS:

LARA – She's 29 anc autiful, but the clock is ticking and she knows it.

DUDLEY – He's 22, i istic and, like all guys at that age, absolutely certain that he's verything figured out.

SETTING: A weekend e upstate.

TIME: Present.

(LARA COMES STOR G out of the bedroom, DUDLEY close behind

her. LARA is half-dressed and begins to put the rest of her clothes on. DUDLEY is wearing only a T-shirt and boxer shorts.)

LARA: This will NEVER happen again!

DUDLEY: But—

LARA: Promise me.

DUDLEY: But—

LARA: Promise me! Say the words, Dudley, say the WORDS.

DUDLEY: I promise … to love you forever and ever.

(Short pause.)

LARA: Those aren't the RIGHT words, Dudley!

DUDLEY: I know.

LARA: Those AREN'T the WORDS I wanted to HEAR, Dudley!

DUDLEY: I know, Lara, but—

LARA: Those words aren't even CLOSE to the WORDS you should be saying to me RIGHT NOW!

DUDLEY: I know, but—

LARA: THOSE WORDS, those are the words that are fucking us up. It is those particular words that are at the heart of our problem, Dudley, those are the PROBLEM words. Now, I need you to listen to me, right now, because this is very important. Look at me. You can't ever, ever say that to me, ever again. Promise me that you will never speak those words to me, Dudley, please. Promise.

DUDLEY: I can't do that.

LARA: God DAMN it, Dudley!

DUDLEY: I can't and I won't.

LARA: Honey—

DUDLEY: I won't. I'm done pretending.

(Short pause.)

LARA: Why are you trying to ruin this? We got a good thing going here, don't you think? Don't you enjoy our weekends together?

DUDLEY: I do enjoy them, more than anything else in the world.

LARA: Then why are you so bound and determined to fuck the whole thing up?

DUDLEY: Lara, I you.

LARA: Stop it. I'n ng to pretend you didn't say that.

DUDLEY: And I k that you love me.

LARA: You don't l half of what you think you know.

DUDLEY: I feel it I know you feel it.

LARA: You can fe ll you want, you just can't say it.

DUDLEY: Why ca say it?

LARA: Because I c do this then, Dudley, that's why. I can't.

DUDLEY: Why no 's real, you know it's real.

LARA: Well see, ley, here's the thing, if we don't say it, then we don't really v for sure, do we? You can suspect it's real, and I can suspec real, and in the back of our hearts and minds when we're ou ing dinner or holding hands or making love, we can maybe n suspect and pretend that it's real together, we can do tl a safe, unspoken way. We can do that. It's safe, because it m or might not be real. We can pretend it is and we can also pre l that it isn't. That's very important. But once you say the wc once you put it out there, there's no pretending anymore. you say the words it's either real or it's not real.

DUDLEY: So?

LARA: So in ord or me to do this, I need to be able to pretend.

DUDLEY: Pretenc pretend that it is or that it isn't?

(Short pause.)

LARA: I need to b e to pretend that ... it isn't. I have to.

DUDLEY: That's you want me to promise I don't, even when I do.

LARA: You have t mise me.

DUDLEY: I'm tire promising that I don't and won't. I said it. I mean it. It's real.

(Brief pause. LARA)

LARA: Well. It is r

DUDLEY: Where ou going?

LARA: I'm leaving

DUDLEY: But we the whole weekend yet.

LARA: You should have thought about that before you opened your mouth.

DUDLEY: You're leaving, does that mean … are you saying … it's over, everything, the two of us?

LARA: What do you think?

(Short pause.)

DUDLEY: You don't want to go, you don't want to leave me.

LARA: I do a lot of things I don't want to do, Dudley.

(Very brief pause.)

DUDLEY: I'll tell.

LARA: Who are you going to tell?

DUDLEY: Who do you think I'm going to tell?

(LARA lets out a scream.)

LARA: Oh MY GOD, I can't believe this is happening, I am such a Goddamn fucking IDIOT, I should have KNOWN THIS WAS GOING TO HAPPEN! We should have never gone to the gym and worked out together that time, that's what did it, you in those workout tights, me and my endorphin rush. God damn it! I knew it would be a mistake, I knew it! Fucking younger men! FUCK!

DUDLEY: I'm sorry, but I can't let you do this. This is too real to walk away from.

LARA: You are twenty-two years old, Dudley, twenty-two! The sum total of what you know to be real is jack-fucking shit! Goddamn it, why am I such a dumb bitch, why!

DUDLEY: You're not that much older than me.

LARA: The difference between twenty-two and twenty-nine is a lifetime, Dudley.

DUDLEY: You were twenty-two when I met you.

LARA: And like I said, the sum total of what a twenty-two year old knows is jack-fucking shit. This is all my fault.

DUDLEY: Don't leave. Stay with me. Not just tonight or the weekend. Stay forever.

LARA: I can't leave him.

DUDLEY: He doesn't appreciate you. He doesn't treat you right.

LARA: Listen to n can't leave him.

DUDLEY: I don't ‹ he even likes you.

LARA: Listen to vords coming out of my mouth. I can't leave him. I can't and n't. I'm ending this. I should have ended it a long time ago. I sh n't have even let it start. It's my fault.

DUDLEY: You ca id it, you can't.

LARA: I have to, l y.

DUDLEY: No! I'll

LARA: You won't im.

DUDLEY: I swear od I'll tell him, I fucking mean it!

(Brief pause.)

LARA: And what you think he's going to do, Dudley, clap you on the back and s Well hell, thanks for telling me you were fucking my wife, let's a drink?" This is a confrontation you're proposing. He's going angry. He's going to be really angry.

DUDLEY: I can h him angry.

LARA: I don't thi ou're ready for this kind of angry. We're talking anger of biblic oportions here, we're talking the wrath of Moses on the Egypt here. Thunder, lightning, locusts and plague, that's how he's ig to descend on you and me, both of us. That's the reality. He v ever forgive you.

DUDLEY: He'll fo me.

LARA: He's a hus l whose wife you've been having an affair with, he can't forgive y He's my husband, he'll never forgive you.

DUDLEY: He's m ier, he has to forgive me.

(Short pause.)

LARA: He won't. von't forgive you or me.

DUDLEY: He will just tell him that we're in love, real love.

LARA: And that's he won't.

DUDLEY: He will thought about it. He will.

LARA: Dudley.

DUDLEY: What?

LARA: I don't love .

DUDLEY: You do.

LARA: No Dudley on't. I don't love you.

DUDLEY: You do iean that.

LARA: Listen to the words. I said it, now it's out there and it's real. I don't love you.

DUDLEY: You're just pretending. This is one of your safe pretend things.

LARA: It's not pretend.

DUDLEY: You even said that you needed to be able to pretend that it isn't, which means—

LARA: Which means I had an excuse. Listen to me. I don't love you I never did. This was just a fling, a Mrs. Robinson fantasy fling I had because I was bored and lonely. I'm a miserable, sexually unfulfilled woman taking advantage of an attractive younger man. I'm your stepmother, for Christ's sake! If I really cared about you at all I wouldn't have put you in this position. So don't do this. Not for me. I'm not worth it. Telling him is not going to change the fact that I don't love you. I'm sorry. I was pretending that I did because it was fun and felt … good, it felt really good. Pretending to be in love with you was a real rush and thrill, but the reality is that I am not. I'm sorry. I am very sorry.

(Pause as he processes all of that. DUDLEY gets up and slowly walks toward the bedroom door. He stops and looks at her.)

DUDLEY: You should go. Go.

LARA: Honey—

DUDLEY: Don't call me that. *(Short pause.)* I won't tell. I should but … I won't.

LARA: Dudley—

DUDLEY: I'm just going to pretend that this whole thing … never happened. That's what I'm going to do. Pretend.

(DUDLEY slowly exits. LARA puts her head in her hands.)

End of play

PRETEND IT IS NOTES:

THIS WAS another SPONTANEOUS COMBUSTION play at

Manhattan Theatre Sc [illegible] , written in one night, rehearsed the next day, and opened to an [illegible] ence the day after that. I was fortunate in that I had a couple o [illegible] eat actors in it, Christy Klein and Peter Stoll.

THEY WERE FANTA [illegible] . They both later performed it at No Shame Theatre New Y [illegible] City sometime in 2003, as well.

THE PLAY HAD to s [illegible] with the line "This will never happen again" and Moses had [illegible] e mentioned in there somewhere.

8

The Forgiven (1m, 1f)

CHARACTERS:

LARRY – A gay man in his thirties.

JENNY – All American girl, late 20s.

SETTING: Larry's apartment, present.

(LATE ONE NIGHT in LARRY's apartment. JENNY enters the living room carrying a cup of tea and sits primly. LARRY follows her eagerly.)

LARRY: I don't fucking believe it!

JENNY: It's true, I swear to God!

LARRY: When did this happen?

JENNY: Six months ago!

LARRY: I don't fucking believe it!

JENNY: Believe it!

LARRY: And look [illegible] ou! You're sitting there laughing your ass off about it!

JENNY: I am now. [illegible] isn't back then.

LARRY: Why'd yo[illegible] it? Were you drunk?

JENNY: Nope. I w[illegible] ber.

LARRY: Well, it w[illegible] t an accident, you didn't just FALL into his bed, right?

JENNY: Oh no, I [illegible] what I was doing, I was just so pissed at Seth, and I wanted to [illegible] ack at him.

LARRY: But with [illegible] OOMMATE?

JENNY: His BEST [illegible] nd and roommate!

LARRY: Oh my [illegible] D. You and your fiancé's BEST friend. That, in my book, that [illegible] lled getting back at him. I can't believe it, you of all people, Littl[illegible] ss Monogamy. Did you ever tell him?

JENNY: Oh no, I'l[illegible] er tell him.

LARRY: What? If [illegible] never tell him, how does that qualify as getting back at him?

JENNY: I got bac[illegible] t him on a sub-conscious level, he was fooling around with h[illegible] x-girlfriend, he didn't think I knew but I just knew. So when he[illegible] s out of town, I went over, it happened, and I knew that somel[illegible] I had evened the score on a subterranean emotional level.

LARRY: Holy shit. [illegible] s has totally rocked my world.

JENNY: I just had [illegible] ll you, I had to get it off my chest and tell somebody I could tru[illegible] fore the wedding. But this is between us, strictly between us. Th[illegible] my deep dark secret.

LARRY: Just betw[illegible] us girls. I can't believe that you slept with your fiancé's best frien[illegible]

JENNY: Well, I di[illegible] EXACTLY sleep with him.

LARRY: What?

JENNY: I said I di[illegible] exactly sleep with him.

LARRY: Wait a mi[illegible]. You spent the night in his bed?

JENNY: Yes.

LARRY: You were [illegible] ed when this happened?

JENNY: Oh yes.

LARRY: You were naked, in his bed, and can I assume that certain sensitive body parts were being rubbed against other sensitive body parts?

JENNY: You can assume that, yes.

LARRY: So how can you say you didn't EXACTLY sleep with him?

JENNY: Well, we did all that, but we didn't …

LARRY: Fuck?

JENNY: We didn't do that.

LARRY: There was mutual climax?

JENNY: Yes.

LARRY: But no fucking. So what did you do?

JENNY: Umm … oral pleasure.

(Pause.)

LARRY: I don't fucking believe it. Well, well. Hail to the Chief.

JENNY: I didn't want to have sex with him because that would be too cruel to Seth, I thought, and Ray understood.

LARRY: Not have sex with him? You had sex with him.

JENNY: Oh no, I didn't, it's not the same thing.

LARRY: You gave him a blowjob, Jenny, what would you call it?

JENNY: It was just fooling around, it's not real sex, it's not intercourse. Those things don't count.

LARRY: Don't get presidential on me, Jenny. There's a reason it's called oral SEX. Blowjobs might not be the same as fucking, but they are both forms of sexual expression!

JENNY: It's not, it's not, one is serious, the other is not serious.

LARRY: Now you listen to me. You're speaking to a dedicated homosexual, Jenny, and if there's one thing dedicated homosexuals are serious about, it's chugging cock. Blowing a man and blowing him WELL is serious business.

JENNY: Let's not get crude, Larry, that may be how it is for you over on your team, but it's different game on my side. It's just a silly non-serious thing.

LARRY: You put someone's sexual member in your mouth and you really believe that there were no serious sexual connotations involved?

JENNY: That's rig [illegible]

(Pause.)

LARRY: Nobody [illegible] d fucking believe this.

JENNY: You can't [illegible] nybody.

LARRY: Who wou [illegible] elieve me?

JENNY: I'm seriou [illegible] u cannot tell anyone, it has to be our cold hard secret. Seth can [illegible] find out.

LARRY: Well Doll [illegible] there were no serious sexual connotations involved, then what di [illegible] nce does it make?

JENNY: He would [illegible] understand that it wasn't serious, he just wouldn't.

LARRY: Would yo [illegible]

JENNY: I would u [illegible] stand.

LARRY: Oh CO [illegible] N. If you found out Seth got a blowjob from somebody, you [illegible] d FREAK and lose your SHIT all over the place.

JENNY: No I wo [illegible] 't, I wouldn't be happy about it, but I would understand. So [illegible] nes silly things happen during a relationship, and plus, we're n [illegible] arried YET. After marriage, it's different, that's what separates [illegible] om the White House. Marriage is sacred.

LARRY: So tomo [illegible] Seth comes up to you and says he just has to get something o [illegible] s chest before the I DOs. He tells you that a couple months ago [illegible] moment of drunken weakness, he asked for and received a ver [illegible] nd hummer from an equally drunk girl in the bathroom of a b [illegible] st for kicks and giggles, he did that and now he wants your for [illegible] ess. The question. You give it to him?

JENNY: Yes. Yes, I [illegible] ld eventually forgive him.

LARRY: What ab [illegible] er?

JENNY: Who?

LARRY: Her, she, [illegible] the woman on the receiving end of Seth's silliness.

JENNY: Why shou [illegible] forgive her?

LARRY: Why not [illegible] forgive the BLOW-EE, why not forgive the BLOW-ER?!!

JENNY: That's di [illegible] t! I don't know her, I have no reason to forgive her.

LARRY: Let's say you did know her.

JENNY: None of my friends would do that to me.

LARRY: So say someone you knew did that very thing to you.

(Brief pause.)

JENNY: I would forgive her.

LARRY: You would forgive her.

JENNY: I would. I would be hurt but silly things happen. I would forgive her.

LARRY: How about him, would you forgive him?

JENNY: I already told you I would forgive Seth.

LARRY: Not Seth.

JENNY: Then who?

(Short pause as they look at each other.)

JENNY: You DIDN'T.

LARRY: We were drunk.

JENNY: Oh MY GOD! I don't fucking believe this. You're making it up.

LARRY: No. We were drunk. Super Bowl Sunday. Fucking around in the bathroom of a bar while we were taking a piss. He was teasing me, waving his cock at me, daring me to do something about it. So I did.

JENNY: You are a horrible person.

LARRY: Why am I a horrible person?

JENNY: Because that's horrible thing to do to somebody, that's why!

LARRY: You did it! You BLEW his BEST FRIEND!

JENNY: That's different, I did that for balance and justice and it wasn't even that serious!

LARRY: It's a bit more serious now, isn't it?

JENNY: I don't really think we can be friends anymore, Larry.

LARRY: And I guess forgiveness is out of the question.

JENNY: My friends don't take advantage of my husband-to-be like that when he's drunk.

LARRY: He was only drunk the FIRST TIME.

JENNY: What?

LARRY: You heard what I said. There were other head to head

encounters. I expect t will be more. I told you, if there's one thing I'm serious a , it's chugging cock. Especially HIS cock, baby.

JENNY: I can't fuc believe this.

LARRY: If it mak ou feel any better, I think I'm falling in love with him.

JENNY: That do make me feel any better. I will never forgive you for this.

(JENNY exits.)

LARRY: But I ... d oose ... to forgive you.

(LARRY takes a drin n exits.)

LIGHTS FADE

THE FORGIVEN NOT

FIRST PRODUCED by e Defiant Ones at Manhattan Theatre-source, directed by S Zavieh, featuring Anthony Wood and Melissa Picarello.

THIS WAS FIRST PR JCED in 2002 or so, something to that affect. Sam Zavieh, w ad acted in a number of my plays, did a great job directing it a e actors were perfect.

IT STARTS off as a co iece and goes to a dark, clearly unsympathetic place by the pl nd, which Sam and I both found interesting and unexpected

9

Three Times (1m, 1f)

CHARACTERS:

THURBER – A scientist and mathematician.

WINNIE – a professor of literature.

SETTING: Thurber's apartment

TIME: Present

(THURBER STEPS INTO HIS STUDY, *a calm passive look on his face. At a loss for a moment,* THURBER *looks around the room as if seeing it for the very first time.*

Suddenly he bursts out in a frenzy of energy, ripping and tearing things from his desk, shelves and wall [illegible] *ough his movements contain a frenzied fury, the expression on his face is sti* [illegible] *of innocence. He stops in the center of the room, looking at the mess he has* [illegible]

WINNIE enters. TH [illegible] *ER looks over at the doorway where WINNIE has entered and stands look* [illegible] *t him.)*

THURBER: Oh, [illegible] Winifred.

WINNIE: Hello T[illegible]er.

THURBER: Umm [illegible] you can see, I've just experienced one of my very rare emotiona[illegible]bursts.

WINNIE: I can se[illegible]t.

THURBER: Woul[illegible]u like some tea?

WINNIE: Tea wou[illegible]e lovely.

THURBER: *(after* [illegible]*ment)* I … uh … I'm all out of tea it looks like, bad news, I apolo[illegible] I apologize for the mess and disarray—

WINNIE: Thurbe[illegible] all right—

THURBER: Pleas[illegible], have a seat, I just wasn't expecting you quite so quickly.

WINNIE: Thurbe[illegible]

THURBER: Goo[illegible]ws, the good news is that all of your personal effects surviv[illegible]e … outburst quite intact. I have them here in this box, your [illegible]tact lens case and disinfectant, bath oils and incense, bathrobe[illegible]vel, the Winnie the Pooh socks that you, that you …

WINNIE: I love th[illegible]ocks.

THURBER: Yes, [illegible] I knew that. Um, also your blue blouse that you left here last [illegible]ter, your feminine hygiene products, the autographed copy of [illegible]dges To Infinity: The Human Side of Mathematics that I ga[illegible]ou for your birthday, your earrings, one gold necklace, two pai[illegible] paisley panties, one aqua-colored sports bra and last but not le[illegible]ll of your CDs, I arranged them in order alphabetically by artis[illegible]know how you feel about that but I just couldn't help myself.

WINNIE: I can se[illegible]t you went to a lot of effort and I appreciate it.

THURBER: I … [illegible] that … that it was the very least I could do, after all … after all

WINNIE: Yes. It's very kind and sweet of you. Most people would not be so gracious were they to find themselves in your position.

THURBER: Really?

WINNIE: Yes.

THURBER: *(after a moment)* Mother always said I was a bit of an over-achiever.

WINNIE: I think you're a really great person.

(Short pause as they look at each other.)

WINNIE: Thurber?

THURBER: Yes?

WINNIE: Are you … are you going to be all right?

THURBER: Oh yes. Yes, absolutely. No question about it.

WINNIE: You don't … um, I'm very concerned about you.

THURBER: You are? Why?

WINNIE: I worry about you, how you're going to take all this, how it will affect you, I worry so much I can barely breathe sometimes.

THURBER: Winnie, don't worry about me, I … know appearances are a bit off at the moment, but I will be fine, I have no doubts. I've identified the problem and I am set to finding a solution. Don't worry about me, I'm a scientist, that's what I do. I solve problems.

WINNIE: Remember what you once said to me? There are no problems, only—

THURBER: Only probabilities, yes. I remember. Got me, I used a figure of speech that was inappropriate. Good catch. But I feel confident of an early resolution.

WINNIE: It isn't always that simple, Thurber. Life isn't that simple.

THURBER: Sure it is, it's all science, all numbers, all math, all the time. That's life, it all breaks down to numbers, pure and simple, sooner or later. There's always an answer for any question you have and always a question to any answer you have that doesn't have a question attached to it as of yet. It's all a matter of study, work and dissemination. What are you smiling at?

WINNIE: Nothin 've just always liked listening to you. Talking with you has a 's, from the very beginning, been an electric experience. So wh ve you discovered so far?

THURBER: Well. ere's just a WEALTH of information on this issue, thousands thousands of books, I've managed to gather some of the be m the best in the field. Let's see, we have HEALING & HELPI BROKEN RELATIONSHIPS – LOVE YOURSELF BEF E ANYONE ELSE – LETTING GO, SPLITTING AMICA IN AMERICAN SOCIETY - HEARTS BROKEN, HEARTS RE - LOOK AT THE BRIGHT SIDE, SHE'S GONE – CO G UP FOR AIR, LIFE AFTER LOVE – KICK THE BITCH THE CURB, A SURVIVIORS GUIDE FOR HOMEBOYS L IN LOVE– BREAKING UP IS HARD TO DO, SO DO I ST – STITCHES, REPAIRING THE DAMAGE AFTER S S GONE – and finally, THE IDIOT'S GUIDE TO GETTI VER HER. These are just a few of the titles.

WINNIE: My. Ha ey been of any help?

THURBER: Actu no. But it is a start, I have to narrow down the field some m but it's simply a matter of time. I can do it. I can do it.

WINNIE: I know. worry about you.

(Short pause.)

THURBER: It's n fling, is it?

WINNIE: No. No, not.

THURBER: I tho not, I'd hoped ... but I thought not. So but this is certain, isn For the record, as an absolute certainty, our romantic relations s over. Correct?

WINNIE: Yes.

THURBER: Ah. I

WINNIE: Thurbe ou are, quite possibly, one of the most fascinating, loving an lliant men I have ever known. Ever day, every moment I spen h you was like an exotic adventure. I'd never met anyone tha ved the world quite as you do, and when I'm not with you or a o talk to you on the phone I miss you so terribly. I miss sharing ngs with you. You touch me in places in my soul and my life that no one does or ever has. I've never loved anyone like you before.

THURBER: *(after a moment)* This is quite an unusual way of breaking up with me.

WINNIE: I just wanted you to know that I love you.

THURBER: *(thumbing through the books)* I mean, this wasn't covered in any of the literature.

WINNIE: Thurber. Thurber!

THURBER: Yes?

WINNIE: I never wanted to hurt you, Thurber.

THURBER: Well, it's ... you didn't ... it ... this is just a setback, you know, an unfortunate event, but it's not a cancer or a terminal brain lesion, it's an evolving relationship, it happens, it happens, untold numbers of people all over the country go through this kind of thing everyday and survive it, according to the books, anyway. It happens, it's a break-up, it's not a hurricane.

WINNIE: *(looking around the room)* It's not?

THURBER: Well, visible evidence aside, it's not a tropical storm that kills people, it's a breakup. It's difficult but percentage-wise rarely fatal according to the charts and graphs. People survive them. The numbers are on our side.

WINNIE: I don't care about the numbers, I care about you, I want you to be all right after this.

THURBER: I'll be all right, I'm telling you, the numbers don't lie, math is on our side—

WINNIE: I don't care about the numbers, I don't care about math, there's a lot more to life than math.

THURBER: More to life than MATH? What are you talking about? There is nothing more, that's what LIFE is! Science is the process of examination and breaking down of systems and MATH is the tool used to do so and the only poetic language CAPABLE of EXPRESSING the TRUTHS DISCOVERED THEREIN – it's the ONE way all cultures communicate, the ONE thing we ALL have in COMMON, the ONE TRUE ABSOLUTE IN LIFE AND THERE ISN'T ANYTHING MORE THAN THAT! THERE IS NOTHING ELSE! THERE IS NOTHING ELSE!

(Short pause as THU R and WINNIE look at each other.)

THURBER: Wini I'm sorry.

WINNIE: I'm sorr). I didn't mean to upset you. I caused yet another very rare outb of emotion.

THURBER: You ight, that's TWO in one day, this is unprecedented, I have nake a note of this in my logbook. What are you smiling at?

WINNIE: Nothing … I was just remembering the first time we … made love. You re so ... enthusiastic. The first emotional outburst out of you I'c iessed.

THURBER: Yes. nember. I hadn't been that excited about anything since I first st l studying Calculus.

WINNIE: You wer even all that INTERESTED in sex in the beginning, I'd never m man like that, you said, you actually said, "all that effort and exe for a two second physical contraction? A waste of time better nt in study and vibrant conversation," That's what you said.

THURBER: I did i't I?

WINNIE: Then w I actually GOT you into bed and did the deed, you were like a boy at Christmas, jumping for joy, "Let's do it again, let's do it a !"

THURBER: I did 'as, I had miscalculated, I failed to figure in the unknown factor hared sensuality and thus it's affect upon shared intimate physic lations. I erred.

WINNIE: You we mping up and down on the bed, going "I get it, I get it, now I ge at all the excitement was about!"

THURBER: Like ic when the apple fell from the tree on his head.

WINNIE: You wer adorable.

(Short pause.)

THURBER: So, u o if all of what you've told me thus far is fact, why … why …

WINNIE: Why an aving you for Richard?

THURBER: That

WINNIE: Well. I' ot going to pretend he's as smart as you are, or as interesting o n as cute. He's not any of the things that you are. But there's something about him that draws me, makes me want to touch him, feel him and it pulls me, magnetically. I feel a pull from him physically that I don't feel from you, or anyone else. I fought it for quite some time, because I do love you and want to be with you. But I can't. I can't, I think of him, too. He pulls at me. I hoped he could only be a fling, I hoped maybe I could get him out of my system, but I couldn't. I can't. He's not the man you are, and I wish, wish desperately that he were. He may not the man you are, but he may be the man for me. The man I will love and live with the rest of my life. That may not make sense, but it is what it is. I'm sorry Thurber. I'm really, really sorry.

THURBER: I see.

WINNIE: I keep having this silly dream, of the three of us someday becoming friends, sitting on a porch sipping tea and talking, maybe when we're all retired, and the dream makes me so happy. But I know it's just a dream, I know how you feel about him, and I understand. I just wanted you to know how I felt about him. And you.

THURBER: I understand. Pulled, drawn, almost magnetically.

WINNIE: I just want you to be happy, and someday someone will make you happy.

THURBER: Pulled.

WINNIE: Happier than I ever could.

THURBER: Wait a minute, I got it! I got it!

(THURBER takes out his notepad and scribbles on it furiously. He shows it to WINNIE proudly.)

WINNIE: What is it?

THURBER: The answer! In 1831 Michael Faraday proved with a series of simple experiments that, and this is the historic statement – whenever a magnetic force increases or decreases, it produces electricity; the faster it increases or decreases, the more electricity it produces. Get it?

WINNIE: What?

THURBER: The two of us, you and I, we had an electric connection because we were drawn to each other, and electricity can be a good thing, it gives us light and power and illuminates. But it's also a dangerous entit ectricity, they still use it to kill people in certain barbaric states u have to be careful with it. Now as our magnetic attraction g and increased, so did the electricity it produced and the m hat was illuminated. But suddenly you found yourself drawn another, and the magnetic force of our relationship decreased a startling rate, decreased faster than it increased. The electri ılse produced from that decrease, that's what it is, that's what c d it.

WINNIE: Caused t?

THURBER: Caus .. caused the pain. It's right here in the formula, right down ir l hard true math. Which means … which means …

WINNIE: Means ?

THURBER: Noth It means I still have more work ahead of me. I need to get to wc

WINNIE: Wait, wa hurber.

THURBER: Wha

WINNIE: I'm not entist or mathematician. But I remember another thing you told for every action ...

THURBER: Ther n equal and opposite reaction, yes.

WINNIE: We fee d because we have the capacity to feel good. You feel horrible ause we felt …

THURBER: Grea

WINNIE: And I l horrible now, Thurber, so horrible because at how this tu d out, what I've done to you, how much I'll miss the little thing hared with you, so horrible that you have no idea.

THURBER: I hav retty good idea.

WINNIE: But I wo do it again, because the joy I got out of it was worth the pain. A know there is more out there waiting for me. And for you. The so much happiness out there waiting for you, there is, I know tl is and I know it without a formula. Some day, I wish, wish, wish SH we can be friends again. I really do. I do.

(Short pause.)

WINNIE: I have t y good-bye now, before I start having an

emotional outburst of my own. I just wanted to tell you how special you are to me.

(WINNIE moves to him and kisses him softly.)

WINNIE: Good-bye Thurber.

THURBER: Good-bye Winifred.

(WINNIE picks up the box and leaves as quickly as she can. THURBER looks dazed for a moment, then brings his finger up to his eye, feeling the moisture gathering there. He tastes it.)

THURBER: Look at that. Three times. Three times in one day.

THE END

THREE TIMES NOTES:

FIRST PRODUCED at Manhattan Theatre Source in 2000, featuring Mahlon Stewart and Luisa Battista, directed by the author.

LATER PRODUCED by Common Factor in 2002 at the D2 theatre with Sam Zavieh and Heather Dilly, directed by Karina Miller.

ALSO PRODUCED by the All You Can Eat Theatre Company, among others.

PERSONAL NOTE, though this is an early work of mine, it's specifically one of the first that moved away from just sex and dick jokes and into more personal territory, that of loss. It very nearly made my top five. This would be right up there.

10

News (1m, 1 f)

CHARACTERS:

DARYL – A very calr ave It To Beaver type of husband who remains calm in the fa everything … except one thing.

MERYL – Daryl's wife, itable and with impulse control issues.

SETTING: Their living n.

(DARYL SITS in his loun air reading the evening paper.

Special note, DARY he very picture of zen calm and patience until the very end, but once the belt off, look out.

DARYL's wife MER ters.)

DARYL: Meryl, w have you been? You didn't come home last night.

MERYL: Daryl, I have a confession to make.

DARYL: You do?

MERYL: It's a rather upsetting confession.

DARYL: What is it, Meryl?

MERYL

It's going to make you angry.

DARYL: It's going to make me angry?

MERYL: Really angry. Really, REALLY ANGRY. You're going to be furious. You're going to be livid with rage, you're going to be homicidally pissed off, you are going be incredibly, incredibly angry to a degree that the actual temperature in this room will rise once you hear what I have done, that's how angry you are going to get.

DARYL: Wow. That's pretty angry.

MERYL: But I can't keep it to myself anymore, I have to brave the violence of your temper and confess what I have done.

DARYL: Goodness. Maybe I should take my Zoloft now as opposed to later?

MERYL: No, no, I can't wait any more. I must confess. I have to tell you. Daryl. I'm leaving you.

DARYL: Leaving me? But why?

MERYL: It's a long story. I've been cheating on you.

DARYL: Cheating on me? With who?

MERYL: With your boss at work.

DARYL: Oh.

MERYL: And your co-worker Ben.

DARYL: Oh.

MERYL: And his secretary.

DARYL: Oh.

MERYL: And his secretary's husband.

DARYL: Ah.

MERYL: And his secretary's brother. All at the same time.

DARYL: Hmmm.

MERYL: We filmed it, the orgy. And they showed it at the last office Christmas party after you passed out. We even had popcorn.

DARYL: Popcorn.

MERYL: We used real butter on the popcorn, too, I know, we're

terrible people. And the party, I had sex with the building
custodian just because omplimented me on my thighs. Basically,
I've had sex with near eryone you see while you're at work. And
your brother. And also boy that delivers the morning paper.

DARYL: The pape ? But he's only thirteen.

MERYL: Fourteen just turned fourteen. But before you lose
complete control, ther ore.

DARYL: More?

MERYL: I wrecke ur car, your treasured Jaguar, I got high
and totaled it last ni Actually, that's not true, although I was
high, I wasn't driving. I had to let the paperboy drive, he's been
dying to drive it and mised him that once he got his learner's
permit I would let hin ad to let him drive the car otherwise he
was going to tell his r that he and I were showering together
every afternoon. So h s driving and while he was driving I was
… servicing him, I gu ou could say, servicing him orally, and he
got so excited during s ervicing that he ran right into the back of
a school bus. That's w didn't come home last night, I was in jail
for molesting a minor. kid's still in the hospital in critical condi-
tion. But there's more. ortgaged the house and sold your motor-
cycle in order to mak . I plan on skipping bail, so start looking
for another place to liv h, that reminds me, you're flat broke.

DARYL: Broke?

MERYL: You're b I emptied your savings accounts, cashed
in all the CD's and and emptied your 401K. I did this last
week, unfortunately, b I knew I was going to need bail money. I
spent the money on x treatments for my thighs, they really
needed the work, and ne rest on heroin, I've recently developed
something of a habit, the way you need to get an HIV test, I
forgot to tell you.

DARYL: HIV?

MERYL: There's . Your dog Skippy didn't run away, I had
him put to sleep, I did ke the way he was looking at me so I had
him put him down. A lly, that's not true, I didn't have him put
down, it costs a lot of ney to put a dog to sleep, like about two
hundred bucks, so inst gave him to some farmer who killed him

by hitting him over the head with a shovel. That way only costs five bucks. Oh, that reminds me, your mother didn't pass away peacefully in her sleep at the rest home. I smothered her with a pillow and then sold all of her vital organs on the black market. Also, I've been lying to you, my real name isn't Meryl, my real name is Mayreagonnoyustof and I'm here illegally from Lebanon.

(Brief pause as DARYL lowers his head and purses his lips He sighs.)

DARYL: Well Meryl, I have to say that I am very, very disappointed in you.

MERYL: I know, I know, you have every right to be furious with me.

DARYL: Well. I am pretty upset by all this. But I think that you've seen the error of your ways and appear to be genuinely contrite so … why don't we just let bygones be bygones?

(DARYL brings his paper back up.)

MERYL: I'm afraid that there's more bad news.

DARYL: More bad news?

MERYL: With uh … with everything that's been happening, I … I haven't … uh … I haven't paid the cable bill in quite awhile. Months and months.

(DARYL lowers his paper. MERYL hides her face in her hands.)

DARYL: You don't mean …

MERYL: It's true. They've cancelled our subscription.

(Very brief pause. DARYL slams his paper down on the floor.)

DARYL: Fuck! Motherfuck! SHIT!

MERYL: I'm sorry! I'm sorry! I'm sorry!

(DARYL stands and takes off his belt, looping it around his hand.)

DARYL

Now you've gone too far.

(MERYL screams.)

Blackout

BAD NEWS NOTES:

13

le Details (2m)

CHARACTERS:

BILL – a beer-drinking ılar type of guy.

BOB - BILL'S best frier lso a beer-drinking regular guy.

TIME: Present

SETTING: Bill's apartn

(BILL AND BOB are dri beer and watching TV.)

BILL: Speakin' of ails, Bobby-boy, there's somethin' I gotta tell ya.

BOB: What is it?

BILL: I like girls.

BOB: Atta-boy, Big Bill.

BILL: I like 'em a LOT. I LOVE WOMEN!

BOB: WOMEN YOU LOVE!

BILL: All types of females, all shapes, all sizes—

BOB: Females, skinny, fat, short or tall—

BILL: I love 'em Bobby-boy, I love 'em all.

BOB: Yep. Yep. Yep.

(Brief pause.)

BILL: I just felt the need to establish that with you, Bobby my boy, as a roommate and friend, I felt the need to express my, you know …

BOB: Hey, I understand—

BILL: My VALUES, my hierarchy of DESIRES, the crown at the tippy-top of my totem-pole of NEEDS. I just had to say it out loud.

BOB: I'm with you, Big Bill, I'm with you all the WAY!

BILL: I mean, we've known each other, how long?

BOB: YEARS. We've been friends for YEARS!

BILL: And we know each other pretty well.

BOB: Oh yeah.

BILL: And we been roommates now for—

BOB: Three big days.

BILL: Three big days. So the POINT to all this, what I'm leadin' up to, Bobby my buddy, Bobby my best friend, now we live together, now we share space and down-time with each other, now even more intimate little details of our lives are going to pop up and make themselves known to one another, 'cause that happens—

BOB: Yep, that happens, that happens.

BILL: Happens as a PART of the NEW ROOMMATE process, and we should be prepared, we should be READY for it—

BOB: Ready and prepared!

BILL: So that we are not caught unawares and with our pants down at any sudden surprises, so that when a dark secret corner of one of our personalities is unexpectedly brought to light, we can go AHA!

BOB: AHA!

BILL: I knew that gonna happen, I knew that I would eventually discover someth unexpected about my old friend and new roommate that I woul t have believed had I not seen it with my own eyes, but here it see it, AHA, and I was prepared for it, because I know these gs happen when you're sharing intimate space for the first tim all a part of the NEW ROOMMATE process, you hear what sayin?

BOB: Loud and cl 'm readin' you loud and clear.

BILL: And we don nt these little DETAILS to fuck us up. So to cut to the chase, th tom line, Bobby my boy, in honor of this process and our frien , to get things off on the right foot, I wanted to look you e eye, and explain this very important fundamental facet of rsonality.

BOB: Which is?

BILL: I LIKE GIR

BOB: That's great. 's just great.

BILL: I just had to t.

BOB: I always kne at about you, but it's comforting to hear it out loud and clear.

BILL: I know, Bo know, and it is the ONE thing that you should keep in mind a times, lest the … little details of my daily life begin to sow seeds oubt in your mind, REMEMBER what I said to you at the very nning. I like girls.

BOB: You like girl l, I have a confession to make to you as a new roommate and ol nd.

BILL: What is it, B what is it?

BOB: I like girls to

BILL: THAT'S M OY!

BOB: I like 'em a le lot. I try and be with 'em as much as humanly possible. Wh ey let me. I think that girls—

BILL: Women.

BOB: Chicks.

BILL: Broads.

BOB: Tomatoes.

BILL: Babes

BOB: Female species, whatever, I think they're just … great.

BILL: Me too, Bobby-boy, me too. I'm glad we're havin' this talk.

(Brief pause.)

BOB: In fact, I like EVERYTHING about them! Completely EVERYTHING!

BILL: I don't just LIKE everything, Bobby-boy, I LOVE everything about women.

BOB: Oh yeah, oh yeah.

BILL: The way they walk, the way they talk—

BOB: Everything!

BILL: The way they dress—

BOB: The whole kit and kadoodle!

BILL: Everything. From the soft dusk-colored evening gowns complete with gloves and a feathered fan to rowdy gingham skirts and checkered blouses, I … I … I love it all.

BOB: You do. You do. You do.

BILL: I share this with you knowing that the thought foremost in your mind is—

BOB: You love girls.

BILL: I do, I do. Don't let the little details distract you from that basic belief.

BOB: I won't, I won't.

BILL: So if by accident, you happen to stumble across something in one of my drawers, for example, something like …

BOB: Like a black lace negligee with silk stockings and garters.

BILL: Something like that, yeah, or maybe something like …

BOB: Like little polka-dotted panties with the days of the week sewn in, one for each day.

BILL: Yeah, yeah, or maybe even …

BOB: Dozens of pairs of leather high-heeled pumps in various colors.

BILL: Stuff like that, yeah, if you were stumble across something like that ...

BOB: Accidentally.

BILL: Accidentally, your reaction, your instincts would be to …

BOB: Pay it no mi [illegible]

BILL: That's my b [illegible] ecause deep in your heart, you know …

BOB: You like girl [illegible]

BILL: That's right [illegible] e girls. And the details, the little details in life, you shouldn't even [illegible] k about them, 'cause all they can do …

BOB: Is fuck every [illegible] g up.

BILL: Fuck every [illegible] g up. Very good. I'm glad we had this talk, Bobby.

BOB: Me too, Bill [illegible] too. Little details, they're a real bitch.

(They both chuckle an [illegible] e a big drink of their beers.)

LIGHTS FADE

LITTLE DETAILS NOT [illegible]

PREMIERED in 2002 [illegible] Manhattan Theatre Source as part of TASTY, an evening o [illegible] ort plays, featuring Josh Casaubon and Sam Zavieh, directed b [illegible] e author.

JUST A FUN, foolish p [illegible] that still makes me laugh.

14

The Dance (1 m, 1 f)

CHARACTERS:

JANE – A club girl in her 20s.

LEON – A Frenchman around the same age.

SETTING: A club.

(LEON STANDS WITH A DRINK, *listening to music. JANE crosses over to him.)*

JANE: Hi, my name is Jane.

LEON: Hello. I am Leon.

JANE: Leo?

LEON: Leon. Leon.

JANE: Okay. Where are you from, are you Italian?

LEON: French. I'ı ench.

JANE: French. Ok rench works, good. Cool. I'm American.

LEON: I got that.

(Brief pause. JANE at him, up and down.)

JANE: Okay then. Let's get out of here, shall we?

LEON: Sorry?

JANE: Let's go, le ogie, it's loud and obnoxious here. Let's go, let's get out.

LEON: To go whe

JANE: How about place?

LEON: My place?

JANE: We can go y place, but if yours is closer …

LEON: You want to my place?

JANE: All right, al it. My place then. Come on.

LEON: Wait, wait. y are we going to your place?

JANE: Leon, pay ition. We've met, we've exchanged pleas-antries, now we're goi omewhere and swap bodily fluids. That's how it works. Come o

LEON: Wait. Bod ds?

JANE: Intercourse ual intercourse, we are going somewhere close and quiet to hu each other, jump each other, do the wild ting, make Mr. Slapp ppy, do the naked tango, make the beast with two backs, slip i omebody comfortable, WE are GOING fuck each other's brai it, I'm assuming you know what at least one of those phrases it, right? Because it's ten-thirty, I have to work in the morning, pect to be in mid-orgasm by eleven and asleep by eleven-thirty

LEON: You want ve sex with me?

JANE: Uh … YE hy do you think I've been talking to you for all this time? I t ht this was supposed to be a universal language or somethin ne note, I expect good hygiene so if you haven't showered yet y then you will before you get into bed with me and also, I ex and demand oral gratification, I get mine and then you get you at's how it works, it's called trickle-down economics, okay? Go)rop your socks and grab your cock, it's time to hit the road, Ja

LEON: My name's not Jack, and what makes you think I want to have sex with you?

JANE: What?

LEON: What makes you think I want to have sex with you?

JANE: What is this, some kind of joke? Of course you want to have sex with me. Look at me! I'm a hot babe. Even gay men want my body. Oh God. You're gay?

LEON: No, I am not gay.

JANE: Then why wouldn't you want me? I'm attractive, don't try and tell me that I'm not attractive, because I am. I could have any man in here if I wanted, I KNOW I've got a hot bod.

LEON: It's true that you are attractive, but—

JANE: Then what's the problem here, Jean-Claude? We're are wasting some serious WHAM-BAM time here with the chatter.

LEON: Listen. I'm not about to run off with some woman I just met. You're very attractive but I just don't do that.

JANE: Are you serious?

LEON: I'm sorry, but I don't do that kind of thing.

JANE: Then what the fuck are you doing in THIS place?

LEON: I just come for the music.

JANE: Oh give me a fucking break, nobody comes here for the music! This place is a major meat market, EVERY person in this bar is here to hook up. Look, look, he's here to fuck, she's here to fuck, and him, and her and him and especially her, look at the outfit, would a normal person wear that to church? The back of her dress is cut all the way down to the middle of her ass, the only reason to wear something like that is to get fucked, end of story. That is why everyone is here!

LEON: Not me.

JANE: What kind of freak are you? I can't believe you turned me down. I can't believe it. I shot down three guys on my over to see you just to get rejected by you, this is un-fucking-believable. NOT only that, you're supposed to be FRENCH!

LEON: What does that have to do with anything?

JANE: Come on, the French INVENTED weird kinky sex stuff, you're French and I expected BETTER.

LEON: We didn't [illegible] it the kinky sex stuff—

JANE: Uh, excuse [illegible], but what about the Marquis de Sade, French kissing, French [illegible] lers—

LEON: Wait a mi [illegible] —

JANE: The Louvre [illegible]

LEON: The Louv [illegible] a museum!

JANE: With a ver [illegible] ual name! With lots of naked paintings and naked statues and [illegible] round sexual artifacts.

LEON: The Fren [illegible] ave TASTE, which is more than you can say.

JANE: And WH [illegible] we're on the subject of all things FRENCH, why are yo [illegible] ople so rude? I was kind enough to come over here, introduce [illegible] lf, offer up my body and you have the nerve to sniff and re [illegible] me? It is true what they say about the French then, isn't it? ([illegible] ey, I'm French and from France, I'm too cool for anyone else in [illegible] room. You from France? Oh, you're not from France, then you [illegible] fuck off, hey, I'm French and I'm too cool for words.

LEON: Now TH [illegible] funny! Americans INVENTED rudeness! Let me ask you [illegible], why do YOU people always have to announce everything [illegible] loud fast empty talk like a TV commercial? Hey I'm Americ [illegible] ook what I'm doing over here, Hey I'm American, look what [illegible] scovered over there. Hey, I'm American from America, land of [illegible] free and I know you want to be just like me, what do you mea [illegible] u don't speak English, doesn't everyone over here speak Englis [illegible] hat do you mean, you don't serve French fries here, this is Fran [illegible] sn't it? But I'm from America, the most important place in the [illegible] ld, you have to listen to me, I don't care if you don't speak Englis [illegible] u have to listen to me! Oh, look at that, they won't listen to me [illegible] n though I'm from America, these people are so rude. I got ne [illegible] or you, if someone doesn't speak your language, talking LO [illegible] R doesn't make them understand you ANY BETTER!

JANE: Laugh it u [illegible] ut if it wasn't for us RUDE Americans, you'd be speaking GE [illegible] N!

LEON: You never heard of a little thing called the French Resistance?!

JANE: I'm feeling it RIGHT NOW!

(Short pause.)

LEON: Look Jane, this is silly and stupid. You are a very attractive woman and of course I am drawn to you. But I can see that you only want one night, and one night only, and that I cannot give that to you.

JANE: Why not?

LEON: What it comes down to is this. What the French, and myself, have to offer up to the world of sexual culture, is something that cannot be contained in only one night of carnal celebration. That is why I must refuse you. In America you celebrate the assembly-line. Cars keep coming down the line and you keep screwing on the tires, one after another. That is what all these people here are, factory workers tending to their bodies, and that's hard and cold, that's not what I have to offer. Not in one night. Given time, I could offer you something else entirely.

JANE: Like what?

LEON: Passion. Romance. Taste. It's begins like this—

(He leans down and kisses her hand.)

LEON: With a kiss. And when the kiss is planted correctly, with the exact amount of passion and tenderness, it can blossom fully. But it takes more than one night to bloom, it can demand the entire year or more from you to fully flower. Once it does, it opens into something that tastes so lovely and beautiful, it can take your breath away.

(Short pause.)

JANE: My name's not really Jane.

LEON: Really.

JANE: That's just a name I use in the clubs.

LEON: I thought so.

JANE: My real name is Beatrice.

LEON: How do you do, Beatrice?

(The song, "Deep Inside" by Third Eye Blind, begins to play.)

JANE: I hate this song.

LEON: I don't kn very well.
(Brief pause.)
JANE: Would you o dance?
(Very brief pause.)
LEON: Absolutel
(They begin to dance, y.)
End of play.

THE DANCE NOTES:

PREMIERED at Surf ty in 2001, featuring Franck Raharinosy and Carrie Keranen. I produced in 2002 at Manhattan Theatre Source featuring Fran harinosy and Liani Riccardi.

I WROTE this specific or Franck, I was friends with his manager at the time.

THERE WAS an even f plays going up at Surf Reality and his manager asked me to e a couple things for him, as that he was French and it was diffi o find material for him. This was one.

SURF REALITY WAS great theatre on the lower east side that sadly does not exist an ger, like many others of its kind (NADA, Manhattan Theatre e, etc) having been priced out. In fact, that evening was one last shows in that space, if I recall.

THAT'S THE THEATR , man.

15

The Taste (1m, 1f)

CHARACTERS:

JON – A nice, normal guy, the exact kind of guy that woman always say they want to date but almost never do.

TAMI – A businesswoman in charge of everything whose life is falling apart.

SETTING: A bus stop.

(JON STANDS AT BUS STOP, with a briefcase and a newspaper.

TAMI walks up, carrying a suitcase. She drops it angrily and crosses her arms.

Her cell phone rings. She answers it.)

TAMI: What? Wh ... you want? Stop calling me.

(She hangs up. It rings ... n. She answers.)

TAMI: What? I sa ... p calling me.

(She hangs up. It rings ... n and she answers.)

TAMI: What? Ca ... sk you something? Let me ask you something, shut up, I'm ask ... ou something. Are you ready? Okay, here it is. What part of stop ... ing me did you NOT understand? What? No, I am not coming ... and yes, I do mean it. I'm GONE, baby, I'M HISTORY! Well ... be you should have thought about that before you stuck your ... gue up the crack of that girl's ass! Now stop fucking calling m...

(She hangs up. She lo... JON, who is staring at her.)

TAMI: Can I HEL... u with something?

(JON shakes his hea... tely and goes back to his paper. TAMI's phone rings again and she answe...

TAMI: What?! Fu... f ASSHOLE!

(She hangs up and sta... here, steaming mad.)

(It rings again and sh... vers it.)

TAMI: STOP C... ING ME YOU LYING CHEATING SHIT-EATING MO... R-FUCKING PEDOPHILE PRICK! ASSHOLE ASSHOL... SHOLE! *(She hangs up.)* That should take care of him for awhile.

JON: May I sugge...

TAMI: What?

JON: Could I poss... make a suggestion?

TAMI: About wha...

JON: Perhaps, if y... on't wish to speak to him, it might be best if you TURNED your ... ne off.

TAMI: Well, PE... PS it ain't none of your God-damned business, now is it?

JON: If I have to ... d here and listen to it, than I would say that it is.

(Brief pause.)

TAMI: I can't tur... phone off, I'm waiting for my mother to call me back.

JON: Well then. I guess that's there's nothing we can do.

(TAMI's phone rings.)

TAMI: Jesus Christ. I'm sorry. Really. *(She answers.)* Would you stop FUCKING calling me, it is SO over, it is dead and fucking buried. Stop calling me you worthless piece of beetle shit!

(She hangs up.)

JON: Beetle-shit?

TAMI: I'm running out of nasty shit to call him. *(TAMI's phone rings.)* God-DAMN IT. Wait, I know what to do. *(She rummages in her purse and comes out with a whistle.)* He gave this to me, just in case anybody tried to bother me. *(She answers the phone.)* Hi Honey. *(She then blows the whistle into the phone as loud as she can and then hangs up.)* There. It should be about an hour before he gets his hearing back. I'm sorry for all the fuss, really. I'm sorry I was rude earlier.

JON: Don't worry about it. You want me to flag a taxi for you?

TAMI: I have a car service coming to pick me up. Unless you need one?

JON: No, I'm waiting for the bus, I usually take the bus home from work.

TAMI: You work around here?

JON: Yeah.

TAMI: What do you do, you're not a Goddamned actor, are you?

JON: Uh, no. I work at Digi-Corp, I'm a systems analyst. Computers.

TAMI: Thank God you're not a fucking actor, I swear if I ever talk to another actor ever again in my life, I'm going to kill myself.

JON: So you got a place to stay, you're going to stay with your mother?

TAMI: What? Oh no. I'm going to my condo on the west side. My mother, well, I had promised her when we got married that if anything happened between us that I would let her handle the divorce. She's an attorney and she hated his ass from day one.

JON: So you're married, then.

TAMI: Not for much fucking longer. You married?

JON: I'm afraid nc

TAMI: You're luck ıank God for Mom, she insisted on a pre-nup and thank Christ hat. And I even argued with her about it for weeks, I said, we'r love, Ma, we ain't gonna divorce, this is some forever shit. She if we don't divorce then it shouldn't be a problem, just make hi gn the papers and shut up about it. And he PUT it off for week :e he was hoping we'd forget about it. Not my mother, no sir. She on the phone every fucking day, after his ass. Fuck! Thank you na! See, I got all the money, I got a job and a career, I take ca business, he don't have shit and now that he's fucked this up, he t getting a God-damned dime out of me. Penniless free-loading :h! That's a good one, I gotta remember that one if he calls aga God, why did I ever get mixed up with an actor, fucking actors! (ıis, I was in Miami, I was supposed to get back tomorrow, but w sed the deal a day early and so I took the morning flight to com me and surprise my baby, right? I didn't know anything funny going on, shit, I trusted his ass up until about twenty minutes . So I get home, complete with presents for him, I'm smelling t and looking good, I walk in the door of MY house, go into M lroom, and there he is right there, on MY bed, naked as a jaybir icking his tongue up the ass of a girl that couldn't be more tha xteen, seventeen years old! I catch him doing this, and do yo ıow what he has the BALLS to try and tell me?

JON: What?

TAMI: He tries tell me that the two of them are REHEARSING some .e from a play!

JON: Really?

TAMI: No shit. G e fuck out of here, what kind of play is it where you have to sh your tongue up somebody's ass? Is it an audition for Last Tan n Paris, the musical? He didn't have an answer for that, the fu

JON: What'd you ıen?

TAMI: What else yelled, I screamed, I threw shit, lamps, chairs, anything I cou et my hands on I threw at the both of them. Let me tell you something, there was some furniture moving in that house. Fuck! I can't fucking believe this has happened to me! *(Her phone rings again. She answers it.)* I'm not believing you got the balls to call me after I told you NOT to, you fucking freeloading …

JON: Leech.

TAMI: Leech. Leech! You motherfucking, cock-sucking—

JON: Ass-licker, call him an ass-licker.

TAMI: Ass-licking child-molesting piss-poor George Clooney wanna-be with no talent, no brains and no fucking DECENCY OR RESPECT FOR THE SANCTITY OF MARRIAGE! ASS-LICKER ASS-LICKER ASS-LICKER!!! *(She hangs up.)* Thank you.

JON: You're welcome.

(Brief pause. TAMI puts her hand over her face. Her shoulders start to shake.)

JON: Hey. Hey, are you going to be all right?

TAMI: It's just … I didn't see this coming, you know? Up until twenty minutes ago I thought I had everything pretty well figured out. I got a great job, I got money, family, couple condos and a house, I had a husband I loved and who I thought loved me, we were planning to have a family and … in the space of a couple minutes it all fell apart. Three years with that man, a man I thought I knew pretty well, and it turns out I didn't know the first fucking thing.

JON: I'm sorry.

TAMI: I had everything mapped out, retire at thirty-five, manage my portfolio and play house, have three kids, maybe four, they all go to private schools, he gets a supporting role on a sitcom or some simple shit like that, finally makes some of his own money, we get to go to all the award shows, pictures taken of us hand in hand, both of us and our house on the cover of Good Housekeeping, kids go to college, we travel the world, our kids have lots of kids and then the next thing you know, both of us are ninety years old, still holding hands, still making hot love and so comfortable with each other we never have to say anything. I had it all mapped out, I knew everything that was going to be anything in my life, and in just a couple of minutes, ju ke that … *(TAMI snaps her fingers.)* Just like that, and now I don't h any idea what's going to happen to me.

(Brief pause. JON ha TAMI a handkerchief.)

JON: My grandmo ; she was a great lady, lived through three wars, two husbands, our different countries, survived poverty, wealth, health, cancer n health again, then cancer again. She told me, last time she to go into the hospital, I was upset, and she told me, that's the g about life, it can change at the drop of a hat, just like that, but t also what gives it spice. The fact that you don't have any idea w s going to happen to you is what adds a taste to life. That's wha e said. The unexpected is the taste of life. I'll always remember t he said that.

(Brief pause. TAMI her eyes.)

TAMI: There's my . *(TAMI's phone rings.)* And there's my ass-licking soon-to-be ex- band. You know what? I'm turning this fucking phone off. I ca l Mama tomorrow. So listen.

JON: What?

TAMI: Would you to have dinner with me?

JON: Sure.

(TAMI reaches to pi her suitcase, but JON gets to it first, picking it up.

They smile at each oth en walk off to the car.)

The end.

THE TASTE NOTES:

FIRST PRODUCED at Reality in 2001, this is the other piece I wrote for Franck for t urf Reality evening of short plays (but I lost the program an on't recall who the actress was, but I remember she was ver od) … this was before caller ID, obviously, but it's still a lot of fun.

ALSO PRODUCED by All You Can Eat Theatre Company, again cast list not available, directed by Jamie Taylor.

LATER PRODUCED at Manhattan Theatre Source as part of TASTY, an evening of short plays, featuring Franck Raharinosy and Alexis Raben.

18

The ꞡ Question (1m, 1f)

CHARACTERS:

ZED – A normal looki ·llow.

ZOIE – Zed's girlfrienc

SETTING: A park.

(ZOIE IS WAITING for) in the park. He sneaks up behind, startling her. They kiss each other carefu ı the cheek and smile happily.)

ZED: You know, I ‹ women are just wonderful.

ZOIE: I am in tota ·eement with you on that.

ZED: Of course yo ;ree, you are one.

ZOIE: I am, that's , but I still think women are wonderful.

ZED: And I think ıre wonderful.

ZOIE: Oh Zed.

ZED: And we've been together for how long?

ZOIE: Six months today.

ZED: Six months today. Fell in love at first sight in line at the hamburger stand, never looked back.

ZOIE: We did, we did, true love.

ZED: So there's something I gotta ask you.

ZOIE: There is?

ZED: A big, BIG question.

ZOIE: Oh my god, Zed, oh my god.

ZED: But before I ask it, I need some preliminary information.

ZOIE: Anything, Zed, anything.

ZED: If I were in any taller or any shorter, would you still love me?

ZOIE: Of course I would.

ZED: If I accidentally got my face mangled in a machine, would you still love me?

ZOIE: Oh darling, you know I would!

ZED: If I were a woman, would you love me?

ZOIE: *(Brief pause)* A … a woman?

ZED: HYPOTHET CALLY, if I were in an accident, suddenly, and I were to lose my, y know, my masculine objects, and become by process of eliminati woman, but I was still the same person inside, would you still lo ?

ZOIE: Well Zed, I'v thought about it before.

ZED: In THEORY ry of course, I would still be the same lovable Zed, I w be Zed minus the usual manly equipment.

ZOIE: Well, it woul of a shock at first.

ZED: Of course, of

ZOIE: I mean, I am that manly equipment of yours.

ZED: So am I.

ZOIE: I'm sure that I wo

ZED: I know that I would.

ZOIE: But I do love you.

ZED: And I love y [illegible]

ZOIE: So I guess [illegible] nswer Zed, is yes, I would love you, even if you were a woman.

ZED: Hey, that's w [illegible] erful. That's simply wonderful.

ZOIE: But boy, I s [illegible] would miss it. We would have to … invest in some spare parts. Ju [illegible] r play.

ZED: Spare parts?

ZOIE: You know, [illegible] uh … hard plastic substitutes for fleshy male vital parts. You k [illegible]

ZED: Oh yeah, ye [illegible] hose things, yeah, I never thought of that, I guess we would.

ZOIE: Not that I' [illegible] to toys or anything weird, it's just that if you were a woman, I [illegible] w that I would miss the little prince so much, that we'd have t [illegible] SOMETHING!

ZED: Of course. [illegible] bians do that sorta thing all the time, don't they?

ZOIE: Lesbians? [illegible] does that have to do with anything?

ZED: Well Zoie, I [illegible] to break it to ya, but if I were to lose my spare part, and becon [illegible] woman, and we were to be in love and making love, that woul [illegible] ke us lesbians.

ZOIE: Yeah, but y [illegible] ere originally a man.

ZED: But my cu [illegible] status would be that of woman, thus making us lesbos.

ZOIE: I never tho [illegible] about it that way before.

ZED: Would it bot [illegible] ou, being a lesbian?

ZOIE: I've just ne [illegible] considered it before, Zed, whenever I've thought of homosexu [illegible] before, which isn't very often, it's always been about men. I've [illegible] er envisioned women getting in the act. But of course they do.

ZED: Sure they do [illegible] ink about them all the time.

ZOIE: You do?

ZED: Oh yeah. [illegible] nk lesbians are wonderful. I think all women are wonderful [illegible] t I think lesbians are wonderful most of all. I really identify wit [illegible] em.

ZOIE: Wow Zed [illegible] at's great. I never knew you were so sensitive.

ZED: If I were a woman, I would have to be a lesbian. I don't think I could make it with a man, I find the idea of a man's penis, other than my own, I find the penis somewhat threatening.

ZOIE: Oh not me, not me. I love the penis.

ZED: In fact, to be brutally honest, I sometimes find even my own penis somewhat threatening.

ZOIE: Oh I love the penis, I think it's the greatest invention since sliced bread.

ZED: You do?

ZOIE: Oh yeah, there's somethin' so cute and cuddly about it, somethin' that just says HOLD ME, that I just love about it. I'm under no illusions about why you guys grab yourselves so often. If I had a penis, I would be holding it all the time.

ZED: Not me, as a female, I would have to be a lesbian.

ZOIE: I understand.

ZED: In fact, I'm gonna go one step further. I'm gonna say that I am a lesbian right now.

ZOIE: But Zed, you're a man.

ZED: But INSIDE, inside I am a lesbian. I have all the inner lesbian wants and desires.

ZOIE: But Zed—

ZED: In my heart I've got this little inner lesbo that's just yearning to be free!

ZOIE: But Zed—

ZED: Free to stand up and shout at the world … I AM A LESBIAN!

(Brief pause.)

ZOIE: But Zed, what about me?

ZED: Honey, you know I love you.

ZOIE: I know.

ZED: And I know you love me.

ZOIE: I do, I do.

ZED: And I want to stay with you forever and ever.

ZOIE: Oh Zed. I want that too.

ZED: I'm just asking these questions to be sure of our loyalty together. Love that wi ce us to the grave and beyond. I've been leading up to one big c ion.

ZOIE: Oh Zed.

ZED: Are you reac r me to pop the BIG question?

ZOIE: Oh Zed, I 't believe you're doing this, oh my God! Okay, okay. I'm ready. ready.

ZED: Zoie, love of life, would … would … would it be okay if I became a woman?

(Very, very brief paus

ZOIE: WHAT! AI OU NUTS!

ZED: It's just a littl eration—

ZOIE: GET OUT U FREAK OF NATURE!

(ZOIE beats ZED w r handbag and chases him out of the park.)

End of play.

THE BIG QUESTION ES:

FIRST PRODUCED at Riant Theatre in early 1997, the cast list lost in time and space, cted by the author.

LATER PRODUCED t same year at the Loft in Soho, featuring Michele Ammon and J s McCauley, directed by the author.

A PERSONAL NOTE a bit dated, but this is the first play of mine that I also direct n New York City. So I included it here. I was very young when I te it.

BUT OF COURSE I sti e lesbians, I mean, who doesn't?

Solo, Yo

I have a few solo w that are ten minutes long or less, like EXTREME EUGEN

Most of the following ces premiered in the evening called LIP SERVICE at Manhatt heatre Source. In that show, a silent man (played by Boris Kievs ould listen to different people he encountered, never saying a d, playing a different role for each one (sometimes a patient, etimes a doctor, etc). It was a successful evening.

But these short plays vork as stand-alone pieces and have been done that way, too.

19

Pa On The Plane (f)

(Pauline sits on a plane. S aks to a MAN next to her on the plane.)

PAULINE: I'm sc to death of flying. I was scared of it before, you know, b e THAT THING, the THING that happened as it happe I was scared enough before then, as if flying isn't frightening igh as it is, flying a machine thousands of feet in the air with a m n working parts on it and thus the potential for a million things o wrong, it's pretty fucking frightening on ITS OWN, now add t at we have to worry that some demented fruitcake is going to w out his toothbrush and commandeer the flight, crash it into his irlfriend's house as a way of getting back at her, and the corpor owers-that-be will sit back and let him do it, write it off as an ins ice loss and another reason to hike up the price of fares.

I can see that happ g, can't you see that happening? I can see that happening.

Not that it's much er on the ground. Bullets flying everywhere, stores being r d, cars crashing into each other, bricks falling from buildings, n bodies falling from buildings. I heard about this guy, comm d suicide because his wife was leaving, jumped from his offic ndow, fourteen stories high, landed on a woman who was just walking by. Killed the woman, the guy survived. She died, he lived. You're not safe anywhere. I'm scared to death even to walk the street anymore. When I'm walking around, it's like I know something horrible is gonna happen at any second. I see some messenger zipping along on his bike, coming my way, and I just get a picture in my head of him whipping out an axe or baseball bat, braining me with it and then peddling along his merry way, nobody stopping him or even noticing. It doesn't happen, he usually just bikes on by, but I'm sure that it could happen, and that's enough to scare me to death. I try not to walk around by myself if I can help it. Now when I have to go to the store, I call a friend. Not that THAT would do any good, I guess.

I knew this guy, got struck by lightning. Walking around talking to his boyfriend, minding his own business, bang, lightning strikes. Kills him. Wasn't even raining yet, started raining sometime after, but wasn't even raining. No warning, just boom. His boyfriend didn't even realize what happened, kept walking for awhile, looked back and there he was, lying on the sidewalk, sizzling. Horrible.

Somebody somewhere's got a sick sense of humor.

You know what it is? I'm scared to death of death. That's what it is.

That's why I stopped smoking pot, I used to smoke pot once in awhile, I wasn't a druggie or anything, just on the weekend, here and there, it's really good for relaxing a person and I often need all the help I can get when it comes to relaxing. So I would do it, once in while, I would smoke some weed, and it's pretty good, you get high and just sort of let loose, float above your body for awhile and watch all the pretty flowers and colors. But once when I was stoned, I got, like this really bad vision, you know how when you smoke pot sometimes time slows and sometimes it speeds up, that ever happen to you?

Well usually it slows for me which is why I like it, but the last time I got buzzed I went fast forward, like on a VCR I zipped forward in time, really fast, in my life, and I was brought to the end of my life, to my last moment of breath, to my death. I don't know exactly how many years I went forward because I was stoned and not really paying atte ı, but I do know that it was real, it was fucking real, with all letails, who I got married to, number of kids, house, the whol ıow. And I'm floating above my body, looking down at me ahead, me on my deathbed, and that's when it hits me, I'm g ı die. I am definitely gonna die, someday. There was no escape, ıegotiation, no way around it, someday I am gonna kick for goo ıd it FREAKED me out.

I haven't smoked p ıce then. I'm still freaked out.

Doesn't it freak yoı ? I think I'm freaking out a little bit right fucking now.

Excuse me.

(She gets up, squeez ıst the MAN to the aisle and heads for the rest room).

Lights out.

PAULINE ON THE PL NOTES:

PREMIERED in 2002 anhattan Theatre Source as part of LIP SERVICE, featuring A ebster, directed by the author.

ALSO FEATURED in hame Theatre New York City, performed by Maggie Bell, and N ame Theatre Los Angeles, among others.

20

Paul On The Plane (m)

(Paul sits on a plane that's in flight. He speaks to the MAN seated next to him.)

PAUL: You okay? You look a little … you know. A little queasy. Afraid of flying? It's okay, perfectly normal, most folks are. We're thousands of feet in the air, who wouldn't be a little concerned, right?

(The plane hits some turbulence, rocking them both.)

Whoa, that was a rough one, wasn't it? You okay? Just turbulence, that's all. A lot of people are afraid of flying, aren't they? Seems pretty common. It's always struck me as funny, folks saying that they are afraid of flying. Because when you think about it, it's not the flying part of the process that's frightening, it's the possibility that at some point in the process, maybe even mid-flight, the possibility that you might find yourself on a plane that is suddenly NOT flying, only falling. That's the scary part, the falling is the scary part. I'm not, myself. Afraid of flying, I mean. I think the reason I'm not afraid of flying is because the first I ever flew in a plane was when I was going through my suicidal phase, so there wasn't really anything to be scared of. The only thing I was scared of at the time was killing myself, so getting on a plane was something of a relief, because if the plane blew up, BING BANG

BOOM, suddenly I n nger have to worry about either suicide or life, it's out of my nds. Taken care of. Great time to start flying, when you're s dal. It was the most relaxed I'd been in years.

I've grown past m cidal tendencies, but luckily I'm still not afraid to fly.

(More turbulence.)

Really bouncy fligl lay, isn't it? I kind of like flying, myself.

Actually, I really it. I find that flying is a good time to contemplate death.

I mean, why not, r ? Contemplating death is a good thing. It could happen at any ti so why not think seriously about it? What else is there to do on a e? The movies always suck, there is never anything to do once ve plowed through your magazines and don't get me started ie food they serve here. It's poison. You ever think about death o. I think about it a lot.

I don't think enou eople think about it, I mean really think about it. Consider it, f moment. That is the one true link we all share with each othe e one thing you know for certain will happen is that you anc omeday we will die. We will close our eyes and existence as we kr t will cease. Or maybe we WON'T close our eyes, maybe we p off with our eyes open, that happens, it happens, right?

Here's a thought, s a great thought, see that exit door over there? If you were to n that door and jump out with no parachute, right now, thre ousand feet over Wyoming, that means you'd have a good two hree minutes to think about things before you landed. Now then nat do you think would be going through your mind before you ie ground?

(More turbulence.)

That reminds me joke my Grandpa would always ask us kids, he'd go, "What's last thing that goes through a mosquito's mind right when it h our car windshield?" "What Grandpa?" we'd ask, and he'd say ass!"

And he would slap nee and laugh and laugh.

Grandpa's dead n lrank a little too much Wild Turkey one

night while driving and hit a telephone pole. Wasn't wearing his seatbelt, went right through his windshield.

I really think that he'd find that terribly amusing.

Now seriously, what do you think is going to happen once you die? Any idea? Me neither. Lots of people, a LOT of fucking people have theories, oh there are a lot of theories on what happens after death, but no one really knows for sure, do they? They say they do, people SAY they know for sure, but nobody does and nobody will until they hit that big exit door, right? Nobody really fucking knows. That's something to think about. That's what I think about. That's what kept me from committing suicide. Thinking hard about death kept me alive. Grandpa would have appreciated that irony, I think. Long flight ahead. Why don't you give it a shot? I have to go to the bathroom. Excuse me.

(Paul gets up, edges past the man to the aisle.)

Lights down.

PAUL ON THE PLANE NOTES:

PREMIERED in 2002 at Manhattan Theatre Source as part of LIP SERVICE, featuring Anthony Wood, directed by the author.

ALSO FEATURED at No Shame Theatre New York City, performed by Adam Devine.

21

·rry In Jail (m)

(JERRY comes over to a *and morose Man sitting on the bench. The Man never speaks. Jerry never s* *p.)*

JERRY: Hey. Hey dy. Hey man. You got a cigarette? No?
Fuck. I was hoping yo 1 one. Those fucking things are expensive
these days man. Can e them away all nonchalantly anymore
right? People are getti lesperate now you know? I was in a bar
last week and this fuck ıot chick tried to bum one off of me. You
know, she comes up t all sweet and pouty-like. Flashing some
major fucking chest h are. And let me tell you something. She
was hot. I mean she w ɔrn star hot. I mean fucking hot. And she
goes "Hey stud, can n a cig?" All smoky-like. And you know
what I said? You know ıt I said to this chick that I would happily
kill my own mother fo

I said: "Only if yc ɔw me, honey. And I'm talking blow. I'm
talking the kind of bl b that you go to hell for. And I want to
videotape it. And sell eBay. For posterity. You know what I'm
saying? That's the o way you're getting a cig from me." I
said that.

Hey, cigarettes are fucking gold now. Funny thing is, that, for a split second, I think that she actually considered it before she kicked me in the balls.

These are desperate times, my friend. Desperate fucking times. You scared? You look scared. Don't talk much, do you? I don't blame you. That's the safest thing to do. Lay low and shut the fuck up.

Wish I could do that. I don't shut the fuck up. I can't shut the fuck up. Shutting the fuck up is not in my nature what-so-fucking ever. I get it from my mom. She could make your ears bleed she talks so fucking much. That's how by dad died. He bled to death through his ears. It's true. And I have the same problem. I talk too much. I talk too fucking much. I talk way too fucking much. I mean I'm a talker. Talk. Talk. Talk. That's what I do … talk. That's how I ended up in here, you know. Talking. Talking to a couple of cops.

I'm standing on a corner, waiting for a friend of mine. I put a cigarette in my mouth, light it, toss the match into the gutter with the rest of the shit and garbage. Couple fucking cops see me, point at the match, and say, "Pick that up."

Can you believe that, can you fucking believe that? Like there's not a hundred people walking by, dropping butts and matches all over. The blue asshole points at the match, says it again, "Pick that up." I look at him, grab my crotch and say, "Pick THIS up!" Pretty good, right?

Course, next thing you know, he's bouncing the business end of a nightstick off my skull and I'm in for resisting arrest and obstruction. Don't know why I said that, but I did.

Just can't help myself.

I remember once, when I was in high school, just a shit-eating-wet-behind-the-ears freshman, ninety pounds dripping wet, wouldn't say shit even if I had a mouthful, get the picture?

I was walking down the halls with a couple of my dork buddies, walking in that freshman way, sliding quiet next to the walls to avoid any seniors waiting to beat our ass, you know? And we're walking along, class bell rings so we know we're gonna be late, when the football coach comes out of the bathroom, buckling his pants up.

He was also our biology teacher, but everybody called him

Coach Paulson, the fc ll coach. At least to his face. Behind his back, different story.

Behind his back, w led him Psycho.

Psycho Paulson. G as forty-five, been lifting weights since he was two and was stack ke a brick shithouse. Stacked and mental, fucking mental case, ybody in the school was afraid of him. Fucking everybody, m eriously. Our fucking football team took about five conference mpionships and it wasn't because they were any good, it was inly because they were scared shitless of Psycho Paulson. They ught if they lost he'd literally fucking eat their nuts for breakfast

So me and my do ddies are slinking along, Psycho Paulson comes out of the shitt oks at us, grunts and says, "You boys get your butts to class, on double!" Can you believe that? On the double, like we was fuc in the army, something like that.

So he says that, m rk buddies turn white as a fucking sheet that he even spoke to he says that to us and before I can even blink, my mouth is o ng wide and deep and I'm falling right down into it.

I look at him an "Why don't you go FUCK yourself?" That's what I said.

Psycho Paulson do even get it at first, he's halfway down the hall when it finally sir to his gorilla head, what I actually said, and he spins like he's ging a linebacker and looks at me, disbelief in his eyes, and he , "What did you just say to me?"

He was even givi ne an out, Psycho Paulson was actually giving me a chance tc e my skeevy ass and proclaim that I did not say what I had inc said to him, giving me a choice, a choice between lying for hum ng life and extreme honest pain, possibly even death. He aims h ggy eyes at me, asks me again, "What was that you just said?"

And I think for a nent, savoring the choice ahead of me, then I open my moutl d say, "what I said was, why don't you go FUCK yourself, Psych back to your classroom and just FUCK yourself."

Took three teache d five varsity starters to pull him off my ass. Cracked open my skull, broke my hand, four ribs and knocked out at least half my teeth. I was in the hospital for two months. Psycho Paulson went stark-raving looney-tunes, they had to buckle him up and take him away. Never came back to the school, not while I was there. He's probably still locked up, somewhere. Shit, I hope so.

Don't want to run into him in a dark alley somewhere.

I was a hero, really. Even the other teachers were glad he was gone. But a lot of people wanted to know why I did it, why I opened my mouth not once, but twice, sealing my fate. Did I have a grudge against Psycho, was I setting him up, did I have Tourettes? All sorts of shit. I never had a good answer.

Now though, I think I know. I know what it is.

The thing of it is, I enjoy the words.

That's what it is, I just fucking enjoy saying the words.

Lights out.

JERRY IN JAIL NOTES:

PREMIERED in 2002 at Manhattan Theatre Source as part of LIP SERVICE, featuring Keith Chambers, directed by the author.

ALSO FEATURED at No Shame Theatre New York City, featuring Chuck Bunting.

IN ADDITION, Ato Essandoh contributed to the writing of this monologue.

22

octor (m or f)

(The DOCTOR approach MAN, looking at a chart.)

DOCTOR: Okay, , here we go. I am going to lay it on the line for you. We're bc rofessionals, we're in different fields, but we are both intelligent sonable men and we've known each other for quite some time. Si ninety-nine, isn't it?

You came to me fo dney stone, right? Something like that.

Point being, you'v n my patient for a long time, not only do I have your history, medical history, you and I, we have a personal history, the tv us, send each other holiday cards and I see you once every six nths at least, if not more during the cold and flu season.

So it is with great tance that I am find myself in this position, having to say to what I am going to have to say. Are you ready for what I have t ?

All right then. He e go. Here is, in my medical judgment, what is wrong with you

YOU ARE A STU FUCKING MORON!

Got it? Let me rep at.

YOU ARE A STU FUCKING MORON!

Now then, do you wish to be healthier, want to get better? Here's what you HAVE to do.

STOP BEING A STUPID FUCKING MORON!

That is my judgment as a medical FUCKING professional. Fucking WISE your ass up. Stop what you are doing or die. That's it. Goddamn dumb fucking asshole. You've been coming in here for years, I've been giving you your physicals, running the bloods charting your adventures and the whole time I've been calm, quiet and polite but enough is fucking enough. I'm through being civil, I'm here to tell you that you are a dumb fucking numbnut ASSHOLE!

You drink EVERY night, in excess, you drink a bottle of wine every night, throw in a few gin or vodka tonics into the mix, No exercise, bad diet, if you've got a date then you usually snort coke, once or twice a month, you combine cocaine and illegally prescribed Viagra, driving your blood-pressure through the roof and fucking up your immune system, you are a walking advertisement for a heart attack.

Fucking shit-for-brains-fuckhead.

But all this I could live with, really, let me tell you what's really got my ass-hairs burning. This is what really pisses me off.

You smoke two, three packs of cigarettes a day, with your blood pressure and no exercise except to take a piss once in awhile, you smoke like a fiend and not just any cigarettes mind you, you smoke Camels, fucking Camels, one right after the other, you can't even get up on the exam table without wheezing stale nicotine right into my face.

Why not just put a loaded gun into your mouth? You've been to fucking medical school, you've been there, you know what those cocksucking CANCER-STICKS do to a person, and yet still you LIGHT 'em up, suck it in and blow it out. ASSHOLE!

You have abscesses in your throat and nasal passages, pus-filled abscesses, you cough up bits of phlegm and blood, even your cat died of lung-cancer, you didn't think I knew that, but I knew that, we go to the same vet, shithead. Cat lives with you, gets sick, dies of lung-cancer and you are somehow surprised, "Hey, how can my cat get lung-cancer, he ı't smoke, I'm the one that smokes," ASSHOLE!

I've been telling yı r years that you have to stop, you simply MUST stop abusing) ody and you are still are too much of a pussy to try and quit. / [OLE!

Shit, I saw you ou ront of the building with the rest of the mental defectives, puf ıway even though it's at least five below and it's raining out, y out there, sucking it up. And the worst thing about that set-u ı's the entrance to the building, everyone has to slide past you o get it. Pediatrics is on the third floor, which means that ther steady stream of kids, sick CHILDREN, that have to walk thro the gauntlet of smoke from you and the rest of the tobacco ret n order to get into the building.

ASSHOLE ASSH ASSHOLE! You little fucking TURD!

I've had it, I've ha ugh. I'm your doctor, and I'm here to tell you, you either stop b ı dumb fucking moron or you will die. In six months. That I ca arantee. Because if the booze or smoke doesn't do you in, I w rsonally kill you myself just for being an insult to my profession

That's my professi udgment.

Have a nice day.

Lights down.

The end.

THE DOCTOR NOTE

PREMIERED in 2002 anhattan Theatre Source as part of LIP SERVICE, featuring J Klatsky, directed by the author.

ALSO FEATURED at ıame Theatre New York City, performed by Lou Carbonneau.

AND IT IS STILL a complete mystery to me why anyone smokes cigarettes.

23

Lanna (f)

(LANNA, a guest at a w… stands next to a man watching the ceremony. She speaks to him, sotto m… the time, and he tries to ignore her.)

LANNA: You kno… always right about now that it hits me, at this point here, wh… see the bride coming down the aisle, all dressed in white satin … ilk, with the wedding march playing and all the aunts and gra… thers crying, it's always RIGHT at this moment that it's all I c… NOT to fall to the ground screaming in maniacal laughter.

From this point on … ntil the "I do's" it takes all the strength I have not to break into … erics. Look at this, my lip is bleeding, it's bleeding because I hav… bite it just to keep quiet.

Wait, wait. Lister… that preacher. "We are gathered here together to unite the … vo souls in holy matrimony." What a pompous ASS. You kn… think that's why they do this whole thing up like this, with the … and the tuxes, the pomp and the ceremony, they dress it … disguise what a big JOKE the whole thing is.

Seriously. The wh… dea is one big fat hairy lie. I'm sorry, I mean, how can you … se in front of God and the rest of the world to love, honor a… bey one person for the rest of your life?

How do you know how you're going to feel twenty years from now? You could be a completely different person by then. People grow and change.

How can you be absolutely positive you will still love the same guy for the next forty years once he gets fat, old and lazy and only cares about football? What are you gonna do when you run out of things to talk about? What are you gonna do when you've tried every sexual position there is and there are no surprises anymore? Nothing.

All that's left is to crank out a few kids, wipe their noses and pick up after them. Don't get me started on childbirth, don't get me started.

Do you know how much your vagina dilates when you give birth? Ten centimeters. TEN centimeters. Not me, buster, uh-uh NO WAY. Once you stretch something like that it loses its elasticity. I'm not doing that to my vagina. I like my vagina just as it is, thank you very much.

Do you know how many of these weddings I've been to in the last year or so? Nine. NINE weddings. It's like every woman I went to school with hit thirty and started panicking. Oh My God, I'm over thirty and I'm not married I gotta do something, I gotta get a man I gotta get a man NOW! Take the bride and groom, for example. You know how long they've known each other? Six months. Less than that, five and half months.

That's it. She says it was love right away. Bullshit. They met over the Internet, in a CHAT room. She was just so relieved to find somebody she could live with she couldn't wait. She just felt old and desperate, that's what it is. Trust me. I know. She was frantic.

Would you listen to that windbag preacher go on and on? Come on, cut to the I dos, kiss the bride and let's all go get drunk. I can't stand here in these heels all night. Is he getting paid by the word, or what? Cut to the chase, Pops.

Still, I got to admit, there is something about this whole thing that is a turn-on. The church, the dresses, the suits. Gets my juices flowing. Makes me feel, you know, sexy.

You seeing anyone, involved with anybody right now?

Wait, don't answe[illegible]. Never mind. Nothing personal, I keep grabbing one-night st[illegible]at every one of these deals and it always ends horribly. He get[illegible]d, I get hung-over. Plus, no offense, but you guys NEVER loo[illegible]ood the next day as you do today. Never. It's a simple wedding [illegible]ge. Sorry, I can't have sex, besides, this is my week to bleed any[illegible]You are SO lucky not to be a woman, let me tell you.

Look at that gro[illegible]ook at him up there in his tuxedo, all shaved and shining. [illegible]ng at him you'd never guess that he's unemployed, would y[illegible]know what it said on the announcement, he was identified as [illegible]aphic artist" but trust me, he's unemployed. He's no graph[illegible]ist, he does tattoos in his garage for cash and that's it. I think h[illegible] a cartoon published in Penthouse once, but that was years ago[illegible]t me, he's unemployed.

And her in her W[illegible] dress.

White dress? Pleas[illegible]gest slut in junior high, believe me. She's a close personal frien[illegible]you have to call a spade a spade and she was a class A slut. Firs[illegible] of us to kiss a boy, touch a penis, give a blowjob, you can do th[illegible]t of the math.

Not that I think [illegible] a bad thing, oh no, I admired her in school, she was consi[illegible]l a pioneer. Why do you think we are friends? But a white d[illegible]come on! Oh it hurts, I'm cramping up, trying not to break int[illegible]ghter.

White. What a jok[illegible]o should wear white, anyway?

What kind of idio[illegible]s a virgin until marriage? You'd have to be three kinds of a m[illegible] to save yourself until then, I mean, my God, what if you wa[illegible]nd then he sucked in bed, and I don't mean sucked in a goo[illegible]?

What would you d[illegible]n, you're stuck? You're stuck and you're fucked, and not in a g[illegible]way. Then again, if you're a virgin when you get hitched, how [illegible]d you know if you're having bad sex or good sex? I guess you [illegible]ln't know.

What a horrible th[illegible]t.

Such bullshit. On[illegible]real mental defective wouldn't have sex before marriage. You [illegible] car, you take it for a test drive, right?

The whole idea o[illegible]ring white and staying pure is simply an insult to women, that's what I think. Men want you to stay simple, pure and stupid. That's what I think. It's a marketing plan, it's advertising, to hook you in to the whole idea of everlasting love and marriage, that's what the white dress is all about. It's a billboard.

I get married, I'm not wearing white, I tell you that much.

IF I get married, and that's one big fucking IF.

(She starts to laugh.)

Me. Married. What a joke. Oh my God.

I don't see that happening for me. I just don't think anything in the whole institution works. At all.

I remember something my mother once said, she said getting married was great, it was the living together afterward that was hell.

I think the idea, the idea of true and everlasting love is a great ideal, but that's all that it is, an ideal. It's not connected to our live reality here. It's not REALITY.

I've never seen it with my own eyes, and the people I've met who said they had it, were living it in their own relationships, I've never believed them. Relationships have always looked to me to be a combination of mutual delusions and needs.

That's not love. I'm not entirely sure love actually exists. Not really.

But the idea, the idea of true and everlasting love is a great idea. I would like to, I want to, see it with my own eyes.

I'd like to believe it might exist.

I'd like to believe in the billboard.

I'd like to believe in the white dress.

I would.

Lights down.

LANNA NOTES:

PREMIERED in 2002 at Manhattan Theatre Source as part of LIP SERVICE, featuring Constance Boardman, directed by the author.

24

Ryc nd the Beaver (m)

(TAYLOR, a regular dud s out and speaks to the man.)

TAYLOR: The si funniest thing that I've ever seen in my entire life had to be my e brother taking a shit on a beaver dam.

See, we grew up o arm in Iowa, nothing but corn and bean fields for miles. This w fore cable television, so there was exactly fuck all to do, especial the summer. All we could really do was get into trouble. Fuck nd in the barn, break something, get our ass beat. This was wh anking was in, and let me tell you something, Dad made good of corporal punishment.

Summer I was elev nd my brother Ryan nine, our family was going through some times, money wise. Dad was working during the day at co ction to make extra money, then doing chores and stuff at n Mom had taken a part time job as a checker at the grocery ten miles away.

So me and Ryan w alone most of the day. We had chores to do, course, but we a managed to do them in the last ten minutes right before th ks got home.

So what we did d play games, starting usually with army man, then as the co t higher we moved on to cowboy and

Indian, planet of the apes, all kinds of shit. Our farm covered a few acres, and as long as we didn't leave our land, we avoided a licking.

Sometimes Joe Berger, kid lived next farm over, he'd ride his bike over and join us, but he usually had his shitty kid brother with him, Darin, who was six and a whiney little fucking brat. God, I hated that kid. Tell his folks fucking everything you did, and let's face it, a kid has got to have his secret adventures, you know what I'm saying?

This was this creek that twisted through our property, just a little one, few feet wide with no decent fish in it or nothing, and if you followed it about a mile into one of our fields you came to this little island of trees and brush, almost like an oasis, and it was right there that some beaver built a very large dam and pooled the water up some. That was the Beaver Dam. The Old Man was always gonna clear it out, but he never got around to it.

Now Ryan was obsessed with the beaver dam that summer, part of it was the name, beaver dam, beaver DAM. He got a kick out of just saying it, he'd say, let's go to the beaver DAM, you wanna go to the DAM? Tickled the hell out of him, it was like he was cussing but couldn't get in trouble for it.

Course, we were expressly forbidden to go near the beaver dam, water was too deep, too dangerous, all the usual dumb excuses adults throw at you which never work and so of course we went out there whenever we could.

It was fun, there were lots of trees and brush right around there, one big low hanging branch that crossed the creek right over the dam, if you were real brave, you could hang on the branches and swing over the water like Tarzan of the Apes.

We never saw any beaver there of course. There weren't much beaver in Iowa back then, almost all trapped out. Still, Rye would drag me there every chance he got, we'd stay on the side of the creek, reading comic books or something, and every once in awhile Ryan would go "Shh, did you hear that, was that a beaver?" and we would stop and listen and never hear anything except the wind going through the corn.

Ryan would set tr or it, you know, big box held up with a stick on a string, that of thing. I told him, I said, beaver can chew through an entir , that old cardboard box won't stop him.

"I don't wanna kee n," he said, "I just wanna see him."

I just shook my he d went back to what I was doing, he was crazy, he'd put out littl es of wood on a plate, 'cause that's what he thought they ate, e wood, he'd call it, come and get the prime cuts of wood, M aver. Beaver never showed, not once.

Come August, tim the family went from tight to terrible to about as bad as it can Ma and Pop were fighting a lot, and were quick to give us a sm f we even looked like we were thinking about trouble.

One night, after w nt to bed, we lay there listening to our folk's fighting like all out. It got pretty rough that night, the yelling. We could hear ll of it. Ryan gets up out of bed, goes to the window and starts mb out.

Where are you goi ask him.

"For the damn bea he says.

You mean the beav m, I say.

He stuck his tongu at me and hops out the window.

I jump out the wi after him and we spent a large part of the night out there, ing the stars, listening to crickets and searching for that dam ver.

Caught a licking fc e next day, but it was worth it.

We ended up los he farm to the bank. Lost everything, house, land, tractors, furniture. Toys. It all got auctioned off. We were all gonna ha move, leave the only place Ryan and I had ever lived, go up t sconsin and stay with some relatives after everything got sold.

Dad couldn't look dy in the eye at the auction, he just sat in the shade with Uncle and drank Bud out of the can, not talking. Ma was inside cry ith her sister Betty. Piece by piece, everything we owned was sc f in a single afternoon.

I'd been following auctioneer around, because that was a pretty interesting job ught, get paid to talk real fast, but I lost interest after he sold my bike. Joe Berger's dad bought my bike, bought it for Joe's little snot-nose shit brother Darin. Only paid five dollars for it, too. I had to leave after that.

I knew where Ryan was, folks had told me to keep my eye on him but he was where he always was, where he wasn't supposed to be. Standing on the bank staring out at the dam.

I come up next to him, I could tell he'd been crying. We stood there quiet for a minute.

"Shit on this beaver!" he said. I knew he was real upset to say that, he never said the word shit 'cause Ma made he chew on soap if she caught him.

"Shit on this damn beaver!"

And so my little brother runs up the tree and goes out on the big branch that hung over the damn, takes his shorts down and sits, bare-assed, right over that beaver dam.

"Stupid beaver, I just wanted a look! Shit on him!"

And damned if my little fucking brother didn't actually drop one, he dropped a grade A corn-fed turd right on the exact center of that beaver dam. PLOP!

And then he started giggling, giggling like you wouldn't believe, his giggling causing the branch he was sitting on to bounce with his giggles.

"Shit on you beaver, shit on you!" he yelled and we were both laughing now, my stomach hurt, I was laughing so hard, his little white butt was on that branch, going up and down, up and down, spitting out little tear-dropped turds and we were screaming with laughter.

Joe Berger and snot-nose Darin came wandering over, wondering what we were doing, saw my little brother's butt bouncing up and down on that branch and fell to the ground laughing.

Joe was laughing so hard he couldn't breathe, he was squeaking, actually squeaking.

Suddenly there's this big crack and the branch Ryan is sitting on sags halfway down to the dam. Ryan looks at me, bug-eyed and scared, and starts pulling his shorts up.

Don't move! I yell im, but he doesn't listen and next thing you know, branch br and down he goes right on top of the beaver dam, rolls forw nd plops right down into the water. The whole time he's falling still trying to pull his shorts up.

I can see him do nderwater, flapping his arms, trying to come up for air.

I jump into the w trying to get to him. I'm getting scared now, I can't figure ou Ryan won't come up for air, he knows how to swim. I finally ver to where he is and dive down to him. I grab him and pull, b an't get him to move, he's stuck or something, I think his foot i k.

I go down deeper ry to find his foot, the water's murky but I can just make it out, nnis shoe is caught on some branches. I run out of breath and for more air.

Ryan ain't movin much as before and I'm beyond scared now, I'm at that type ared where everything is cold and tight, you know?

I can hear Dad ye and I take another breath and go down to his shoe. I pull an , trying to get it off or untie it, but Rye always double-tied hi s. I try to break the branch, something, Rye ain't hardly movi v and I am ter-ii-fucking-fied.

I'm seeing spots n an't breathe and I start back up. I ain't gonna leave without h o I grab him under the armpits and pull like I've never pulled b and a funny thing happened.

Rye looks up at m he water he turns his head up to me and he smiles. Smiles at n ext thing you know he's free and up we pop to the top of the r like corks. Dad's in the water by now, screaming and splashi vard us.

Grabs up by the of our necks and hauls us to the bank, where Uncle Terry an Berger and little shit Darin are waiting.

I'd never seen Dad that, he was almost crying. Ryan was still smiling, the little fuck d he was awake, he was actually awake. He looks at me and sa

"I seen 'em Taylor ally seen 'em."

Pop threw us dov the bank, started checking Ryan out, making sure he wasn't ding or broke or something, whole time promising us we were in for the beating of our lives and what the hell were we thinking?

"Just wanted to see the beaver, I saw the beaver," Ryan said.

"What the … WHAT the hell for?!" Pop was yelling, now that he knew we were okay he was feeling free to be seriously pissed off.

"Because. Because Uncle Terry said getting to see a beaver was a real good thing," Ryan said.

Pop stared at him for a second, all the blood going to his face, than he looked at Uncle Terry and back again at us.

Then he started to shake and smirk, and damned if he didn't start laughing, something he hadn't done in good while, laughed long and hard from the belly, Uncle Terry joined in and all us kids, though at the time we didn't really get the joke.

We laughed because we were glad to be alive.

Funny thing was, seeing that beaver did turn out to be a good thing. After we moved Dad got a great job, everything got better, we bought another house and things were never as tight and fierce as they were that summer. We didn't know it then, but that day was the beginning of the best time in our family. Thanks to Ryan and the beaver.

Another funny thing, after we went back to get cleaned up I got a look at Rye's tennis shoe, the one that'd been stuck. Sure enough, he'd double tied them and he liked them big thick laces as well, so I would have never gotten them untied.

Lucky for us, I didn't have to. They'd been cut clean in two, right under the bow, like someone taken a knife and slit right through them.

A knife or a powerful set of incisors.

Seeing the beaver turned out to be a damned good thing.

Lights out.

RYAN AND THE BEAVER NOTES:

PREMIERED in 2002 anhattan Theatre Source as part of LIP SERVICE, featuring T r Ruckel, directed by the author.

NOTE: In Iowa, creek onounced "crick". I don't know why. But it is.

25

Wally In The Waiting Room (m)

(WALLY sits in the waiting room of a doctor's office. He notices an unseen person staring at him from the audience and leans forward.)

WALLY: What the hell are you looking at?

Would you like to know what you're looking at? I'll tell you what you're looking at. You're looking at a dying man.

That is the unfortunate truth of my situation. I am dying.

Don't look so surprised. Who did you expect to run into in a hospital waiting room?

Of course, we are all dying, aren't we? Nobody lives forever. We're all on a collision course with death, it's as unavoidable as the clap was in Korea during the war. The real tragedy is when a person discovers just how close they are to the final checkout, when you're told that it's happening today or tomorrow, that's when it's shit-your-pants time.

I don't know why you're here, I'm sure it's not good but even without knowing what exactly is wrong with you, I'm willing to bet hard cash money that I'm closer to dying than you are. Bet you right now, give you three to one odds, too. Not interested? Smart. I'd of taken your money even though I don't have the time to spend it.

You know how far I am from death?

(He holds his fingers u ut an inch apart.)

That far. Yessir. S ny pants? You bet. Just found out, too. Last week.

Shit the pants, and I spend what little time I have left sitting in these fucking waiti ooms, waiting for a test, waiting for the doctor to look at the , waiting for the nurse to stick her head out the door and ask n come in.

You'd think they'd o pick up the pace a little bit, seeing as that I'm on a limited t of days left. Don't even know why I'm here, should just say fi and go to a bar. What's the difference if it's tomorrow or the d ter tomorrow, right? But I guess nobody wants to go before the e to.

I'm not even old. a fairly young man, really. Just beat my body all to shit, basical rewed the internal engines up beyond all repair. I guess it was th nking, drugging, fucking and all the fried food, that's what did n

Had fun, though, did I have some fun. I was a merchant marine, I've been ever re in the world. Top to bottom. I've seen sights that'd frost you trust me. I've had so many adventures, seen so many perfect t , it's almost unbelievable.

In my circle, I'm s hing of a legend for all the scrapes I've gotten in. I've brawled chased and been chased, I've gotten the girl more than once 've saved many a day with my buddies when they were in a ja can honestly say that I've lived a life full of excitement and adv e.

Of course, sitting l vaiting to die isn't nearly so exciting as it is nerve-wracking. Mo my friends are out at sea, won't even know I'm gone till afte funeral. My mother passed away while I was at sea. I never mac o her funeral. I should have gone.

Always thought ab vriting them down, my adventures, when I retired, write a book mething and maybe sell it to the movies. You could make a bun movies out of stuff I've done, get Bruce Willis, make a pile o oney. And I'd be immortalized forever on film.

Always thought about maybe doing that. Now it's too late.

Reminds me of something, something I haven't thought of in a long time. I remember when I was a kid, long time ago, I was eight or nine, I went to the beach with my mother. Private beach, owned by some fella my mother was dallying with, so I had the whole beach to myself while they had their lemonade in the shade.

Hadn't really been to the beach before, my first time, and so I set myself to making the king of all sand-castles, I mean I created a beautiful monster, that sand-castle, it was elegant in design and detail, had a drawbridge and moat, five towers and a flag, it was a work of art. I spent the whole afternoon on that castle.

Went looking for Mom so I could show off what I'd done. Ran everywhere, up and down that beach, looked around the fella's house, couldn't find her anywhere. Ran around looking for quite awhile, started to get scared.

Finally she heard me yelling and came running, her and the guy, afraid I was drowning or something. Both looked a little flushed. I grabbed mom's hand and dragged her down toward my sandcastle, pretty damn proud of what I'd done.

Of course, being that young, I didn't yet know anything about tides. Tide had come in while I was looking for her and washed the whole castle away. I was pretty upset.

Mom just ruffled my hair, said she was sure it was beautiful and I could build another one whenever I wanted. Then she went back to the fella, standing over in the shade.

It always frosted me that I'd made something so beautiful and yet the only one that seen it was me.

I did it and then it was gone. I remember that.

(A NURSE gestures for WALLY to come in.)

There she is, the nurse. Guess it's my turn to walk down to the room of doom.

(He gets up and begins to exit, stops and looks at his conversation partner.)

You should have seen my sandcastle.

It was something, it really was.

(WALLY exits.)

Lights fade.
End of play.

WALLY IN THE WAI G ROOM NOTES:

PREMIERED in 2002 anhattan Theatre Source as part of LIP SERVICE, featuring R l Hamilton, directed by the author.

26

Happy Wendy (f)

(WENDY enters and talks to her unseen therapist.)

WENDY: Okay, this is SO fucking stupid. I shouldn't be here, I say that every week and every week I mean it, I shouldn't be here. I don't belong in THERAPY. I don't. Therapy is for unhappy people, I am not unhappy people. I am happy people.

Don't say it! Don't say a goddamn word, listen to me. LISTEN TO ME! You always do the talking but not today, buster, today you're gonna listen!

I am a happy person. Shut up! I mean it, just sit there and shut the fuck up. Therapy is for miserable, twisted, sick, unhappy losers with nowhere to go or nothing to do with their lives. I am none of the above, so I shouldn't be here.

Okay, you could make an argument for twisted, I'll grant you that. I will admit to a healthy dose of twisted running through my personality, but it is a good twisted, it's the healthy-eccentric-sexually-exciting-kind-of-twisted, not the sick-catch-stray-cats-and-torture-them-in-my-basement-kind-of-twisted. I am the GOOD kind of twisted, not the BAD kind of twisted, I LOVE animals, I don't even wear leather for crying out loud.

I am a HAPPY PE)N, and if it weren't for the court order, I wouldn't even BE HE]

This is all my ex-b end's fault. He is such a pussy. He is! He used to LIKE it wh left him obscene phone messages. He LIKED IT, it turned on, it was his fucking idea in the first place, the kinky prick would call each other and leave dirty messages ALL THE . I'm serious, don't roll your eyes at me you QUACK, I am y and completely serious. He loved it, SHUT UP, he fuckin)VED it when I called him and left a message that said, "Y iry PIG! WHERE ARE YOU? I want you to GET your AS r here and FUCK ME and you'd better FUCK ME HARD! I t at least THREE ORGASMS and if I don't get them I will your sorry, lying ass until it's BLOODY! Get over here you FU R!"

He used to love it I left messages like that.

So now that's it's " he decides he doesn't like it anymore? He's such a big puss nean, who calls the police after a few hundred phone calls? Christ.

You know what? not even that good in bed, really. Seriously, He has major d cies in his overall technique. One move, in-out, in-out. That's i did have good endurance, but it was still only the one move. In in-out. And oral? Forget about it. I tried everything, I had him ng the alphabet and singing French love songs down there, non it worked. He just didn't have the feel for it. Despite what you n think, our relationship wasn't about the fucking. It was more t hat. The only reason I kept seeing him was because I liked sl g him. And he liked being slapped. He DID! He LIKED it. w he liked it because he TOLD me he liked it.

Oh, and now bec it's "OVER" I'm not allowed slap him anymore, and Oh, le ll the COPS on Wendy just because I smacked him and gav a bloody nose just like in the old days? He used to fucking lov hen I did that, now I get arrested for it.

Such bullshit.

It's because he got ied, that's what it is.

It's that cunt of a wife he's got now, she's to blame for all this. She's the one that should be in therapy, she was stupid enough to marry HIM, she needs therapy. A LOT more than I do. I'm the happy one. I'm happy, I'm telling you.

Oh, and the resisting arrest charge? That's bullshit too, see what happened was I was trying to explain everything to the arresting officer, explain exactly what I just now told you, and the big pig wouldn't listen, if he had just LISTENED to me, he would have understood that there was NO reason for him to be there or even to arrest me. But the big blue prick wouldn't listen to me, he just kept saying, "put your hands on the hood of the car, put your hands on the hood of the car" and as you can see, I USE my hands when I talk, I'm very expressive with my hands while speaking, and how am I supposed to explain everything completely and fully if I'm required to keep my hands placed on the hood of the car?

Then when he grabbed me, well, my reaction was purely instinctual, seriously, I'm a woman, you have to take into account that I'm a woman and when a man that I DO NOT KNOW grabs me without being invited to, whether the man's wearing a uniform or not, I get grabbed by an unknown man, I'm going to react just as any woman would.

That's why I kneed him in the crotch. It's what any woman would do, it doesn't make me sick, miserable or unhappy. I'm a happy person and I didn't deserved to be maced, beaten with a nightstick and arrested for assaulting an officer, resisting arrest and obstruction of justice.

What a crock of shit. HE assaulted ME. I should sue. And listen. Obstruction of justice? What is that, anyway? My EX-BOYFRIEND is the major obstruction of justice.

And can I ask you, WHO just up and gets MARRIED out of the fucking blue? Who does that? Only a week before I was humping his hairy ass in the back-seat of his Toyota, then ten days later "Oh, by the way Wendy, I got married last weekend, Heh-heh, so I guess we're gonna have to stop seeing each other, heh-heh", I mean, what the FUCK is that?

And I'M the one ir ·apy?
HE'S the ONE w ıe major fucking OBSTRUCTION, and
it's stuck RIGHT up ;s! He should be here, not me. I'm basically a happy person. I appy!
Okay, now look, I ;e what you're thinking, you're looking at
my file and you're thir "Oh but Wendy, what about the suicide
attempt?" Here's the c

What normal, rati well-adjusted person DOESN'T attempt
suicide at least once ir · life? Every happy person tries it at least
once. No, it's true, it's E, if you have any brain at all you try it
once, it's only natural. ·rable mental defectives, LIKE MY EX-
BOYFRIEND, are th ly ones that seem to be able to avoid
suicide.

Don't you ever no ow the people that SHOULD off themselves NEVER do? H folks such as ourselves have to give it at
least one shot.

Look at the Ami ·ople, they look happy, right? A lot of
suicides attempts in tl nish community. Really. It's true, I read
about it in the Times.

So I gave it a shot, empted suicide, so what? It doesn't mean
I'm unhappy, it's does ıean I belong in therapy. And not only
that, it was an attem n attempt, a suicide ATTEMPT, not a
suicide ACHIEVEME ı suicide ATTEMPT.

If I wanted to achi uicide, it would have been achieved, trust
me, but there is NO w vould give that asshole prick EX of mine
that sort of satisfactio ɔt a chance. That would make him very
happy, which would m ıe unhappy.

I am not unhappy, at this face, look at the smile on this face.
I am one HAPPY ıg girl. I'M FUCKING HAPPY!

Lights fade

The end.

PREMIERED in 2002 at Manhattan Theatre Source as part of LIP SERVICE, featuring Karina Miller, directed by the author.

27

e Futility (m)

CHARACTERS:

JIMMY – a man in his wenties, early thirties, an obvious case of arrested development.

GIRL – a cute girl in h nties.

TIME
Present

SETTING
A Cafe.

NOTES: It's possible, urse, to do the play without the girl, as a solo piece.

LIGHTS UP.

(A GIRL in her early twenties sits at a table, sipping coffee and reading the paper.

JIMMY, a young man in his late twenties, comes running into the café desperately. He runs up to the table and sits down with the girl. JIMMY speaks very fast.)

JIMMY: You won't BELIEVE what just happened to me, you won't believe it! First of all, I am so, so sorry. Please, please forgive me, it's not like me, doing something like this, it's completely out of character for me to be this late. Punctuality is a priority of my life. Without punctuality, it all falls apart, everything. But you're not gonna believe what just happened to me, it was something right out of the papers, right out of the tabloids. I left my apartment early, because I'm always on time, always always always. And I'm walking down the street, whistling away because I'm really looking forward to meeting you, when all of a sudden all these huge cops wearing body armor come busting out of nowhere, yelling and screaming and jamming guns in my face. They grab me and throw me on the ground, going "Hands where I can see 'em, Hands where I can see 'em! Don't move motherfucker, don't move, I fuckin' mean it don't you fuckin' move!" And I, of course, wasn't moving, I had NO intention of moving and even if I WANTED to, I couldn't, I was lying-face first, spread-eagled on the ground, hand-cuffed with five cops standing on my legs. Now the guy in charge, the one with the Glock automatic, he screamed, "In his mouth, he put something in his mouth!" and the guy that was sitting on my back, he reached around and stuck his fingers into my mouth and grabbed my tongue. And he had a big hand, a big huge hand like a canned ham and it was stuck in my mouth. "Spit it out, spit it out fuckface, spit it out and you better not fuckin' bite me!" he was bellowing this, not two inches from my e: d banging my head against the sidewalk. I was trying to spit, bu ›uldn't get anything past his canned ham of a fist and not only t ıave you ever tried to do any kind of spitting without involving tongue? You can't do it, you can't spit unless you use your t e, it's impossible. This big ape had my tongue, what was I s sed to do? Finally, my gum fell out, I always chew Dentine (ng gum because fresh breath is a priority of my life, and that's w hey were after, they saw me put the gum in my mouth and they : after that like rabid dogs in August. My gum falls out on the g d. The ape with the canned ham hands grabs my gum, going ' it I got it I got it" and they pop my gum into a little baggie an ıisk it away. Then they all relax, smoke some cigarettes while t tand around on top of me. And there we sat, for forty minutes, l somebody figured that it was chewing gum in the baggie an t I was NOT the person that they were looking for. It was a ca mistaken identity. They thought I was a drug dealer, can you b that? Is that fucked or what? Me, a drug dealer? Do I look like : g dealer to you?

(SHE SHAKES HER H)

JIMMY: That's what I' ing! I don't look like a drug dealer, what drug dealer looks like Nobody! Thank GOD I didn't have any pot on me today, I wo ave really been fucked if I'd had a roach tucked away somewh ı case I needed it. Anyway, it was all a case of mistaken iden Would you believe that there is a drug-dealer out there som re with the same exact shoes that I'm wearing right now? T ; what it was based on, my shoes, my goddamned shoes. Fir ng when I get home, I'm throwing these fucking shoes OUT t oor. They're fucked now, jinxed. Sixty bucks for these shoes : ıow I can't even wear 'em. What a mess. But, what can you do, :now?

(SHE SHRUGS.)

JIMMY: Anyway, back to the present. Sorry I'm like, so late, but I'm here in one piece and that's the important thing. I made it, finally I'm here. God I'm thirsty, I gotta get something to drink, you want something to drink? You got something already, right, listen I'm just gonna grab a couple of coffees cause I'm parched, getting strip-searched is thirsty work but I'll be right back. Okay?

(HE STANDS)

JIMMY: You know what?

(SHE LOOKS AT HIM QUIZZICALLY.)

JIMMY: You're much prettier than I expected. I mean, I expected pretty cause I was told pretty, but you really are pretty. I just wanted you to know that.

(JIMMY WALKS OFF, but keeps talking.)

JIMMY: I mean, you never know what's out there. There are some real monsters swimming out there in the dating pool. I'm talking monsters, I'm talking Bigfoots, I'm talking Legend of Boggy Creek Sasquatches that Steve Austin would have trouble with. They're out there and they're hungry. And dishonest too. I met this one girl, set up through the internet, she had wrote to me that she was a stunner, that's what she wrote, that she was a CURVY stunner. And when we finally meet, I see that 's about five foot two and three hundred pounds. Now, I don't l anything against large women, my moth-er's a large woman, do believe in truth in advertising and damn it, there's a big ence between calling it curvy and calling it three hundred poun onesty, it's a priority of life.

(JIMMY RETURNS *wi e large cokes. He sits down and starts to drink one of them.)*

JIMMY: Anyway, we s probably get on with this. Well, as you know, my name is Jim work in the Internet industry but I really want to do something ic with my life. I really would, I think it's important to do some artistic, I was thinking along the lines of performance art, I c be a performance artist. When I was younger I thought ab eing an actor or a stand-up comedian, but I couldn't do it. this thing, this thing about speaking in public or even to mo n one person at a time. I can't do it, I hyperventilate and get , it's really disgusting. I can't even talk to more than one person ork at any one time, otherwise I'm liable to break out, seriousl n do it if they're sitting down and I'm sitting down, but if so dy stands up to do something, it kicks in. Is that weird or what? what can you do, it's who I am. Which is too bad, because I thi ot a lot of personality that I could share, if only I could figure ow to get it out there without suffocating myself. That's why I' en thinking performance art, something artistic that I could d ublic that won't involve me speaking or anyone seeing my fac yway, I'm working on it, me and my pal Chucky, we got a coup ngs in the hopper. So how are you doing, you doin' okay, you ne ything, a muffin or something like that? I can get you a muffin u want. You need something you let me know, all right? I just to do a good job at this, even though it's probably futile, I wan my best. I'm not trying to be negative, it's just … I really ain't l at this kind of thing, you know, meeting people, I don't know, impressions, I always fuck them up, but you gotta keep tryin' even though it's usually hopeless. It's a jungle out there, don't you think? I met this one girl once, we went out to dinner, real nice place and all that, ordered the meal and before the food even got there, she deleted me, BING, right in the trash bin, she said something like, "You know what, we shouldn't waste each other's time. It's either there or it's not there. And guess what? It's not there." I was like, how do you know, you just met me, we don't even know each other yet? And she just goes, "I just know," picked up her bag and walked out. What a rip-off, I mean, if you agree to have dinner with someone, you should stick to your word and eat the fuckin' dinner, not walk out and stick him with the meal and the check. I mean, that's cold. Don't you think that's cold? I think that's cold. I'll tell you something though, that food came and I ate it, every bite. I paid for that meal so I was goddamned gonna eat it. Fuck her, anyway. Dating sucks, don't you think it sucks? I think it sucks. I keep doing it and it keeps sucking. It's futile, I mean, how can we ever really know anybody? Do you think you're gonna know all that I am in this one brief casual encounter? Or I you? It's not gonna happen, it's not. People never really get to know each other. Take my girlfriend, my EX-girlfriend, take her, for example. Three years, we went out three years, practically LIVED together, might as well have, she was always at my apartment cause she hated her place. So one night, she just up and breaks up with me. We're eating popcorn, getting stoned and watching Lost Boys when she stands up and says, "it's over," and I was like, whatta talkin' about, it ain't over, Jason Patric just found out he was a vampire, we gotta long way to go yet! And she goes, "Not the movie, you goof, us. You and I, we're over," and she goes to get her coat. And it took me a minute to catch up cause I had a hell of a buzz working, then it hit and I jumped up, I said, what are you talking about over, what happened, what'd I do? "Nothing," she says, "you didn't do nothing, don't worry about it." Don't worry about it, you just dumped me in the middle of my favorite movie, you ruined my favorite movie! And on a side note, let me just add that I think Joel Schumacher is an under-appreciated cinematic GENIUS. That's right, I said GENIUS, he's an artistic genius. St. Elmo's Fire, don't get me started. Anyway she's out the door, I'm chasing her n the hall, yellin' if I didn't do anything wrong, why was she br ' up with me? And she stops, looks at me for a minute, and says cause I don't like you." You don't LIKE me? After three years)ON'T like me? "Yes," she says. Just like that all of a sudden ou he fuckin' blue you don't like me? "Yes," she says. When did TI appen? When did you DECIDE you just didn't like me? Just to ? "No," she says, "I've never liked you. I just finally decided to something about it," and with that she turned and walked ou my life. It all was very emotional, I still can't watch any mov ith Keifer Sutherland or either of the Coreys without gettin choked up. I'm all right with Jason or Jamie Gertz, they dor ther me, but those guys … I can't even LISTEN to the Lost soundtrack without bawling like a baby. Three years, she date for three years and she didn't even like me. It's like I said, you never really know people, you can't. It's futile.

(SHORT PAUSE as JIM looks at her.)

JIMMY: I suddenly ju membered, you're not supposed to talk about your ex-girlfrien hen you're on one of these, it's supposed to be a big jinx. I'm I fucked up again. Okay, so listen, just forget I said any of tl kay. Just forget all of it. Tell me a little about yourself, where rom, what you love, all that jazz, talk to me, talk to me, talk to

(BRIEF PAUSE, then a opens her mouth to speak, JIMMY interrupts her.)

JIMMY: You know wh ou are beautiful, you are truly beautiful. Too beautiful to be o one of these things. And I just had a revelation. I suddenly a flash. You and I, we could go out, we could date and have a lot of fun, the two of us. We would have great sex too, we would, I can feel the physical chemistry in the air between us, we would be on fire together. And I'm good at it, I am great at sex, believe me. I got all the books, all the training videos, I've done my homework when it comes to sexual prowess. I figure a person can only be GOOD at a couple of things in life, and so I decided one of mine would be sex and I've put in the practice time. And you, just looking at you a person can tell you're a tiger in bed. I can see this and more, all this with us. And it wouldn't be only sex, we would be pals, friends, buddies that hold hands. We could do things together, great things, live together, maybe even get a dog or cat, I could see us doing that. We would be great. But you know what? Sooner or later, the little things would get to us, sooner or later my career as a performance artist would start to eat away precious share time between us, and the little things, how I eat popcorn would bug you, my habit of turning my socks inside out so I can wear them twice as long, my obsession with Diane Sawyer, all that after awhile will begin to really bug you, I can see that. I could entertain you for awhile, I could give you a lot of laughs, but at some point you're gonna realize that you're too beautiful for me and that I'm a making you crazy. I would drive you absolutely fucking crazy. But you know what? I ain't gonna do that, I ain't gonna drive you to the point where you look at me and tell me you don't like me. I can't take it, I'm losing all my favorite videos to break-ups. AND I don't want to do that to a beautiful person such as yourself, I know from your profile that you're a sweet, sweet very nice person and I don't want to do that to you. You really shouldn't be doing this kind of thing anyway, all you're gonna meet on these deals are freaks like me that will make you nuts. I ain't gonna do that to you, I am taking a step toward integrity, integrity is the new priority of my life. I've decided that one good date is better than three years of bad ones and so this is it, I'm calling this one right here, right now, don't try to argue with me on this, I think I know myself pretty well and I believe that the right thing to do in this case is to shake hands and walk away, don't look back, and go on with our lives. That's it. I'm out of here, I'm walking and I don't want you to say anything, not a word. You and I both should get out of this game, we should, computer dating is ma ;, pure madness. Dating itself is futile, it's all futile. We should al walk away.

(JIMMY GETS up and s her hand formally.)

JIMMY: Cathy, it was a sure meeting you, no, don't say anything, don't. It's going to tak he strength I have just to walk away from you, I know it's hard t n't make it harder on me, please. Don't. Nothing more. Please.

(JIMMY TRIES to let her go, but is overcome. He kisses her hand gently.)

JIMMY: In another u e, another time and planet, you and I could have been more great, I know it. Let's honor that futile missing dream by walk way from this with … integrity. Farewell, Cathy, Farewell.

(JIMMY TURNS and w t resolutely. She stares after him.)

GIRL: My name is San a.

LIGHTS DOWN

END OF PLAY

THE FUTILITY NOTES:

FIRST PRODUCED in 2001 by The Defiant Ones at Manhattan Theatre Source as part of their evening of one acts entitled CLOSE ENCOUNTERS, directed by the author, featuring Chuck Bunting as Jimmy and Tara Platt as the Girl.

I WROTE this piece for my good friend Chuck, who is a walking whirlwind of a human being, a tremendous person and talent.

FOR YOU, Chucky.

Pc ;, Satire And Shit Like That

As mentioned previo began as a writer in the early 90s by contributing sketches O SHAME THEATRE while a grad student at the univer f Iowa. Mostly dick jokes, the kind of thing a young guy in h ly 20s finds funny, so on.

In the fall of 2002 No ne started up a branch in New York City for a year. It was a he ime, then, with the WTC attack on our city still fresh and raw.

I was never political b that sad and tragic event; I don't think I even voted. The WTC g down affected a lot of people in many different ways. Me, I to politics, I wanted to know how something like that could h ppened. Now I vote, definitely.

2002 and 2003 was a y time, man; hundreds of thousands of people were protesting upcoming invasion of Iraq in New York City and across the co .

Many of the sketches I wrote during that time became plays that were produced across the country as part of a tour called NO SHAME GOES TO WAR, a theatrical movement protesting the invasion of Iraq. Time has proven us, sadly, all too right about that.

I've included the ones that stand as plays in this collection. So here we go.

28

I A merica (4 m or f)

CHARACTERS:

FOUR PEOPLE (CAN ale or female) designated thusly as –

AMERICA
LIBERTY
TRUTH
JUSTICE

THE CHARACTERS A ESS the audience directly. I will admit that I've always thoug Liberty as female (something to do with the statue, I guess) an ice as male (something to do with Judge Moore in Alabama) so may come through in the dialogue a bit, but you should feel fre ast whatever sex, age or race of actor as you please. You can gi m signs or t-shirts to designate character or leave it up to the a ce's imagination in terms of their individual names.

AMERICA: I am America, land of the free.

LIBERTY: And we only had to kill and subjugate four or five million Native Americans to do it.

TRUTH: It wasn't completely free, I mean, we had to give some of the little buckskin-wearing buggers a bunch of shiny beads and whiskey, I think it set us back about three bucks or so, just for Manhattan alone. So it wasn't THAT free.

JUSTICE: Land of the free, but not land of the free health insurance, that canker sore on your face, that's going to cost you.

AMERICA: I am America, where all men are created equal.

LIBERTY: And women get to do the dishes.

TRUTH: America, where it took only two hundred years for a civil rights movement, a movement that met with much resistance, in fact there are people in office as we speak who still doubt that it was a good idea.

JUSTICE: In fact, some elected officials think that Strom Thurmond retired far too early.

LIBERTY: Even though he's dead.

AMERICA: I am America, where the separation of Church and State is the law and freedom of religion is sacred.

JUSTICE: As long as you pagan pig-fuckers remember that we are one Nation, UNDER GOD, that's what it says in the Pledge of Allegiance and don't you fucking forget it. UNDER GOD.

TRUTH: You have the freedom to believe what you want as long as you believe in Jesus.

LIBERTY: And please keep in mind that Jesus was white, blond and blue-eyed.

JUSTICE: I don't care where he was born, he's the son of God, he had to be white, don't give me any of this garbage that there weren't any white people in the Middle East back then because I don't give a good crap. America's Jesus is WHITE.

AMERICA: I am America, where any child can grow up to be President someday.

JUSTICE: As long as he's either a Republican or Democrat,

reads the bible every day, comes from family money and attended an Ivy league school where he was able to achieve at least a "C" average, then he can be President.

LIBERTY: And as long as HE is a HE and not a SHE, then your child can be president.

TRUTH: Our corporate sponsors tell us that we're not going to be ready for a female President for quite some time, HOWEVER, in forty or fifty years we could very well see a Jewish President (because they believe in God, too) or maybe, just maybe, even a black President.

LIBERTY: As long he or she only looks black, but is still able to think rich and white, i.e. Condoleeza Rice.

AMERICA: I am America, where every vote counts.

TRUTH: They do COUNT the votes.

LIBERTY: They don't mean anything, but they do COUNT them.

JUSTICE: Your vote does count, unless one of the candidates is the son of a previous president who also ran the CIA and therefore knows where a lot of bodies are buried, than that counts more than your vote counts.

TRUTH: And if one of the candidates is related to a Governor of a swing state, then that counts more than your vote counts.

LIBERTY: And if one of the candidates happens to be VERY good friends with the guy that owns the machines that counts the votes all across the country, then that counts more than anything else counts.

AMERICA: I am America, where freedom of speech is guaranteed.

JUSTICE: Hey, it's America, you can say what you want. Now shut the fuck up.

TRUTH: You can say what you want. Just be careful of what you're saying.

LIBERTY: And who you're saying it to.

JUSTICE: And don't criticize our leaders, regardless of how badly they may read the teleprompter or how poorly they equip our troops.

TRUTH: And don't burn the flag, let it touch the ground or turn your back on it.

LIBERTY: You can protest in America, just don't protest about America.

AMERICA: I am America, and I support the spread of democracy around the world.

TRUTH: Except in Saudi Arabia, China, Lebanon, Jordan, Turkey, Taiwan, Tibet, most of Central and South America and parts of Africa.

LIBERTY: And Texas.

JUSTICE: We make too much money there to bother with democracy.

AMERICA: I am America, and I fight for those that cannot fight for themselves.

TRUTH: Except in Saudi Arabia, China, Lebanon, Jordan, Turkey, Taiwan, Tibet, most of Central and South America and parts of Africa.

LIBERTY: And Texas.

JUSTICE: We make to much money there to bother with human rights.

AMERICA: I am America and I invaded Iraq to bring freedom to the Iraqi people.

JUSTICE: There was a lot of money being made there and we weren't seeing one red cent of it. Not only that, that Saddam was an evil prick. He imprisoned, tortured and killed his own people.

TRUTH: He can't do that to his people.

LIBERY: Only we can do that to his people.

AMERICA: I am America, and every citizen of America has the inalienable right to freedom, life and pursuit of happiness.

TRUTH: Unless you're poor and you need health-care.

LIBERTY: Unless you're a woman and you want equal pay and opportunities.

JUSTICE: Unless you're a homo and you want to serve in the armed forces or get married.

TRUTH: Unless you're neither a Republican or a Democrat and yet would still like to be represented by Congress.

LIBERTY: Unless you're over the age of sixty-five and you need affordable prescription medication.

JUSTICE: Unless you refuse to believe in God.

TRUTH: Unless you're eighteen years old, able to get drafted but not able to get a drink in a bar.

JUSTICE: Unless you suddenly find yourself classified an "enemy combatant".

TRUTH: Unless you're lacking in corporate sponsorship.

LIBERTY: Unless you're in Texas.

AMERICA: I am America, and I am at War.

JUSTICE: We are fighting a war for our way of life.

LIBERTY: We are fighting a war for truth and justice.

TRUTH: We are fighting a war overseas to avoid having to fight a war here at home.

AMERICA: I am America and I am at War.

TRUTH: If we don't fight this war, than sooner or later everyone is going to wonder why we haven't caught the people responsible for destruction of the World Trade Center and we can't have that.

LIBERTY: If we don't fight this war, sooner or later everyone's going to realize just how dumb and ineffective the guy sitting in the White House really is. Sooner or later mistakes our leaders made that cost the lives of Americans at home and abroad will have to be accounted for and we can't have that.

JUSTICE: If we don't fight someone else, then sooner or later we're going to have to fight each other. And our corporate sponsors can't have that.

TRUTH: We need this war.

LIBERTY: We need this war.

JUSTICE: We need this war.

TRUTH: War is a good thing.

LIBERTY: War is a good thing.

JUSTICE: War is a good thing.

AMERICA: I am America and I am at War.

BLACK OUT.

I AM AMERICA NOTES

I FIND that the piece works best when delivered like an upbeat "Rock The Vote" commercial or like what you see onstage at a typical Republican Convention.

THE FIRST PERFORMANCE of the piece at No Shame Theatre No York was February 28th, 2003, with the following cast:

MAGGIE BELL as Liberty
Dan Brooks as Justice
Joshua Peskay as Truth
Joshua James as America

PERFORMED at No Shame Goes To War (Los Angeles), on March 8, 2003. Directed by John James Hickey, with the following cast: Tory Seiter, Mike Rothschild, Jenn Cousin

PERFORMED at No Shame Goes To War (Charlottesville), on March 21, 2003, by Vanessa Brown, Chris Estey, Todd Ristau, and Seth Silverman.

PERFORMED at No Shame Goes To War (Charleston), on March 21, 2003. Performed by Amber, Betsy Johns, Rachel Lewin, Hilary C.

PERFORMED at No Shame Goes To War (Austin), on March 22, 2003, by Jonathan Morrow, Kate Caldwell, Keely Williams and Wetzel Parker.

I AM AMERICA received its professional world premiere in the summer of 2005 at The City Theatre in Miami, Florida, as part of their Summer Shorts Festival. J. Barry Lewis directed the production.

WHEN I READ this piece today, in 2013, I'm taken aback, I mean, I wrote that the country would be ready for a black President before a female President and look where we're at now, I mean, yikes. It's just amazing to look back at this, ten years later.

WHEN IT WAS PRODUCED in Miami, they only used one actor for all four parts (I don't agree with that choice, myself, I see them as all separate characters) and the actor refused to say the line "only we can do that to his people" referencing America torturing Iraqis, because he thought it was in poor taste, I guess, and because America would never, ever torture.

IRONIC, given what we know about the war today.

BUT I CONSIDER it a significant accomplishment that this play was produced in Jeb Bush's back yard in 2005.

IF ANYONE WISHES TO do the play today, you have my permission to change or cut the specific line "Unless you're a homo and want to serve in the armed forces or get married" because happily, gays can openly serve in the military and get married today.

AND YOU MAY TWEAK the lines regarding catching who was responsible for the WTC and how dumb the guy in the President's office is, etc… since that has changed. That's the thing about writing these political pieces, if we're lucky, we make progress.

PROGRESS IS ALWAYS A GOOD THING.

29

Diplomacy (2 m or f)

CHARACTERS:

MAN ONE – Career Diplomat in a suit.

MAN TWO – Career Diplomat in a suit.

SETTING: Outside the United Nations

(MAN ONE STANDS OUTSIDE, smoking a cigarette to relieve his stress.

He is joined by MAN TWO. They nod to each other politely. MAN TWO gestures for a light for his cigarette. MAN ONE gladly gives him a light.

They both stand and stew for a moment.)

ONE: Those bastards.

TWO: I know, I know.

ONE: Those backstabbing bastards.

TWO: I'm with you.

ONE: You can't trust 'em.

TWO: You said it.

ONE: They're just not … trustworthy.

TWO: Not one bit.

ONE: It's a cultural thing, I think, it's just not genetically possible for them to be trusted, there's just something—

TWO: Something somewhere, in their wiring, something in their—

ONE: DNA, it's in their fucking DNA—

TWO: That's right, in the DNA, something that's programmed to be—

ONE: Untrustworthy.

TWO: Untrustworthy, Yeah. Yeah. I'm with you. Yeah.

ONE: Those bastards. After all we've done for them.

TWO: Those bastards.

ONE: And there's no talking to them!

TWO: No communication!

ONE: You try and be reasonable, you state your case with logic and intellect and fucking … fucking …

TWO: Reasonableness!

ONE: Reasonableness! And what do they do? Drop their pants, turn around and immediately start talking out of their ass!

TWO: I know, I know. It's shameful. Nothing but Ass-talk. It's a Goddamn shame. It's like they think every day is their birthday or something.

ONE: Those bastards.

TWO: Those fucking bastards.

ONE: Where would they be without us, anyway?

TWO: Nowhere, that's where!

ONE: Between you and me—

TWO: Yeah?

ONE: Just between you and I. I sometimes think that the best thing to do in the name of world diplomacy …

TWO: Yeah, yeah?

ONE: Best thing to do, and I wouldn't say this to anyone else on the council but you—

TWO: I hear you, same from me to you, big guy—

ONE: And this is just my opinion, but I sometimes think that the best thing to do with those people, would be to just simply drop a big fucking nuclear warhead right in the Goddamn center of them. I mean, I'm all about peace, I want the peace just as much as anyone, but sometimes, sometimes you just wanna go, okay, you're going to be that way? BOOM! Take that you ungrateful fuckers, BANG! WHOOSH! All gone.

TWO: Between you and me—

ONE: Yeah?

TWO: I feel the exact same way.

ONE: I'm telling you—

TWO: That's not our official policy, mind you—

ONE: Ours neither, of course.

TWO: Our OFFICIAL policy is to TRY and be diplomatic with the stubborn fuckers. TRY TO, anyway.

ONE: Same with us, same with us.

TWO: Because they bring SOME assets to the table.

ONE: A few, a few, that's true, they do.

TWO: But there are days, I'm telling you, there are days—

ONE: I hear ya—

TWO: There are days when I dream of us, our people, doing just that same exact thing to those greedy fuckers. Just go, is that what you have to say? Okay! Bang! Whoosh! Boom!

ONE: BOOM!

TWO: Bang! All gone!

ONE: All gone! Those bastards.

TWO: Those fucking bastards.

ONE: All we've done for them and this is how they treat us?

TWO: It's a disgrace, how're they're behaving, seriously. This is a problem, this is a big serious fucking problem.

ONE: You know what I think? Fuck those guys. You know? Just fuck 'em!

TWO: Fuck 'em! Fuck those assholes and their ass-talk, fuck 'em!

ONE: Fuck those fucking bastards. Just what do they offer the world in terms of culture, anyway?

TWO: Shit. Not much.

ONE: Try nothing! Nothing! They make a few decent movies—

TWO: That they do, it's true—

ONE: But we always remake them for ourselves anyway—

TWO: We do too!

ONE: Other than some cool movie ideas and an okay film festival, they do nothing!

TWO: Fucking nothing!

ONE: Their cuisine is pretty good, too. But other than their food and movies, there is NOTHING that they have to offer to the civilized world, nothing. Those bastards.

TWO: That's right, those bastards. Wait a minute. You said food?

ONE: Sure, the food is good.

TWO: Are you serious? Their ... cuisine?

ONE: Come on, admit it, their food is pretty good, they got good restaurants. I always eat like a pig when I'm over there.

TWO: Wait a minute, wait a minute. Who are we talking about again?

ONE: Who are we talking about? Who do you think we're talking about?

TWO: Aren't we talking about the Americans?

ONE: What? Are you fucking crazy? We're talking about the Goddamn FRENCH, why would you think that we were ...

(Short pause as they look at each other.)

TWO: You're from America, aren't you?

ONE: And you're with the French team, aren't you?

TWO: *Mais oui.*

ONE: Well. At least we're PRETTY MUCH on the same page, save one or two wrinkles.

TWO: Right, right. We should probably—

ONE: Get back to the table, get on with the diplomatic talks—

TWO: Got a lot of work to do—

ONE: You said it, you said it.

(The two men walk off in opposite directions. They stop and glance each other. They turn toward the audience.)

ONE & TWO: Bastards.

Blackout.

DIPLOMACY NOTES

DIPLOMACY DEBUTED at No Shame Theatre New York City on February 21, 2003, featuring:

Adam Devine as Man One
Joshua James as Man Two

PERFORMED at No Shame Goes To War (Los Angeles), on March 8, 2003. Directed by J.J. Hickey.

PERFORMED at No Shame Goes To War (Charlottesville), on March 21, 2003, performed by Chris Patrick and Scott Silet.

PERFORMED at No Shame Goes To War (Cedar Falls), on April 4, 2003, performed by Luke Pingel and Grant Tracey.

DIPLOMACY RECEIVED its professional world premiere in the summer of 2006 at The City Theatre in Miami, Florida, as part of their Summer Shorts Festival. James Randolph directed the production.

PEOPLE FORGET NOW (some deliberately and dishonestly so), but ten years ago not everyone believed Iraq had WMDs (I didn't, nor did hundreds of thousands of others) I mean, after all, remember that we renamed French fries and French toast, called them FREEDOM FRIES, for crying out loud, simply because France didn't want to invade Iraq with us.

AND THE FRENCH WERE RIGHT.

30

New Texas: Or, Now That War Is Finally Over, Party On! (4 m)

By
Joshua James and Joshua Peskay

CHARACTERS:

DUBYA – The President
DICK – The VP and man in charge
RUMMY – The Brains of the Outfit
DELAY – late as usual

SETTING: Iraq.

TIME: Right after the invasion.

SPECIAL NOTE:

THESE BOYS HAVE thick Texas accents and they are not saying Iraqis but rather "Iroquois", pronounced just like it's spelled. All the misspelled words in this piece are intentional.

(LIGHTS UP ON DUBYA, sitting on one of four lawn chairs, gnawing on a toothpick, drinking a beer. A cooler is by his side.)

DUBYA: Ahhhhh. Now this is downright presidentimable. Sun, beer, only one thing missing.

(Enter DICK.)

DUBYA: Dick! You old bastard!

DICK: Junior! You sombitch!

(They embrace.)

DUBYA: Welcome to New Texas, Dick.

DICK: It's a pleasure, junior, about damn time we got this country licked, woulda been sooner if it hadn't been for these damn terrorist liberals.

DUBYA: Tell me about it, I'm so sick of hearin' about that damn Fourth Amendment shit. Who needs four Amendments? There's only one law that counts, and that's that a gun in the hand is worth two in the … in the … hmm.

DICK: Don't hurt yourself, junior, I get what your saying. Toss me a cold one there, tough guy. So, how is it here New Texas?

DUBYA: Suuuhweet. Tons of space, shitloads of oil, and no bill of rights. Dick, this is living. Dick, I need a favor. I wanna be the El Capitan of New Texas. Can I be El Capitan, please, pretty please with sugar on top?

DICK: Well … I suppose you've earned it.

DUBYA: WOO-HOO! Hot diggidy dog! In honor of me declaring myself El Capitan of New Texas, we gonna celebrate, Texas style!

DICK: Execute a few minorities?

DUBYA: You know it! The Secret Service is rounding up some right now! That reminds me, make sure Condi's got her passport. I don't want her getting caught up in the round-up again like last time. Man, was she pissed of.

DICK: Heh-heh. So, what kinda minorities they got down here?

DUBYA: Iroquois, some shit like that, who knows. I swear I can't figure these people out, though. They look like wetbacks, but they don't speak a lick of Spanish and they can't cook for shit.

DICK: If they ain't white and ain't from Texas, color 'em terrorists, that's what I always say.

DUBYA: Where's Rummy?

DICK: He's gassing up his Hummer. He couldn't believe the prices down here.

DUBYA: Amen to that. Gas is so cheap here it's like Jesus himself is pumping it into your soul.

DICK: Fuckin' A. Here's Rummy.

(Enter RUMMY.)

DICK: Rummy, you sumbitch!

DUBYA: Rummy, you old rat bastard. Come on here and have a sit down with El Capitan Big Dubya.

RUMMY: I swear to God, fellas, I've been looking since yesterday and there ain't one Goddamn titty bar in this whole country.

DICK: It's a state now Rummy. We're in the state of New Texas.

RUMMY: State, Country, Church, School. Whatever. They all look the same to a laser-guided hellfire missile. How you fellas doing?

DUBYA: Hot but not bothered. What are you drinking, Rummy?

RUMMY: Petrol, high octane, straight up. Love the stuff. Dick, how's the ticker?

DICK: It's still workin' so don't get any ideas, you ambitious bastard. I know you were the evil cuss that sent that epileptic hooker to my room last night. Lucky for me I had just charged up the ol' pacemaker. That bitch lit me up like a Christmas tree.

RUMMY: Dick, I swear it wasn't me that sent her, I swear on my honor as a member of the United States Government.

(Pause, then they all look at each other and laugh hysterically.)

DUBYA: *(laughing)* Woo!

DICK: *(laughing)* Fuck.

DUBYA: Haw! I can't believe you said that with a straight face!

RUMMY: I didn't know how long I could hold it, I almost broke, I swear to God.

DICK: Haw! It hurts, it hurts!

DUBYA: Next thing ya know, he's gonna be askin' ya to go hunting with him!

(DUBYA and RUMMY laugh, only to stop when DICK stares at them.)

DICK: That ain't funny.

RUMMY: I'm sorry Dick.

DUBYA: I'm sorry too, Dick.

(Brief pause, then DICK busts out laughing. DUBYA and RUMMY join in.)

DICK: Gotcha! You shoulda seen the look on your faces!

RUMMY: Man oh man, woo! I though you was for real!

DUBYA: Hot damn, you really had me goin'!

(DELAY enters, all pissed off.)

DELAY: Damn it to hell!

All: Delay!

DELAY: Shit fuck piss cunt! Damn it all!

RUMMY: Delay, what the hell's the matter with you?

DUBYA: What happened, did ya get slapped with another indictment?

DICK: He catches indictments like a sailor catches genital warts. Often and all over.

DELAY: That ain't funny, Dick. Indictments go away, genital warts is forever. Fuck, fellas, this ain't good.

RUMMY: What ain't good? The war's over, buddy. We won!

DUBYA: We wuz just about to celebrate by zapping a few darkies, just like in Old Texas.

DELAY: We can't.

DUBYA: What?

DELAY: Ya can't fry nobody.

DUBYA: What do ya mean I can't? Of course I can, I'm El Capitan of New Texas, not to mention to the Assistant to the Vice President of the US of A. I do whatever the fuck I want to, ain't that right, Dick?

DICK: Pretty much. So long as I tell you to first.

DUBYA: And right now I wanna execute a few minorities. Killing poor colored folk is the thing I miss most about being Governor of Texas. Why the hell do ya think I invaded this country in the first place? It wasn't for the oil.

DICK: Well, actually … it WAS for the oil, junior.

DUBYA: The oil was for you, Dick, Not me. I just wanted to fuck up some poor minorities. Now what's this horseshit about me not being able to carry on with my Texas-style celebration?

DELAY: It's that Goddamn Jimmy Carter.

DUBYA: Jimmy Carter?

DICK: What's that peanut-pushing liberal cracker doing here?

DELAY: Goddamn cracker started up an ACLU branch in Baghdad.

DICK: We don't call it Baghdad anymore, Delay. The capital of New Texas is now called Dubya Beach.

DELAY: My bad. But he's there an' handing out pamphlets. They actually started voting.

DUBYA: They've BEEN voting, haven't they?

DELAY: Yeah, but this time it's for real, they ain't using our machines. Carter got 'em to vote and fucked us. They decided. The Iroquois want civil liberties.

DUBYA: Civil liberties? What the hell are civil liberties, Rummy?

RUMMY: Means ya can't execute anyone without some kind of reason.

DUBYA: What kind of shit is that? That's the dumbest thing I ever heard of. We don't have no civil liberties here in New Texas.

DICK: We don't have them in Old Texas, why should we have them in New Texas?

DELAY: It's too late, the media's already caught wind of it.

DUBYA: Fuck the media, we own the media. What the hell are we paying them for if they're gonna turn around and fuck us over like this.

DELAY: Not our media, are you high, it's the French media, they got wind of it and now it's been picked up over Europe.

DUBYA: Fucking Carter. Delay, call Jiminy Cricket and tell him if he don't skedaddle outa here pronto that I'll fuck him so hard he'll think he's a virgin on prom night.

DELAY: We can't control it, fellas. Now that the war's over, there's all this sympathy for the poor little Iroquois. Ya can't fry nobody now.

DUBYA: What's the point then? I only went to war so I could execute poor minorities. If I can't DO that one simple thing, what's the point of being El Capitan?

DELAY: But the war's over, Dubya. We can't keep killing people without a war.

DUBYA: Rummy, is this true?

RUMMY: War is over, Skip.

DUBYA: Dick?

DICK: They're right, junior. The war is over.

DUBYA: But I can't have this, I need some bloodshed! I need some death an' destruction just like in the Old Testament. Dick, can't ya do somethin' about this?

(Brief pause.)

DICK: I guess there's only one thing left to do. Rummy, how many soldiers and how much time would you need to take over France?

RUMMY: France? Sheeeet. Maybe a dozen Navy SEALs. Three hours. This time tomorrow, we'll be staging public executions at the Louvre.

DUBYA: The Louvre? He said France, Rummy!

DICK: The Louvre is in France, junior.

DUBYA: Well, fuck me in the ass. When did they move it there?

DELAY: I'll go prep congress.

RUMMY: I'll draft a press release.

DICK: I'll see if the nukes are ready.

DUBYA: Hey wait a minute, what are we doing? Aren't them Francies mostly white people?

DICK: Yeah, but they're liberal.

RUMMY: And peace-loving.

DELAY: And they have universal health care.

DUBYA: Time to bring 'em some war, baby! Texas style. Boo yah! Party on, Dick?

DICK: Party on, junior.

ALL:Party on! Whoo-hoo!

(Music, Quiet Riot's Metal Health, begins to play.)

Lights Down.

NEW TEXAS: OR, NOW THAT THE WAR IS OVER, PARTY ON! NOTES:

THIS PREMIERED at No Shame Theatre New York sometime in early in 2003 and was also part of their BEST OF NO SHAME show, featuring: Dan Brooks, Matthew Peskay, Joshua Peskay and Joshua James.

NEW TEXAS: OR NOW THAT THE WAR IS FINALLY OVER, PARTY ON! received its professional world premiere in the summer of 2006 at The City Theatre in Miami, Florida, as part of their Summer Shorts Festival.

JOSHUA PESKAY and I have been friends for a long time, we were both at the University of Iowa at the same time and both participants during No Shame Theatre's New York's run. We wanted to write something together. So we did this in a few days over email and just wanted it to be as obnoxious as possible. It was a lot of fun to perform. I saw the production in Miami and it was hilarious, too.

They really nailed there, but my program with the cast list for that production is missing.

I SPOKE to Joshua Peskay recently about the play, when preparing this book, and we both felt that, at the time, we may have gone too far with it but with what we know now, in hindsight, we probably could and should have gone a whole lot farther.

THAT'S how crazy the Bush administration was, it made satire a real challenge.

31

Afraid Of The Dark (2f)

An A train Play
Originally presented at New World Stages

CHARACTERS:

ALISON – A pretty, young schoolteacher.

TABBY – A retired housewife.

SETTING: On a subway car, trapped during a power outage.

TIME: August 2006.

AUGUST, 2006

(Subway car. Stops. Lights go out.

Train sits.

Dark. Unmoving.

Two women sit at opposite ends of the car.

Frustrated. Hot.

Squinting in the darkness.

Long pause.)

ALISON: Oh my GOD! How long are we gonna sit here like this? Oh my GOD! Why aren't we moving? What happened to the lights?

(ALLISON, a young woman, stands and paces in the darkness.)

ALISON: Oh my God. I hope everything's all right. No announcement, nothing. They're not even telling us anything.

(TABBY, an older woman, sits quietly.)

TABBY: I'm sure it's going to be all right.

ALISON: Do you think it's … oh my God, I can't take this, it's so hot and dark. I can't take it.

TABBY: It will be all right, I'm sure we'll know something soon.

ALISON: It's not right, just to leave us here in a dark tunnel, no lights or announcement, they should at least make an announcement, don't you think? We deserve an announcement!

TABBY: The power is out. They can't make an announcement without power.

(Short pause.)

ALISON: Do you think it's the terrorists?

TABBY: It's not the terrorists.

ALISON: It could be the terrorists, right? It could be, we don't know it could be *al qway-da* again—

TABBY: It's not al-Qaeda.

ALISON: They attacked us once, they could be hitting us again, right?

TABBY: It's not al-Qaeda, it's Con Edison. Con Edison dropped the ball again, that's all that it is.

ALISON: You're sure?

TABBY: I'm sure, trust me. I live in Astoria.

(Short pause.)

ALISON: Oh God. I don't know if I can handle this. It's so hot in here, there's no air. God. I think I'm going to cry. I'm sure I'm going to cry.

TABBY: Hey. It's going to be all right. Take some deep slow breaths. They'll get us moving soon and we'll be fine.

ALISON: I'm sorry, I'm so sorry. It's just … I'm afraid of dark. I'm sorry, it's so silly, I mean, I'm a grown woman and here I am afraid of the dark. I'm starting to lose it in here, I really am, I'm about at the end of my rope. Oh my God.

TABBY: Honey, it's not silly at all. Everyone is afraid of something. Sit. Sit next to me. Here.

(ALISON sits next to her.)

TABBY: My name is Tabitha, but all my friends call me Tabby. What's your name?

ALISON: Alison, everyone … everyone calls me Alison.

TABBY: Pleased to meet you, Alison. Now listen. I want you to take deep breaths and tell me a little about yourself. What do you do? Where do you live?

ALISON: Okay. All right. I'm a schoolteacher, I teach social studies. I live in Washington Heights with my fiancé', Grant. He's a broker. He's just the best. We're getting married this fall in Florida.

TABBY: That's wonderful. You're going to get married and have a wonderful life.

ALISON: We are. Unless I die right here on this train. What if it's a bomb? It could be a bomb, right?

TABBY: Honey, it's not a bomb, it's Con Ed.

ALISON: The power wouldn't go out like this for no reason, would it? How could something like this happen?

TABBY: It happens all the time. It happened three years ago, remember?

ALISON: I didn't live here then, we were in Florida. I don't remember. But … it can't just go out, for no reason, can it? Maybe someone's trying to do something, maybe a terrorist is attacking us through our power grid, something like that?

TABBY: It's no terrorist, honey, it's simply deregulation.

ALISON: Deregulation?

TABBY: Deregulation and politicians putting the profits of privately owned businesses ahead of public interests. The government leases public assets to private industry. Private industry in turn sells our resources back to us at a much higher cost. Private industry is interested in only one thing, making profits, not in getting power to the people efficiently, so they let their systems become antiquated and run down because to upgrade costs them more for little to no return. What we end up with is, in effect, a monopoly made by the elected officials that are supposed to look out for us.

(Short pause.)

ALISON: What is it you do, again?

TABBY: I'm a housewife.

ALISON: Housewife?

TABBY: Retired housewife, actually. My husband passed away some time ago, bless his heart, so now it's just me.

ALISON: Oh, I'm so sorry.

TABBY: I was, too. He was a good man.

ALISON: I don't know what I'd do if I lost Grant. He's just the best. Oh my God, I hope he's all right, what if … what if something happened to him … oh my God!

(ALISON puts her hands over her face.)

TABBY: Honey, he's all right. It's just a power outage, it's all right. Every year it's the same thing. It gets really hot and Con Ed is, for some reason, shocked and surprised that the eight million people who live here would want to use their air conditioners. He's fine, sitting somewhere stewing in the dark, just like we are.

ALISON: He's afraid of the dark, too. He pretends he isn't, but I can tell. He's so cute. What's your name again … Tabby? Tabby, I'm so sorry I'm such a mess. I'm just afraid all the time, you know. Don't you get afraid?

TABBY: Certainly.

ALISON: I think I'm more afraid now then I have ever been. Ever since … ever since that thing happened, you know, in 2001—

TABBY: In September.

ALISON: Yes, THAT. I didn't live here then, but it had to be the scariest thing ever, I didn't even want to move here but Grant insisted, for his career, Wall Street, you know. I'm just so afraid of terrorist and dirty bombs and everything, so much, I don't know what to do sometimes.

TABBY: I know, sweetheart, I know.

ALISON: I mean, I just thank God every day that George Bush is President, that's for sure.

(Short pause.)

TABBY: I don't FUCKING BELIEVE you just SAID that OUT LOUD!

(TABBY jumps to her feet.)

ALISON: What?

TABBY: DON'T TELL ME YOU JUST SAID, THANK GOD GEORGE BUSH IS PRESIDENT! TELL ME YOU DIDN'T SAY IT! TELL ME!

ALISON: I . . . but . . . I am, I am thankful George Bush is President, and—

TABBY: Stop RIGHT THERE. NOT ANOTHER WORD!

(TABBY grabs her bag and stalks to the other end of the car.)

ALISON: What's wrong with that? He's the only one with the strength and courage to protect us from the terrorists—

TABBY: Honey, save that shit for the tourists, okay? There's a big fucking hole downtown in the financial district and who do you think was in charge when that happened? Who was supposed to protect us and didn't on that September day in 2001?

ALISON: He'd just gotten into the job, it's not fair to blame him for the mess Clinton left him.

TABBY: Oh, I can blame him, he had a memo warning him it would happen and he ignored it, so I can and will blame him. Clinton wasn't a factor, he'd been out of office nine months. And Clinton sure as hell didn't tell Bush to lie to us about WMDs to get us to invade Iraq!

ALISON: He DIDN'T LIE about Iraq, EVERYONE thought Iraq had WMDs!

TABBY: Bullshit! That's corn-fed BULLSHIT! Remember we had to rename FRENCH fries and FRENCH toast because France didn't believe us? Remember the UN saying NO? Remember the half a million people marching in Manhattan prior to the invasion in PROTEST because THEY didn't believe there were weapons there, neither!

ALISON: Grant says—

TABBY: Grant? GRANT??!

ALISON: My fiancé. He says people just want to hate Bush because it's easy, because he doesn't speak as well as some people and he was a C student at Yale. They don't really know how much good he's actually doing for America and democracy around the world. He says the President is making the country safer.

TABBY: I have ONE word in response to that. KATRINA.

ALISON: Grant thinks—

TABBY: Darling, I don't need to hear anymore, because if that's an example of how your fiancé THINKS, then my advice for you is to run for the hills, as far away from him as possible, because GRANT is so full of shit that he probably squeaks when he walks.

ALISON: How dare you! How … how dare you!

TABBY: How dare you, in light of all the terrible things that's gone on in this world, how dare you sit there and say Thank God for George Bush. How dare you promote the sick fairy tale that he's got OUR best interests at heart. With the wars and debt and people killed and tortured, how can you actually believe he's anything but an incompetent sociopath?

ALISON: What do you know, anyway? You're just a housewife!

TABBY: What, a housewife can't watch the news? A housewife can't read the papers? A housewife can't have an opinion or a brain, is that what you're saying? You're a fucking social studies teacher, you should know better!

ALISON: I don't want to talk to you anymore.

TABBY: FINE BY ME!

(Short pause.)

ALISON: I met him. I met him during the last election. In Florida. He shook my hand and thanked me for my support. I looked in his eyes and I saw ... I saw compassion, and strength. I saw someone who would protect me from terrorists and all the other things I am afraid of. He's a good man. I saw it in his eyes.

TABBY: Lots of women looked in the eyes of Ted Bundy and saw love. It didn't make it fucking so.

ALISON: You just WANT to hate him. It doesn't matter what he does or doesn't do, you've decided he's a horrible person and that you hate him, no matter what. I am less afraid of the terrorists and ... and the gays and the Muslims and abortionists because he is there. Protecting me. I'm not as afraid because of him and that's all that matters.

(Short pause.)

TABBY: Honey, I don't hate George Bush. I hate what he's done, but I don't hate him. He's the village idiot, so of course he's going to do terrible things when he's left alone in charge of the toy store. I don't hate him for that. You know who I DO hate?

(TABBY turns toward ALISON.)

TABBY: I hate the people who put him there. I hate the people who refuse to admit the truth, that they fucked up and put a maniac in charge, the people who elected him not just once but twice, TWO TIMES, the people who are smart enough to know they've made a mess but are too proud or too Goddamn scared of the dark and terrorists to admit they're WRONG about George W. Fucking Bush, that's who I hate. People like YOU.

(TABBY leans close to ALISON.)

TABBY: You want to know something, Alison? You shouldn't be afraid of the dark. You shouldn't be afraid of terrorists. You should be afraid of people like me, because someday, someway, people like you won't be in charge any longer and people like me will demand retribution for the death, destruction and debt done in America's name. COUNT ON IT!

(Lights come up. Train starts moving.)

ANNOUNCER: Ladies and gentlemen, we apologize for the

delay but we have the problem fixed and are now under way. We thank you for your patience.

(Train stops. Doors open. TABBY stands, gives ALISON one last good hard look, and then exits the train. Lights fade.)

End of play.

AFRAID OF THE DARK NOTES:

FIRST PRODUCED in 2006 at New World Stages as part of the A train series. Directed by Susan Einhorn, the cast list sadly lost. I looked and looked for that cast list, because the actors in this were fantastic, just superb.

THE A TRAIN plays are fun, you basically travel to the end of one line of the A train, draw actor names and headshots out of a bag, then climb on the train and, AS THE TRAIN travels to the other end of the line, you write a play and it must be finished before the train reaches that point.

THE PLAYS HAVE to be set on the train, too. Written and set on a train. We write them, they're handed off to actors that night, they memorize them and they're performed.

IN THE SUMMER OF 2006, we had a major power failure where I live in Astoria, Queens and lost electricity in large parts of the neighborhood for over two weeks. It was pretty bad, especially considered that Con Ed HAS A PLANT in Astoria, less than a mile from where the blackout occurred. And it was August hot, too. Businesses went bankrupt, etc.

BUT MUCH OF this is based on a real life experience, wherein I heard someone going on about the war and all the terrible things and they ended it by saying, "thank God George Bush is President," it's a sentiment I still find baffling, to this day.

THE WHOLE "I looked into his eyes" thing I got from an actor being interviewed on TV, I think it was Sean Astin, actually. He said that he trusted President Bush because he looked into his eyes and felt something. He felt safe, some shit like that.

YEAH. I know.

32

All Fun & Games Until... (4 m or f)

CHARACTERS:

TAYLOR – Age nine.
LITTLE CHUCKY – Age nine.
DREW – Age nine
LOUIS – Age nine.

TIME: Present

SETTING: An outdoor playground, located just about anywhere in the USA.

NOTE: Meant for adult actors playing kids, not real nine-year old child actors.

LIGHTS UP

(The song SPYBREAK by Propellerheads, begins to play.

TAYLOR, a young lad the age of nine, runs out, a plastic water rifle in hand.

He spins and "fires", making massive machine gun noises with his mouth.

No water, just lots of special sound effects supplied by TAYLOR himself.

LITTLE CHUCKY appears and "dodges" TAYLOR's shots.

LITTLE CHUCKY carries a toy pistol and wears sunglasses. He's also nine.

LITTLE CHUCKY fires, also supplying sound effects himself. Ryan "dodges" the shots.

DREW, big and clumsy and also nine, stumbles in and "fires" at LITTLE CHUCKY and TAYLOR with his toy gun.

LITTLE CHUCKY and TAYLOR "dodge" and return "fire" upon DREW.)

TAYLOR: DIE, ENEMY OF TRUTH AND JUSTICE! DIE!

LITTLE CHUCKY: You're DEAD and you're butt-ugly, too!

(DREW "dies" a horrible and exaggerated "death."

TAYLOR and LITTLE CHUCKY turn and fire at each other.

LITTLE CHUCKY lowers his "gun" in disgust.)

LITTLE CHUCKY: Butt-munch, you're cheating!

TAYLOR: I'm not cheating, ass-face.

LITTLE CHUCKY: I shot you, like, five billion times already.

TAYLOR: I dodged 'em with bullet time.

LITTLE CHUCKY: You can't use bullet-time, you ain't Neo, I'm Neo!

(DREW jumps up.)

DREW: Counted to ten, back to life!

(Before he can "fire" TAYLOR and LITTLE CHUCKY "shoot" him again, his body going into spasms from the many imaginary bullets.

DREW falls in a horrible and exaggerated "death".

TAYLOR turns back to LITTLE CHUCKY.)

TAYLOR: Just 'cause you got your Mom's sunglasses on doesn't make you Neo! You don't even do bullet time right, ass-breath!

LITTLE CHUCKY: Uh-huh! Watch me, butt-wipe.

(LITTLE CHUCKY does his version of slow-motion "dodging" in bullet time.)

TAYLOR: Uh-uh, it's like THIS.

(TAYLOR does his version of slow-motion bullet time "dodging".

They both do silly, slow motion action sequences.

LOUIS, also nine, runs in carrying a case.)

LOUIS: Hey guys, guess what !

(LITTLE CHUCKY and TAYLOR turn and "fire" at LOUIS. He dies a horrible and exaggerated death.)

DREW: Counted to ten, back to life!

(DREW jumps up, is immediately "fired upon" and dies a horrible and exaggerated death.

TAYLOR and LITTLE CHUCKY turn back on each other and fire. Neither goes down.)

TAYLOR: You can't just dodge all the shots, that ain't fair. You gotta die at least once.

LITTLE CHUCKY: Uh-uh, I'm Neo.

TAYLOR: Even Neo died at least once, you ass-face.

LITTLE CHUCKY: You ain't dying, neither, an' I shot you like ten gazillion times.

TAYLOR: I died three times last week.

LOUIS: Ten, back to life!

(TAYLOR and LITTLE CHUCKY swing their guns toward him.)

LOUIS: Wait, don't shoot! I got something to show ya!

(DREW sits up.)

DREW: Ten!

(LITTLE CHUCKY and TAYLOR turn and "fire" upon DREW, riddling him with bullets before he can even stand.

DREW dies a horrible and exaggerated death.

LITTLE CHUCKY and TAYLOR swing their guns back toward LOUIS, who stands and opens a case.)

LOUIS: Look what I got.

(The boys crowd around the case.)

LITTLE CHUCKY: Whoa. Totally awesome.

TAYLOR: Cool. Where'd you get that?

LOUIS: It's my dad's. He's got a bunch of 'em an' he didn't lock the cabinet. I got to get my picture taken with it for a poster, for some thing my Dad's a part of, some group called N-something.

(LOUIS takes a PISTOL out of the case. It's a real fucking weapon, Sig Sauer nine-millimeter. LITTLE CHUCKY takes it from him and holds it.)

LITTLE CHUCKY: It's heavy.

(TAYLOR takes it from him.)

TAYLOR: Lemme. Awesome. Just like the movies.

(DREW jumps up.)

DREW: Counted to ten, back to life!

(TAYLOR swings the pistol around and FIRES at DREW.

A REAL GUNSHOT ECHOES.

DREW takes the shot.

He falls down in a horrible but in no way exaggerated death.

LOUIS, TAYLOR and LITTLE CHUCKY look at each other for a moment.)

TAYLOR: Cool!

LITTLE CHUCKY: Cool!

LOUIS: Totally cool! Just like the movies!

(LOUIS takes the PISTOL back from TAYLOR.

The three of them go into "battle mode", running around in exaggerated stances.

TAYLOR and LITTLE CHUCKY "fire" their toy guns and LOUIS.

LOUIS "dodges" and FIRES at TAYLOR.

A REAL GUNSHOT ECHOES.

TAYLOR takes the hit and falls in a horrible, bloody and non-exaggerated death.

LOUIS swings the pistol around on LITTLE CHUCKY.

LITTLE CHUCKY goes into his "bullet-time" slow motion dodge.

It doesn't work.

LOUIS FIRES at LITTLE CHUCKY, several times.

SEVERAL REAL GUNSHOTS ECHO.

The bullets knock LITTLE CHUCKY down in a bloody and definitely not-exaggerated death. The boys all lay there, dead. LOUIS grins.)

LOUIS: That was like, the coolest thing ever. Totally.

(LOUIS looks at them, waiting.)

LOUIS: Guys? Isn't that ten? Guys?

(LOUIS waits a moment, patiently.)

LOUIS: Guys? You should have counted to ten by now.

(LOUIS pushes DREW's body with a toe.)

LOUIS: It's been ten. Hey!

(DREW doesn't move or wake.)

LOUIS: Guys? Aren't you coming back to life? Guys?

(LOUIS stands alone, waiting patiently for his friends.
He waits a long time.
"Rock Is Dead" by Marilyn Manson, begins to play.)
Lights fade.
End of play.

ALL FUN AND GAMES UNTIL... NOTES:

NOTE, this play has never been produced. It was specifically written for a theatre sometime in 2006, I think, that had asked me for a piece, they were doing an evening called LETTERS TO THE NRA and I was known by then for my political sketches.

SO I WROTE the preceding play as per their request.

THE THEATRE'S artistic director didn't like it; she wanted something softer than this. So I wrote and sent her FAST LEARNER and she produced that one.

I THINK this is a good play, but it's hard for me to read it these days now that I'm a father of two young boys myself, and in light of all the tragic and terrible shootings that appear in the headlines daily. I mean, it's frightening how many mass shootings there has been just in the years since this was written; we're averaging one every other month.

IT SCARES ME, to be honest.

BUT I DON'T WANT to shy away from this work just because it scares me. Fear means there's something real in there. So it's included in this collection.

33

Fast Learner (1 m)

CHARACTER:

ROBERT – Age nine.

SETTING: A playground.

TIME: Present.

NOTE: Robert addresses another kid whom we don't see. And Robert doesn't need to be played by an age appropriate actor.

(ROBERT, age nine, enters and sits on a swing.)

ROBERT: Hi. My name is Robert. What's yours?

(He speaks to another boy, whom the audience cannot see.)

ROBERT: Yeah but I'm not a stranger, I'm Robert.

I'm new. I just moved here.

Can too.

Can too.

Can too move wherever I want.

My daddy is gonna work here. In this city. He's got a big job. He works at the newspaper.

Can too.

Can too.

Can too work wherever he wants. This is America.

What game are ya playin'?

Army war?

No, I can't play with you. I can't. My daddy won't let me play with army men or any kind of toy guns.

Cause he says it's morally subversive.

It means bad. That's what he says.

No, I can't go play Halo with you. I can't. My daddy won't let me play videogames like that.

Cause he says they're ethically compromised.

It means bad. That's what he says.

What do I do for fun? Lots of stuff.

Uh-Huh.

Uh-huh.

I do too have lots of fun. I read books all the time.

It is not stupid.

It is not stupid. My daddy reads books all the time.

No he can't.

No he can't.

No he can't beat up my daddy. MY daddy would beat up YOUR daddy. That's what would happen.

Huh.

Huh.

Yeah but my daddy lifts weights.

Your daddy is a what? A football coach?

So?

I'm not allowed to play football.

My daddy says so.

Cause.

Cause.

My daddy is writer.

It is not stupid. You're stupid.

I am not stupid. You're stupid.

Huh. Uh-uh. He lifts weights.

My daddy is six foot two, over two hundred pounds. He's big and strong.

Your daddy has a gun?

So?

No.

No, he doesn't like guns.

He says they effectively warp our social consciousness. That's what he says.

It means bad.

It is not stupid. You're stupid.

I'm not stupid. You're stupid.

You are too stupid. You … you … you have no ethical sensibility. You're an ignoramus!

It means bad!

Go ahead and go home, I don't care! I didn't like you anyway! I'm going.

(He pouts and stalks off. He looks back, talks under his breath.)

ROBERT: He doesn't know anything. I hate him. He's stupid.

(He looks around, than points his finger at the other little boy and 'shoots' him.)

ROBERT: Bang! Take that. Now you're dead and you won't have any fun. Bang!

End of play

FAST LEARNER NOTES:

This piece premiered in Maine somewhere (I never got the program, but I do believe I got paid) as part of LETTERS TO

THE NRA, in I believe, 2006. There were some big names involved, I remember, David Rabe was one, and there were other very talented writers.

It's definitely softer than ALL FUN AND GAMES UNTIL... but I didn't see the actual show, so I don't know how it went. I think there's an interesting angle to this piece, and that's why it's here.

I had a rather contentious relationship with the director of this play. My recollection is that she wanted the actor to be able to say whatever he wanted, and when I resisted that, she accused me of trying to force my "playwrighting rhythms" on her actor.

Of course ... that's what I do. That's what all playwrights do. But whatever.

I let the show go on, and when there was talk later on about re-staging it after one of the sadly recent mass shootings in our country, I quietly stayed out of it (and the production never happened, if I remember correctly.)

When you have a hundred or more productions of plays you wrote, you're going to run into people who just don't get or care about your work in the same way that you do. And you learn that and move on until you find those that do.

That's the theatre biz, man.

Speaking of which ...

34

F**k You! (3 m or f)

CHARACTERS:

THREE ANGRY ACTORS, can be any age or type.

THEY ADDRESS the audience directly and very specifically.

SETTING: Right there in the theatre.

(THREE ANGRY GUYS, or could be GIRLS, point out various people in the audience that they do not like.)

ONE: Fuck you.
TWO: Fuck you.
THREE: Fuck you.
ONE: You in the front …
TWO: Fuck you.

THREE: And the big mouth fucker in the back …

ONE: Fuck you.

TWO: You, girl with big hair …

THREE: Fuck you.

ONE: The fucker at the door that charged us a twenty bucks to get into this fucking place.

TWO: Fuck you.

THREE: Fuck you.

ONE: Fuck you.

TWO: Fuck you and the horse you rode in on, you fuck.

THREE: And while we're at it, fuck you over there, too.

ONE: And YOU, you fucker, I see you over there.

TWO: Hiding like a fuck, you fucker. Fuck you.

THREE: Fuck you and the guy sitting next to you, too.

ONE: Especially fuck the guy next to you.

TWO: A BIG FUCK YOU to the guy next to you, for not recognizing what a fuck YOU are. Fuck the both of you.

THREE: You. You. You. Fuck you.

ONE: A general fuck you to that entire row of fuckers.

TWO: But especially you on the end, fuck you.

THREE: Don't even try and fucking pretend you don't know what we're talkin' about, you fucker.

ONE: Fuck you for even TRYING to look all innocent-like.

TWO: Fuck you and fuck anyone that even looks remotely LIKE you, you fucker.

THREE: And that guy, that fucking guy that left early?

ONE: Oh man, yeah, fuck that guy.

TWO: Fuck that fucking fucker.

THREE: Fucking rude and fucking inconsiderate fuck. Wherever you are, Mister-leave-early guy …

ONE: FAA-HUUUCK YA-OUUU!

TWO: Fuck you and fuck your whole family!

THREE: And all of you fuckers that came in late and missed the beginning of the show?

ONE: FAA-HUUCK YA-OUUUUUU.

TWO: A BIG FUCK YOU. You know what time it starts, you rude fuckers. Faa-huuuck Ya-ouuuu. FUCK YOU!

THREE: You there, the giggler, you think this is funny?

ONE: Fuck you!

TWO: And that guy there, and the girl there and the guy with her, fuck you.

THREE: Basically, all you fuckers.

ONE: You fuckers.

TWO: You fuckers.

THREE: Fuck you.

ONE: Fuck you!

TWO: FAA-HUUUCK YA-OUUUU!

THREE: Okay. Okay. Okay. Hold on the fuck. Have we left anyone out?

ONE: I think that's everyone.

TWO: I think we got all the fuckers.

(Blackout. Short pause. Scene continues in darkness.)

ONE: Fuck the guy running the lights!

TWO: Especially that fucking guy, fuck him!

THREE: That fucker!

ONE: FAA-HUUUCK YAA-OUUUUU!!

The End.

F**K YOU! NOTES:

Premiered in May 2003 at No Shame New York City, featuring Dan Brooks, Adam Devine and Joshua James.

When doing this play you may, if needed, improvise (depending on the audience). Don't STRIVE for improvisation, but be prepared to do so if it's required. You have my permission. (Somewhere my good friend Chuck is slapping his hands and laughing as he reads that and thinking, "You're giving me PERMISSION?! All right, here we go!")

Personal note: This was, along with many other sketches I wrote for No Shame New York City, published freely online. At some point the Artistic Director of City Theatre in Miami read this specific sketch online and loved it, just loved it. She became a fan and City Theatre would go on to produce a lot of my short plays as a result.

And the AD always promised me that she would produce F**K YOU at some point.

Personally I would have preferred ALL THE RAGE or BURN-MARKS, which were more my taste. F**K YOU is a short, fun blackout sketch, mainly directed at New York audiences (who loved it, because that's how New Yorkers roll.)

Then in 2010, the AD called me and told me it was finally time; she wanted to produce the play. But she wanted it expanded, she wanted it to be five people rather than three, four women and a man, and wanted me to go all out and hold nothing back.

So I took a day and rewrote the play as per her wishes.

What follows is the expanded version.

35

F**k You! Extended Version (4 f, 1 m)

City Theatre Version 2.0, May 6, 2010

CAST: FUCKING FOUR WOMEN DESIGNATED AS ONE, TWO, THREE, FOUR.

FUCKING ONE MAN DESIGNATED AS FIVE

SET: NO FUCKING SET

LIGHTS: BARE FUCKING LIGHTS.

PROPS: ONE UNDERSTANDING AND PATIENT FUCKING AUDIENCE, WE HOPE.

FIVE ANGRY FUCKING ACTORS.

(FUCKING LIGHTS GO UP, MAN.

FIVE ANGRY ACTORS MARCH OUT AND POINT AT VARIOUS PEOPLE THEY OBVIOUSLY DON'T LIKE IN THE FUCKING AUDIENCE.)

ONE: Fuck you.

TWO: Fuck you.

THREE: Fuck you.

FOUR: Faaauuck you.

FIVE: FUCK YOU!

ONE: You in the front …

TWO: Fuck you.

THREE: And the big-mouthed fucker in the back—

FOUR: Fuck you.

FIVE: You, the person sitting way in the back who kept laughing at all the wrong and inappropriate places—

ONE: Fuck you.

TWO: You, with the gum …

THREE: Fuck you.

FOUR: Lady and the crinkly candy-wrappers?

FIVE: Fuck you!

ONE: How hard is it to understand? It's dinner first … THEN THE SHOW. Not dinner DURING the show. We had dinner, during which all necessary chewing was to take place, we fucking finish eating, THEN WE WATCH THE FUCKING SHOW! With no mastication of the molars therein! Okay? Fuck you!

TWO: You, dude with too much cologne on?

THREE: Fuck you, Aqua Velva, fuck you.

FOUR: I mean, can you seriously not see everyone hacking and coughing every time you stroll by? I mean, there is this shit that's called SOAP, you should try that, perhaps, instead of masking your odor with a bucket of chemicals, hmmm? Oh and … Fuck you.

FIVE: Bouncing foot person?

ONE: *(Bounces her foot at them).* Faaaaucck you!

TWO: You, girl with big hair …

THREE: Fuck you.

FOUR: Is this nineteen eighty-nine? Are you for real? Go to a real fucking hairdresser and get a real fucking haircut, for fuck's sake.

FIVE: I think she looks fine.

ONE: *(to FIVE)* You would. Fuck you.

TWO: *(to FIVE)* Fuck you.

THREE: *(to FIVE)* Fuck you.

FOUR: *(to FIVE)* Fuck you.

FIVE: You, who kept checking for messages on your blackberry and lighting the place up …

ONE: Fuck you.

TWO: Fuck you.

THREE: Fuck you.

FOUR: FAAAAAUUUUCKK YOUUUUUUU!

FIVE: Anyone and everyone who has a cell phone, blackberry, iPhone, iPod, MP3 and your fucking laptop … in the fucking theatre … you people …

ONE: Fuck you.

TWO: Fuck you.

THREE: Fuck you.

FOUR: Faaaoouuuckk Yaooooouuu!

FIVE: And fuck Steve Jobs, too, because I want an iPad and I can't fucking afford it. Fuck you, Steve Jobs, fuck you!

ONE: The fucker at the door that charged everyone twenty bucks* to get into this fucking place?

TWO: Fuck you.

THREE: Fuck you.

FOUR: Fuck you.

FIVE: Fuck you and the horse you rode in on, you fuck.

ONE: And the ushers?

TWO: Fuck all of you! Seriously.

THREE: We know you're standing there hoping and praying one of us falls and fractures something on stage so that you can take our place onstage, you just want our jobs, so fuck you!

FOUR: We weren't born yesterday, you know, so fuck you.

FIVE: And some of us were born a LOT farther from yesterday than others.

ONE: *(to FIVE)* Fuck you.

TWO: *(to FIVE)* Fuck you.

THREE: *(to FIVE)* Fuck you.

FOUR: (to FIVE) Faaaaauuuuckkk yaoooooo!

FIVE: You … third from the left, second row?

ONE: Fuck you.

TWO: You, the one in a t-shirt and shorts?

THREE: Does this LOOK like a volleyball match or a bowling tournament? It's a theatre, for fuck's sake.

FOUR: Fuck you.

FIVE: Oh, and YOU TWO, the proper couple in the first row, the wealthy overdressed pair festooned as though this were a wedding or a bat mitzvah? We have a very special message for you.

(ONE, TWO, THREE & FOUR LINE UP AS THOUGH THEY WERE A CHOIR. FIVE STANDS BEFORE THEM, PENCIL HELD OUT LIKE A BATON. HE LEADS THE LADIES IN SONG.)

ONE, TWO, THREE, FOUR: *(sing)*

Faaaaaaaaaaoooooooaaaoooaaaaacccccckkkkkk yaaaaaaaoooooouuuuuu!

Fuck you, fuck you, fuckyoufuckyoufuckyou faaaaaaa … aaaaa … aaaaa … kaaaaaaayouuuuuuuuuuuuuuuuuuuuuuuuuuuu!

(CHOIR BREAKS OFF, THEY GO BACK TO THEIR PLACES AND POINT AT THE AUDIENCE.)

ONE: And while we're at it, fuck you over there, too.

TWO: And YOU, you fucker, I see you over there.

THREE: Hiding like a fuck, you fucker. Fuck you.

FOUR: Fuck you and the guy sitting next to you, too.

FIVE: Especially fuck the guy next to you.

ONE: A BIG FUCK YOU to the guy next to you, for not recognizing what a fuck YOU are. Fuck the both of you.

TWO: You. You. You. Fuck you.

ONE: A general fuck you to that entire row of fuckers.

TWO: But especially you on the end, fuck you.

THREE: Don't even try and fucking pretend you don't know what we're talkin' about, you fucker.

FOUR: Fuck you for even TRYING to look all innocent-like.

FIVE: Fuck you and fuck anyone that even looks remotely LIKE you, you fucker.

ONE: And that guy, that fucking guy that left early?

TWO: Oh man, yeah, fuck that guy.

THREE: Fuck that fucking fucker.

FOUR: Fucking rude and fucking inconsiderate fuck. Wherever you are, Mister-leave-early guy …

FIVE: FAA-HUUUCK YA-OUUU!

ONE: Fuck you and fuck your whole family!

TWO: And all of you fuckers who came in late and missed the beginning of the show?

THREE: FAA-HUUCK YA-OUUUUUU.

FOUR: A BIG FUCK YOU. You know what time it starts, you rude fuckers. Faa-huuuck Ya-ouuuu.

FIVE: FUCK YOU!

ONE: And that actor in the other play I was in earlier in the evening who kept stepping on my lines?

TWO: Fuck you!

THREE: Hey! Are you talking about m—

FOUR: *(cutting her off)* FUCK YOU!

FIVE: And the actor who keeps forgetting her lines and dropping her cues?

(LONG PAUSE. ONE GETS WHO HE'S TALKING ABOUT.)

ONE: Fuck you!

TWO: And the actor who believes she's a "genius" at improvisation?

THREE: Fuck you!

FOUR: Hey! That's highly uncalled for, it's a freedom-based art form of expression and I was merely … look, I'm a bird!

(SHE DOES SOME FREE FORM MOVEMENT IMPROV … IT SUCKS.)

FIVE: Fuck you!

ONE: Anybody who thinks they're good at improvisation almost never is, so fuck you.

TWO: And that reminds me, whoever wrote that weird experimental avante guarde piece that flopped earlier? The sixties are over, pal, learn out to write shit that makes sense!

THREE: Fuck you!

FOUR: And the David Mamet wanna-be playwright who keeps hanging around rehearsal and insists on giving the actors direction?

FIVE: Fuck you, don't tell me how to say a line, fucker! You're the writer, not the director, so fuck you!

ONE: And the director who always shows up late and begins every note with a breathy, "Okay, wow … um … maybe …" and then doesn't say anything for at least ten minutes?

TWO: Fuck you!

THREE: And the ball-busting director who insists on pointing out every mistake in front of everyone, the one who can't go fifteen minutes without a cigarette break?

FOUR: Fuck you!

FIVE: And the egomaniac grad school director who keeps adding props and sound effects to the piece that have nothing to do with the story and then cutting lines he doesn't get because he can barely read and doesn't know what he's doing?

ONE: Fuck you!

TWO: I don't care about your concept, asshole, and neither does anyone else, okay? Your concept is not the play, the play is the play!

THREE: So fuck you.

FOUR: Faaaaooook youoooooo!

FIVE: Fuck you!

ONE: And the actress with the cleavage who keeps leaning over all the men, flirting and pretending they actually have a shot at fucking her when in reality they have zero chance of getting into her pants?

TWO: Fuck you.

THREE: FUCK YOU!

FOUR: Faaaaaaaoooook yaaaaoooooooouuuuu!

FIVE: *(after a moment)* Wait, you mean she … no chance at all?

ONE: *(to FIVE)* She no fuck you.

TWO: *(to FIVE)* No such luck of fuck you.

THREE: *(to FIVE)* Fuck you not at all.

FOUR: *(to FIVE)* Not gonna Faaauuuuuckkkkk Yoouuuuuu!

FIVE: Fuck!

ONE: And most of all, fuck the person who decided do produce a bunch of lame ass short plays instead of something with depth, meaning and drama … fuck you!

TWO: Other actors gets to play iconic roles such as Medea, Electra …

THREE: We get to stand on a bare stage with no costumes reciting profanity over and over until the joke is dead, so fuck you!

FOUR: Fuck you, whoever you are that picked this piece of shit!

FIVE: FAAAA-HUUUUUCKKK YAAAAA-OOOOOOO!

ONE: You there, the giggler, you think this is funny?

TWO: Fuck you!

THREE: And that guy there, and the girl there and the guy with her, fuck you.

FOUR: Basically, all you fuckers.

FIVE: You fuckers.

ONE: You fuckers.

TWO: Fuck you.

THREE: Fuck you!

FOUR: FAA-HUUUCK YA-OUUUU!

FIVE: Okay. Okay. Okay. Hold on the fuck. Have we left anyone out?

ONE: I think that's everyone.

TWO: Yeah, that's everybody, yeah.

THREE: Pretty much.

FOUR: I think we got all the fuckers.

(A QUICK, FAST FUCKING BLACKOUT. BRIEF PAUSE. ACTORS CONTINUE IN THE DARK.)

ONE: Fuck the guy running the lights!

TWO: Especially that fucking guy, fuck him!

THREE: That fucker!

FOUR: Fuck him!

FIVE: FAA-HUUUCK YAA-OUUUUU!!

(THAT'S THE FUCKING END, MAN.)

F**K YOU! City Theatre Version NOTES:

Premiered in the summer of 2010 at City Theatre in Miami, no cast list. As mentioned in the previous version, some improvisation may be necessary with this piece, so performers should be ready and able to do so if called upon. Do either version that you wish.

So I sent this version to the Artistic Director and she loved it, loved it. I worried that perhaps I went too far and she said no, it's perfect. They played it up in the publicity, highlighted it in commercials and in radio interviews and everything.

You see where this is going, right?

My friend Matthew Polly, a bestselling author and martial artist, once remarked to me about one difference between the east coast (where we both live) and where we both grew up (he grew up in rural Kansas, I grew up in rural Iowa) regarding profanity.

In NYC, Boston or Philly it's quite common for folks to say, "hey, go fuck yourself," or "go fuck your mother" as an affectionate way of teasing each other. It happens here all the time (and my memory is that the City Theatre AD was a transplanted New Yorker, which may explain why she liked the play so much).

It's like saying good morning. Seriously.

You do that in rural Kansas or Iowa, even as a joke, it will get you shot. Seriously.

And evidently in Florida, too. Metaphorically speaking, of course.

Yeah, they had to pull the play, long before the run ended.

Two of the actors couldn't handle it when the audience got hostile back at them. And the actors, the director and production staff discussed it and decided to yank the play only a week or so after it opened. Three of the actors were game, but the remaining two refused to do the piece (my dojo friend, known as "Yo" Joe, might say, "fuck 'em, the fuckin' pussies," but as I said, that's how New Yorkers roll, not Floridians.)

They never discussed the problems or difficulties with me, by the way. I found out after it was pulled. I would have happily edited it or gone back to the three person piece. But I was left out of that discussion, and in fact, never even spoke to the AD ever again. It was the Lit Manager who finally called me after the decision was made to yank it.

I still got paid, but that was of small consolation. They were doing another play of mine, THE PAP, at the same time and it was going well. I should have pulled that one, too. But I didn't, I just let it go. They've not done a single work of mine since.

And I'm not sure I'd want them too, now.

The Artistic Director who championed the preceding play, well, she isn't the AD of that theatre any longer, she left right after that. I don't know if the play had something to do with it or what, I've not spoken to her since. She never returned my emails, after the fact. I liked her a lot, too. I hope it wasn't my play that did it. I honestly do not know.

But as I said before, I wasn't even in favor of them doing the piece, they had to push me to do the rewrite. As I said before, I'd have much rather they produced ALL THE RAGE or BURN-MARKS, but … I have no control over what other people choose to do.

And that's the theatre biz, man.

The One Act Plays

These are all my one act plays except for THE FIGHT and THE VIEWING, which are published by Original Works Publishing in the collected titled The THE Plays.

1 – The Beautiful One (3M)
2 – Best Shot (2W, 1M)
3 –Prudence (2W)
4 – Something Situation, extended one act version (3W)
5 – Like The Song (2M, 1W)
6 – Bodily Functions (2M)
7 – Quitting (2M)

All are one set plays, at the most twenty-minutes or so, except for Bodily Functions.

36

The Beautiful One (3 m)

CHARACTERS:

KENNY – Handsome man, in his early thirties but on his way downward, unshaven and sloppily dressed.

KANE – Tall man, same age as Kenny but much better dressed, although somewhat more conservatively.

FIVER – Short man, same age as the others but dressed even better and flashier.

SETTING: Private room off of a bar that is hosting a wake. Present time.

THIS IS A WAKE, not a funeral. A wake. There is NO COFFIN on the stage.

THAT WOULD BE REDUNDANT. It's not a funeral or a viewing. It's a wake. This is a private room off of a bar. There is NO fucking coffin on stage at any time.

I HOPE I've made that clear. No … coffin … on stage.

LIGHTS UP

(Kenny stands in silence with a drink in his hand. KANE, also with a drink in his hand, enters the room. KENNY nods to KANE with a smile of recognition. FIVER walks in right after KANE, also carrying a drink. KENNY nods to him also.)

KENNY: To the Beautiful One.

KANE: The Beautiful One.

FIVER: The Beautiful One.

(They tap their glasses together in a toast and then drink. Short pause as they look at each other, then they all grin.)

KENNY: You guys, you fuckin' guys, I can't believe, it's been fuckin' years, hasn't it? Fuckin' Forever.

(KENNY grabs them both in a big hug, which is returned.)

KANE: It's been a few years, I saw you three years ago at Seymour's wedding.

KENNY: Shit, that's right, that's fucking right, we got shit-faced that night, godddamn. In fact, you and Babe that night …

KANE: Yeah. We did.

KENNY: And FIVER! Fuckin' Fiver back in the old home town!

FIVER: Kenny, good to see you.

KENNY: I couldn't believe it, when I saw you in the back row there, I said, fuckin' FIVER! Shit my pants, it's been too fucking long. How long's it been?

FIVER: Been awhile. Kane, it's good seeing you, too.

KANE: How's life been treating you, Fiver?

FIVER: Life's been good. Except for the last few days, of course.

KANE: Yeah.

KENNY: Fuck yeah. Jesus man, I'm still in fuckin' shock, when Kane called me and told me I dropped the fuckin' phone, I swear to God. Fuck man. Fuck Fuck Fuck. She was fuckin' … She was …

KANE: Special.

FIVER: Special.

KENNY: Special. Fuckin' special. And that's only the beginning. That's only the START with describing her, she was one and only. Fucking special. You guys want a drink, I need another Goddamn drink. Fiver? Kane?

KANE: Sure.

FIVER: No thanks, I'm fine.

(KENNY exits the room.)

KANE: He's gonna get on his ass drunk tonight.

FIVER: He's on his ass drunk already.

KANE: He's taking it hard.

FIVER: Yeah.

KANE: I don't blame him. In fact, I might just lock myself away in the house this weekend, just me and a couple of bottles of good scotch. Get blind, stinking, puking drunk for Babe.

FIVER: I don't drink anymore.

KANE: Yeah?

FIVER: Yeah. Stopped a couple years ago. This is orange juice.

KANE: Were you an …

FIVER: No, I just stopped boozing and started working out instead. No reason. Just had an impulse.

KANE: Uh-huh.

FIVER: But if ever there was a day to get on my ass drunk, this would be it. How'd you hear about it?

KANE: Her aunt. Her aunt, we knew each other. She called me. I called Kenny, few others. So. What you been up to Fiver?

FIVER: Lots of things. Yourself?

KANE: Not much. Well, I just made vice-president at the bank. I guess that's a good thing. Not much else. Not much at all.

FIVER: Hey, congratulations. On the job thing. You married? Got the kids, house and two-car garage, that whole package?

KANE: Not married. Came close once, a couple years ago. Only time.

FIVER: I'm not either. Married, I mean. Divorced. Twice. No kids. Lot of alimony. What about Kenny?

KANE: He's not married, as far as I know, unless he's got a mail-order bride tucked away somewhere. I don't know what he does either. For a living, I mean. I haven't seen him since the wedding awhile back.

FIVER: Seymour got married, huh?

KANE: Three years ago. Some girl from the city, her family owns a hardware store. I saw Kenny at the reception, he was piss-drunk then too. We had to take him home.

FIVER: You were there with …

KANE: Yeah. Fact, he looked pretty blue till he saw us. Perked up and looked happy as a clam. Told us how much he missed us. Took over the dance floor, trying to dance like those Riverdance guys do, took his shirt off, kicking his feet up and down, fell right on his ass. God, he made us laugh. Stomach's hurt, we laughed so hard. 'Specially her. He loved that.

FIVER: He always liked doing crazy stunts.

KANE: Wild child. That was what she called him. The wild child.

(KENNY enters, carrying drinks. He hands one to KANE and another to FIVER.)

KENNY: Here you go, mon-sewers. Fiver, I got you a drink anyway, you look like you need a fucking drink so don't fucking argue. Double Jack straight up. Drink up boys, we gotta burn the funeral blues right out of our system. Jesus, the fucking people that are here, did you see Brenda, Brenda is here.

KANE: Is she?

KENNY: Got five kids, five kids all lined up in a row. Five kids and on her third husband. Can't believe it. And she didn't get that much bigger either. I'd still throw her a hard one, if she wanted. And I saw Anne and Clint and Adam and Margie and what's-her-butt, the girl we all thought was a lesbo even tho' she dated guys, and guess what? She's a lesbian. We were right all along boys. A lesbian. She's still hot, too. I'd fuck her. Who else is here? Oh yeah, Cosmo and Pete and fucking Eric, you remember Eric, Fiver?

FIVER: The ear-wriggler.

KENNY: Yeah, he did that thing with his ears, always wondered how he did that. Wish I could do that. That ear thing was something. I shoulda asked him to do it for me again.

KANE: How you been holding up, Kenny?

KENNY: Hanging in there, big guy. This has been a shitty week, a monumentally shitty day, and an overall shitty thing to happen. Fact, this would be number one on my list of shitty things, this tops the list, but I'm gonna keep a smile on my fucking face anyway, you wanna know why?

KANE: Why?

KENNY: 'Cause that's what she woulda wanted, absolutely. She wouldn't wanted me all Blah-blah-Boo-Hoo, she woulda wanted me still tryin' to make her smile. That's what she woulda wanted. I know it. So I am fucking smilin'. Look at me right now.

(KENNY takes another drink. Then he grins.)

KENNY: I'm fucking smiling my ass off.

KANE: Where you workin' these days, Ken?

KENNY: Been sloggin' my way through the wonderous world of data-processing. But I don't wanna talk about my shitty job. That won't keep me smilin'. Fucking Fiver! It's been … How long has it been?

FIVER: Been a long time.

KENNY: Fucking forever. I don't even remember the last time I saw you, you know.

KANE: It was nine years ago.

KENNY: That long?

KANE: Fourth of July. We went down to the riverbank together. The four of us. Watched the fireworks together, sitting in lawn-chairs in the back of my truck. You were taking off for Europe for the rest of the summer, do one of those hiking things, and then maybe grad school, you weren't sure. Nine years ago this July.

FIVER: Yep. That's when it was.

KENNY: Jesus, the memory on this man. Fucking hell. Could be an elephant, he's got such a memory.

KANE: Got the trunk of an elephant right here.

KENNY: Whoaa-hoo! Fucking Kane hits the big one! Nice. She'd of loved that one. Shit. So what happened with you, Fiver?

FIVER: Fucked off grad school. I stayed in Europe a little longer than I planned.

KENNY: How long?

FIVER: Three years.

KENNY: Whoa, shit. Three years? Doin' what?

FIVER: Uh, this and that. Made a little cash, writing articles about places to go, that kind of shit. You know.

KANE: Where you at these days?

FIVER: Los Angeles.

KENNY: No shit?

FIVER: Been there a few years.

KENNY: Holy shit, Hollywood, you in the movie business?

FIVER: No, no. I'm writing.

KENNY: You write for the movies?

FIVER: No, I write for television.

KENNY: You don't write for the movies?

FIVER: No, just television.

KENNY: Don't you want to write for the movies?

FIVER: No, uh … I like the television work.

KENNY: But you're in Hollywood, you should take advantage, write for the movies, that's the big business there, right?

FIVER: Television's pretty good to me.

KENNY: I always liked going to movies. Know what's best about the movies?

FIVER: What?

KENNY: No commercials. That's what I like about movies. They don't stop once they start. I hate fuckin' commercials, just when you start getting' into whatever it is, along comes some fuckin' ad for a hemorrhoid cream or some shit like that. And usually you're eating when that happens. That's why I like the movies.

FIVER: Yeah, uh … movies are good that way.

KENNY: I never watch television anymore, unless there's a game on. You write for any shows I might know?

FIVER: I don't know. I actually …

KANE: You write that show "The Girl Next Door"?

FIVER: Uh ... yeah, I do write that show. Created it, actually. Who told you?

KANE: Nobody. Watched it, seemed a bit, you know, familiar.

FIVER: I can see how it might. A little.

KENNY: Shit, I'm gonna check this show out now.

KANE: You should. But I didn't see your name in any of the credits, Fiver.

FIVER: I changed my name when I got out there.

KENNY: What? You fuckin' serious? You no-shit changed your name?

FIVER: No shit.

KANE: So your name isn't Fieval anymore?

FIVER: No. It's Ethan Severn now. Fact, no one's called me Fiver in a long, long time.

KENNY: Holy Shit. Fiver isn't Fiver anymore. Why'd you do it?

FIVER: Well, for work, mainly. It's good to be Jewish in LA, but it's not good to be TOO Jewish. The best thing, what everyone wants out there, is to be an undercover Jew. And the name Fieval Schwarzenbaum is not undercover in any way, shape or form. Ethan Severn is.

KENNY: Fucking hell, Fiver. That blows my mind.

FIVER: As the years go by, I find myself doing a lot of things that I never imagined I would.

(Short pause.)

FIVER: When was … I'm sorry, I haven't talked to anyone in years. Did anyone see this coming? What happened, I mean.

KANE: I didn't, but after thinking about it constantly for the last three days, I guess that I am not surprised. She just wasn't happy.

KENNY: She always had trouble that way. Staying happy.

Something always brought her down. Fucking always. Fuck Fuck Fuck.

FIVER: When was the last time either of you talked to her?

KANE: 'Bout a year. We exchanged a few emails, mostly about silly shit, but I haven't talked to her, actually spoke to her, in over a year, I guess. You?

FIVER: It's been awhile.

KENNY: Two weeks.

FIVER: What?

KENNY: I talked to her two weeks ago. She called me, we shot the shit for almost an hour. It was a good time. Seemed that way.

KANE: She say anything?

KENNY: Naw. Maybe. I don't know. I hadn't seen her since that wedding, three years ago, but we talked. We talked pretty regular, always have, couple times a month, whenever she got down she'd give me a buzz and I'd cheer her up. She called me her booster shot for the blues. Told her jokes, shit I'd heard, girls I was fuckin' or tryin' to fuck, she loved stories about that. My love life, that's what she always called it, loved hearin' about Kenny's "Love Life". I told her, I said, this isn't a love life, this is a fuck life. I'm in this for the fuckin'. Someday, she'd say, someday Kenny, you'll meet a nice girl that'll sweep you off your feet and right up to the alter. Just you wait, Kenny, she'd say. I'd always tell her, nice girls know better. And nice girls, they ain't any fun, either, the nice girls. I like the bad girls, waiting for the exact right bad girl. The right one. Last time we talked, she was in a better mood than ever. Teasing me about the nice girls. Laughing, like she used to. She even said …

FIVER: What'd she say?

KENNY: I don't wanna talk about this depressing shit, guys, let's talk about the good things—

KANE: What'd she say?

KENNY: Nothing.

KANE: If she said something—

KENNY: What she said was for me and me only. It didn't have to do with what happened. Shit. Come on, guys. It's fucking hard enough to have to bury one of the fucking best people ever in the world. Let's not get caught in the blues, she wouldn't want that. I'm having a hard enough time. Let's remember the good things, you know. The good times.

KANE: The good times.

FIVER: Good times.

KENNY: Let's talk about the great things she did for us. She did some great fucking things, name them, how about that? Give me one, come on, throw one out there to the fucking universe. She's listening, she always sat and listened while we all shot off our mouths about all the great things we were gonna do with our lives, remember?

KANE: Yeah, she just sat there, smiling. Smiling that smile she had, the one that used only half her mouth.

KENNY: Okay then, put it out there. Baby, wherever you are, this is for you. You know what she did for me?

FIVER: What?

KENNY: She did a lot of great fucking things, but one of the best was she went back with me to my high school reunion. My ten year high school fucking reunion. I didn't want to go to the fucker, shit, I hated high school when I was in it, why would I want to go back? College, college was the good times, right? When the four of us were together, that was the SHIT, right there. So I wasn't gonna go to the damned thing, and I was bitchin' about it to Babe at the bar one night, this was almost five years ago, and I should never have told her. She talked me into goin', she did. Said if I didn't go back and show those cocksuckers I'd always regret it. What am I gonna show 'em? I asked her. I'm fuckin' unemployed, for chrissakes, I'd just gotten sacked again. No job, no house, a car that barely runs, that was my life at that point.

KANE: I didn't know you went to that thing, I remember you bitching about it, but …

KENNY: She talked me into it, rented a limo, bought me a suit, and not just any suit, a primo-Italian tailored sleek-looking MONEY suit, and she made sure I was the shit. AND came up with the greatest story, the most awesome story of what I'd been doing with my life.

FIVER: What was the story?

KENNY: Porno.

KANE: Porno?

KENNY: Porno baby, porno! She turned me into a real porn producer, the real fucking thing, man! I mean, she outlined the whole thing, she created a by-God resume for me, did the research, gave me a porn producer name, had titles of movies I'd done and porno actors who's careers I'd launched, I mean she didn't just give me an idea, she wrote a fuckin' BOOK! She made a movie out of my imaginary life! She even got some autographed pictures of Ron Jeremy to hand out to all the guys! Don't ask me how she did it, but she did. You shoulda seen the faces on those fucks from high school. She turned me into a porn King!

FIVER: That definitely sounds like our Babe.

KENNY: She was balls to the walls, man.

KANE: What was your porn name?

KENNY: Oh shit, that was the best. Kenny Cunnilingus.

FIVER: Kenny Cunnilingus?

KENNY: That was it, man, isn't that the most awesome! She gave me the greatest porno name ever! Kenny Cunnilingus. And Babe went as my date, she put on this red slutty dress, real sexy, no underwear, slutty hair-do and makeup and never let go of my arm the whole night. She was attached to me the whole night. Honey Suckle, that was her porno name, and she was my newest star. Our old prom queen, Deanna Sue Blackburn, she was the stuck-up queen bitch of my class, said something to Babe like, how lucky it was that Kenny had found someone so close to his own interests or some shit like that, and Babe goes, "Honey, I'm the lucky one, 'cause although Kenny's got a great cock, and he does, they don't call him Kenny Cunnilingus for nothing, if you know what I mean. He eats pussy like it was his mission in life and let me tell you something. I've been eaten out by some of the best dykes in the business and none of them, not one of them, ties my twat in a knot like Kenny Cunnilingus. He's the pussy-licking King." And the look on Deanna Sue's face was worth the four years of hell that was high school. Of all their faces. I was the scourge of every wife there and I was the envy of every man at that reunion. Every man, every one of those cocksuckers wanted to be me. It was one of the greatest nights ever. We laughed our asses off about it forever afterward. Thanks to her.

FIVER: That was our Babe.

KENNY: She got me face, man, that what she did, she took me back and gave me fuckin' face for the whole world.

(Short pause. KENNY turns away for a moment. He turns back around.)

KENNY: She was beautiful that way. Fuckin' beautiful. What about you, Kane?

KANE: What?

KENNY: Give us a good thing about Babe.

KANE: There are too many to count, Kenny.

KENNY: Shit man, pick something. Just one thing.

KANE: Kenny—

KENNY: Kane, you lived with her for almost two years, you don't have anything to offer up to the universe?

FIVER: You two lived together?

KANE: Yeah. We did.

FIVER: Not as roommates, but lived together as …

KANE: Lived together as lovers.

KENNY: Two years, two years you cohabitated and you don't got nothing to share?

KANE: Kenny, I like you a lot better when you're pouring the shit into your mouth as opposed to out of it.

KENNY: What does that mean?

KANE: What do you think?

FIVER: I didn't know you two were … together.

KANE: And why would you?

FIVER: I'm just surprised I didn't hear about it from anyone.

KANE: Hear about it from who?

FIVER: Anyone.

KENNY: I woulda told you, Fiver, but I didn't know where the fuck you were. They hooked up sometime after Seymour's wedding. Happened fast, too. One night holding hands and kissing, next night he's moving his shit in.

KANE: Hey Kenny.

KENNY: Hey what?

FIVER: You know what? I need another drink. You guys want another drink?

KENNY: Hell yes. Jack and Coke, baby. Thanks Fiver.

(FIVER exits. KANE looks at KENNY for a moment.)

KENNY: Hey what?

KANE: You talk too Goddamn much.

KENNY: That so?

KANE: Yeah that's so. Maybe you should cool it.

KENNY: Maybe you're too Goddamn touchy.

KANE: Fuck you, Kenny.

KENNY: You know what, Kane? See my face, this face here is smiling right at you. I'm smilin' my ass off and nothing you say or do is gonna change that. I'm smilin' for her and if you don't like it than fuck you. I'm smiling and fuck off if you don't like it.

(Short pause. FIVER comes back with a bottle of Jack Daniels. He pours some in each person's glass.)

KENNY: Thanks, Doctor, medicine just in the nick of time.

FIVER: So Kane. You and Babe lived together for … two years?

KANE: We did. And then we didn't. She moved out over two years ago.

FIVER: It didn't work out?

KANE: It was working fine, that's why she decided to move out. What do you think Fiver, people leave 'cause things are going good?

FIVER: I'm sorry, I don't mean—

KANE: What? To intrude? Hey, what the fuck, with motor-mouth Ken here, you got no chance of that.

KENNY: I'm still smilin' at ya, big guy. Smiling.

FIVER: I'm sorry Kane. I've just been out of touch for so long, I'm naturally curious.

KENNY: When was the last time you talked to Babe, Fiver?

FIVER: Well, it's been awhile.

KANE: How long?

FIVER: I don't know. Awhile. Quite awhile.

KENNY: She didn't tell you, did she? Didn't tell you her and Kane shacked up together?

KANE: Kenny, watch your Goddamned mouth—

FIVER: No, she didn't.

KANE: Otherwise I'm gonna … you were talkin' to her then?

FIVER: Yeah.

KANE: While she was living with me?

FIVER: Yeah.

KANE: And after she left, you were still …

FIVER: Yeah.

(Short pause.)

KANE: So she was calling you while she was living with me?

FIVER: No.

KANE: What? But you said …

FIVER: Letters. We wrote letters to each other. Started about three, three and half years ago. She sent me a letter. I wrote back. Wrote the old-fashioned way, via snail-mail. I got the last one a couple days ago. It's how I knew what was gonna happen. What happened, I mean. By the time I got it, it was too late.

(Very brief pause.)

KANE: You gotta lot of balls, saying that.

FIVER: What are you talkin' about?

KANE: I'm talkin' about how you broke her heart, that's what I'm talkin' about!

FIVER: I broke HER heart? Oh, that's rich!

KANE: Don't try and act all fuckin' innocent, you asshole. You think I wouldn't know? We did live together. When you took off for Europe and didn't talk to her for years, it broke her fucking heart. You wouldn't even return her phone calls. You were a real fucking DICK.

FIVER: She tell you WHY I didn't return her calls? Why do you think I went to Europe for three years instead of three months?

KANE: Sure she did but so what? That was no reason to act like you did! And now I find out you were writing her while she was with me, well hell, that explains fucking everything!

FIVER: Explains what?

KANE: Why she left me, you asshole!

FIVER: Hey, I didn't even know the two of you were together, so don't hang that on me!

KANE: Fuck you Fiver, or Ethan or whatever your Goddamn name is. And if life wasn't tough enough after she moved out on me, every time I turned on the television there was this new show called THE GIRL NEXT DOOR, which is practically the story of Babe's life!

KENNY: Really?

KANE: Kenny, you should be getting fuckin' residuals, you are fucking on TV.

KENNY: No shit? Fiver, I'm honored.

KANE: You might not feel that way after you see the show.

FIVER: I left Babe for one very specific reason. I didn't call her or see her for that same reason.

KANE: And why was that?

FIVER: You mean you don't know? I thought you knew everything?

KANE: Fiver, don't fucking push me, I mean it.

KENNY: Because she wouldn't marry him.

KANE: What?

KENNY: He asked her to marry him and she wouldn't. That's why he left and didn't come back.

(FIVER looks at KENNY, who takes a drink.)

KENNY: Yeah, she told me.

KANE: For that, that's why you cut her off? Put her out of your life? You broke her fucking heart, man.

FIVER: She broke my heart. I loved her. I did. I was devastated when she told me it wouldn't work out. That I wouldn't be able to make her happy. But I loved her.

KANE: Yeah, right.

KENNY: Kane asked her to marry him too.

FIVER: What?

KENNY: Yeah, he proposed. She said no. He took it hard.

KANE: Kenny, shut the fuck up.

FIVER: You asked her too?

KANE: Yeah, I did, so what? I'll tell you something else, when she said no I took it like a man. I didn't cut and run.

KENNY: But it is why she moved out. Because you were so hurt.

KANE: You don't know that you asshole!

KENNY: Sure I do. She told me. She said the same thing to you that she did to Fiver.

FIVER: You asked her to marry you?

KANE: Hey, I LOVED her. I did. I was there for her. I didn't run away. I loved her.

FIVER: Evidently that wasn't enough then, was it?

KANE: Fuck you, asshole!

(KANE pushes FIVER. FIVER pushes him right back.)

FIVER: Fuck you right back!

(Very short pause as they glare at each other. KENNY starts laughing. Laughing hard.)

FIVER: What the hell are you laughing at, you drunk?

KENNY: You two.

KANE: You think this is fucking funny?

KENNY: Both of you, you uptight assholes. Here we are at the funeral of one of the greatest women ever, and you two are in a pissing match over who loved her more. If Babe were here, she'd be laughing too. Jee-sus. You guys don't get it, do you?

FIVER: Get what?

KENNY: You both loved her, but it wasn't enough, you had to have more than that. You wanted to own her, you wanted the paper and the ring and the whole fucking deal and she wasn't about that. She wasn't, she never was. If she'd done that, she wouldn't have been Babe. Hell, I loved her. You think I didn't love her as much as you two? I never even slept with her, and I loved her more than any woman ever. You think it didn't kill me when I saw you together Kane? It did, but you know what? Didn't matter. Or how about when she told me she was back in touch with you, Fiver? Didn't matter. All that mattered to me was that Babe was happy, cause she wasn't happy that often. If living with either one of you two assholes made Babe happy, then hell, sign me up, I'm all for it. I don't care. I loved her, and I didn't require nothing in return for it. I may be an unemployed drunk loser but at least I did that right. I loved her. Hell man, I know I couldn't of made her happy all by my lonesome. I just wasn't enough. I wish I was but I know I wasn't. And I never complained to her about it, either. Babe had enough problems without adding mine. She was a twisted one and she knew it. We're lucky she made it this far. It took the three of us together for her to last as long as she did. You fuckin' guys, you should be happy, fucking happy you knew Babe for as long as you did. You were fucking blessed as far as I'm concerned. Blessed to have known her. I am. You both should shut the fuck up about yourselves and remember who we're here to honor. Fucking remember it!

(Short pause. KANE and FIVER look at each other. FIVER pours them all another drink. They look at KENNY.)

FIVER: You know what she used to do that always made me laugh?

KANE: What?

FIVER: Whenever I was cheesed off at something, she would come right up to me, put her nose right up against mine, and say "But the important thing to remember is that from this distance, you appear to have only a single humongous eye!" And it always killed me when she did that. I loved that.

KENNY: I remember that, I saw her do that to you!

FIVER: I loved it when she did that, I even put it in the TV show.

KANE: She never slept. You could call her at three in the morning and she'd be awake. She liked it when you called her like that. When we lived together, I remember that I'd get up in the middle of the night and she'd be sitting on a chair, naked, painting her toenails. I'd say "Hey, aren't you sleepy?" and she'd say "Not yet," and smile. I'd find her doing different things anytime I got up in the middle of the night, sometimes she'd be baking cookies, naked, and other times she might be making a quilt, always naked. She didn't really like clothing, felt it constricted her, that's why she loved skinny-dipping with us, remember? Very proud of her body and happy to have it hanging free and unbound. Whenever we came home the first thing she always did was take off her shirt. I remember that, but mostly I remember her never sleeping. I would wake up at night and she would be always doing something unusual in the nude and I would always ask her, "Aren't you tired?" and she would always smile and say, "Not yet." She never slept, I remember that. And when we went to bed she'd be awake when I went to sleep and awake when I woke up. Awake and watching me. I'd say, "What are you doing?" "Watching you," she'd say. "I like watching you." She did. I remember. She liked watching all of us.

FIVER: She always said that, watching us three losers was her favorite program.

KENNY: We kept her entertained and smiling.

KANE: As long as we could, anyway. Until she got too tired.

(Pause.)

KANE: Kenny Cunnilingus, huh?

KENNY: Kenny Cunnilingus.

FIVER: Kenny Cunnilingus. That's a great story, there's a great story in there.

KENNY: There is!

(They hold their glasses up in a toast.)

KENNY: To Babe.

KANE: To Babe.

FIVER: To Babe.

KENNY: The Beautiful One.

(They all drink. Lights fade.)

End of play.

THE BEAUTIFUL ONE NOTES:

FIRST PRODUCED at Manhattan Theatre Source, directed by Ato Essandoh and featuring Markus Griesshammer, Adam Rothenberg and Taylor Ruckel.

PRODUCED MANY, many times thereafter around the city, also produced at City Theatre in Miami and an extremely shortened version of this piece, I'm told, was a finalist for Louisville's ten minute play contest in 2005 or thereabouts.

I'M PRESUMING it didn't win (as have none of my other pieces which were finalists) because I never heard from them after getting a letter telling me I was a finalist. They let you know you made it to the finals, and then it's up to you to figure out that you didn't win when you hear nothing after that.

WHICH IS GOOD, because this work was never meant to be a ten-minute play, this version you just read is the perfect length for it.

IF I HAD to choose a favorite one-act play, this would be it (and there's a reason it's listed first in this section.) The first production of it was incredible, a perfect marriage of actors, director and material, enough so it was done again and again.

I AM VERY proud of this piece.

BUT LET'S BE CLEAR, no coffin on the stage. Just three guys and a bottle of booze, got it?

38

Prudence (2f)

CHARACTERS:

MARGIE – 39 years old. A very capable woman who looks younger than she is but sounds much older on the inside.

CATHY – 23 years old. A recent college graduate and still wide-eyed and idealistic.

TIME: Present

SETTING: A quiet café in Chicago.

(MARGIE TAKES her coffee and sits down at a table. She takes her bag off her

shoulders and sets it on the seat of one of the chairs close to her. MARGIE then spreads her paper out in front of her on the table and sips her coffee.

CATHY enters the café, stands and stares at MARGIE. MARGIE slowly becomes aware that she is being watched and gradually looks up. CATHY tentatively approaches MARGIE, who eyes her suspiciously. MARGIE carefully slips her hand into her handbag.)

MARGIE: Can I help you?

CATHY: Are you Margerette Blackburn?

MARGIE: Who wants to know?

CATHY: My name is Catherine Adele Wooley.

(CATHY, who speaks with an Oklahoma accent, sits down at the table with MARGIE.)

MARGIE: Catherine Adele Wooley, do you recall anyone inviting you to sit at my table?

(CATHY jumps back up.)

CATHY: Oh, I'm terribly sorry, I didn't mean to—

MARGIE: What do you want?

CATHY: I'm looking for Margerette Blackburn.

MARGIE: Why?

CATHY: I'm her daughter.

MARGIE: *(Brief pause.)* Have a seat, Cathy.

(CATHY looks at her a moment, then sits at the table with MARGIE. MARGIE takes her hand out of her handbag.)

CATHY: So. Are you Margerette Black—

MARGIE: Call me Margie, everyone calls me Margie. Yes, I am she.

CATHY: I'm uh …I'm your daughter. You gave me up for adoption when you had me … and—

MARGIE: I know Cathy, I was there, I remember doing it. How did you find me?

CATHY: Well, I got your name from the agency, the one I was adopted through . . .

MARGIE: That couldn't have been easy.

CATHY: It wasn't, actually, took a lawsuit and a court order just to get your name released. Your phone number is unlisted, no email address, nothing. I had to hire a private detective to find your home address. I went to your house yesterday morning but this large black woman answered the door and denied that you lived there, denied even knowing you. She threatened to call the police if I came back and slammed the door on me. She was very mean. She didn't even give me a chance to tell her who I was.

MARGIE: That's my roommate, Fran. She's that way. How did you find me here?

CATHY: Well, I saw this café in your neighborhood and thought that it was the perfect spot to stop for coffee in the morning before work. I got up early this morning, waited down the street until I saw you come out of the house and followed you here.

MARGIE: That's very resourceful of you, Cathy. Let's hope Fran didn't spot you following me, she's very protective and things could get ugly.

CATHY: My Lord, she was simply awful. How can you live with someone like that?

MARGIE: Fran has many good qualities.

CATHY: I think she just likes being mean.

MARGIE: So. You found me. What can I do for you?

CATHY: Well, I was hoping that maybe we could get to know each other.

MARGIE: No offense, Cathy, but if I had wanted to get to know you, then I wouldn't have put you up for adoption in the first place.

(Brief pause. CATHY's face bunches up.)

CATHY: Oh my. Oh my goodness. I don't know why … I can't understand why you're being so unfriendly.

MARGIE: I'm not deliberately trying to be unfriendly, Cathy, I'm simply being straightforward and honest. I find life works best for me that way.

CATHY: I don't understand it, your roommate lied about you living in your house, threatened to throw me in jail, when I finally found you and asked you if you are you are you looked at me like I'm some psycho killer, grilled me with questions and with your hand stuck in your bag like you were gonna pull out a baseball bat and hit me over the head with it. What's going on, you got a gun in there or something?

MARGIE: As a matter of fact, yes, I do have a gun in my bag.

CATHY: You do have a gun? Oh my Lord! I'd say that's being unfriendly!

MARGIE: I'd say that it's just being careful. Please keep your voice down. I have a license and permit for it and I'm perfectly within my rights. In my line of work I have to be careful.

CATHY: What are you, some sort of government agent or something?

MARGIE: No. So, what do you want?

CATHY: I just, I just wanted to meet you, that's all, find out a little bit of who you are and tell you who I am. Is that so terrible?

MARGIE: *(Short pause.)* I guess not. All right.

CATHY: Really?

MARGIE: I have about ten minutes. I'll let you have them. So … how's your life? Where did you end up?

CATHY: Well, I was adopted by a wonderful couple, Diane and Russell Wooley, from Lehigh, Okalahoma. I'm twenty-three years old, graduated college last spring with a degree in education, right now I have a job as a receptionist but I'm planning on grad school this fall. I'm hoping to be an elementary teacher someday.

MARGIE: That's nice. Your parents, are they nice people? Did you have a good childhood, get everything you need?

CATHY: Oh, absolutely, very loving parents, I never lacked for anything as a child. Mom and Dad loved me like their own.

MARGIE: Well. Okay then. That's good. That's really good.

CATHY: So do you have any other children, are you married—

MARGIE: No, to both questions. How about you, you married, have a boyfriend?

CATHY: I'm engaged, his name is Rod and he's just the best. He's an engineer, builds grain elevators, we've been together three years. He's the best.

MARGIE: Great. That's great. *(Brief pause. MARGIE looks at her watch and reaches for her bag.)* Well, it was nice to meet you, but I should be going.

CATHY: Wait! Can't we talk some more?

MARGIE: I'm afraid I'm on a rather tight schedule, so—

(CATHY takes out a card from her purse and tries to hand it to MARGIE.)

CATHY: Here are all my contact numbers back home. Is it possible for us to stay in touch? I'd really—

MARGIE: I don't think so, no.

CATHY: It hasn't even been ten minutes yet.

MARGIE: I'm sorry, but I really have to be going.

(MARGIE stands, picks up her bag and starts to walk away.)

CATHY: Do you really hate me that much?

(MARGIE stops.)

MARGIE: I don't hate you. I'm just not ... interested in starting a relationship with you.

CATHY: But you're my mother.

MARGIE: Diane Wooley is your mother. I'm simply the woman that gave birth to you.

CATHY: That's something, at least.

MARGIE: It was something.

CATHY: Isn't it at least worth a whole ten minutes?

(MARGIE looks at CATHY for a moment, sighs and sits back down.)

MARGIE: I suppose that it is, yes.

CATHY: Can I ask you something?

MARGIE: You can ask.

CATHY: Why did you put me up for adoption?

MARGIE: I was sixteen years old when I had you, Cathy. I put you up for adoption because I didn't have the means or the money to take care of you.

CATHY: Why didn't you ask your parents for help? They could have helped raise me, couldn't they?

MARGIE: They could have but they didn't. They kicked me out of the house when they found out I was pregnant.

CATHY: They did what? But ... but they're your parents, why would they do something horrible like that?

MARGIE: Lots of parents all over the world do horrible things to their kids all the time. One thing I've learned for certain is that the ability to procreate doesn't preclude the potential for ignorance.

I managed to survive somehow, and I gave birth to you. I gave you up for adoption so that you would have a happy childhood and not go hungry. It sounds like that's what came to be and for that I'm truly grateful.

CATHY: Didn't you want me?

MARGIE: I wanted what's best for you, Cathy, that's what I wanted.

CATHY: I don't understand why we can't stay in touch.

MARGIE: The time of my life when I had you happened to be a very scary, uncertain time and while it's not anything I'm ashamed of, it not something I look forward to being reminded of, either. I have a different life now. Don't take it personally.

CATHY: Okay. Okay. There was one other big thing I wanted to ask you, um … who was my father?

MARGIE: Again, your father is Russell Wooley and your mother is Diane Wooley. They raised you, they're your parents.

CATHY: But who impregnated you? They said … the agency said that there was only your name on the birth certificate.

MARGIE: That's right.

CATHY: So who was—

MARGIE: I'm not saying.

CATHY: I have the right to know who my father is.

MARGIE: And I told you, your father is Russell Wooley. As far as who I was involved with when I was sixteen, that's my business and nobody else's.

CATHY: But—

MARGIE: There are no buts. I don't have to talk to you. I'm not required by law to tell you anything that I don't want to. I can sit here and not say a word if you want. It's your choice, it's your ten minutes.

(Brief pause. CATHY looks away, clearing her throat.)

CATHY: Okay. Okay. So, um … what have you been doing with your life?

MARGIE: After I gave birth to you, I got a job as a waitress and did that for a long time. I went to night school, earned my GED and after that my college diploma, all while working full time at various jobs. I had some hard times, but I survived. I completed my Masters two years ago and now I work full time as a counselor at Planned Parenthood.

CATHY: You work at Planned Parenthood?

MARGIE: Yes.

CATHY: Isn't that … isn't that where they do ... abortions?

MARGIE: It's one of the places a woman can go for an abortion. We do other things there as well, but we're known for that.

CATHY: Is that why you carry a gun in your bag?

MARGIE: Yes. A doctor and a couple of the counselors have been attacked in the past, and there have been bomb threats, among other things. I also volunteer at a shelter for battered women two nights a week and find carrying a firearm while doing that to be very prudent.

CATHY: So … you do abortions?

MARGIE: The clinic doctors perform abortions. I counsel women that are considering abortion.

CATHY: Do you try and talk them out of it?

MARGIE: I try to help them discover what their very best choice is.

CATHY: Which sometimes means they have an abortion.

MARGIE: It often means that, yes.

CATHY: I could never have an abortion.

MARGIE: All right.

CATHY: I don't know how anyone could ever have an abortion.

MARGIE: How is not too hard, it's usually the why that makes it difficult.

CATHY: You're killing babies, how can you do that?

MARGIE: We don't kill babies, so just disabuse yourself of that notion right here and now. We abort fetuses in the first trimester of a pregnancy. We help women and girls better their lives by terminating unwanted pregnancies, that's what we do, it's a difficult thing but also legal, very necessary and anyone that thinks otherwise is just fooling themselves. Jesus Christ, you sound like one of those crazed Catholics that are constantly picketing us.

CATHY: I AM Catholic, thank you very much!

(Brief pause. MARGIE puts her head in her hands.)

MARGIE: Oh my God. You're Catholic. Someone somewhere has a sick sense of humor.

CATHY: What's that mean? What's wrong with being Catholic, do you have a problem with Catholics?

MARGIE: As a matter of fact, yes I do, I have a problem with any organization that is sexist, homophobic and ignorant and right now as far as I'm concerned Catholicism fits the bill!

CATHY: Oh my Lord, you're one of those atheist lesbian activists, aren't you? That explains everything!

MARGIE: What? No, I'm not a lesbian!

CATHY: You're not married and … oh! You even LIVE with a woman.

MARGIE: Living with another woman doesn't make you a lesbian! What's wrong with you!

CATHY: I should have known! That black woman at your house, she was definitely a lesbian!

MARGIE: Her name is Fran and she's my roommate and yes, she is a lesbian and yes, I am an atheist but no, I am not a lesbian, I'm just her roommate.

CATHY: You're one of those atheist lesbian activists, I was born to an atheist lesbian activist. I can't believe it.

MARGIE: For the last time, I am not a lesbian. Believe me, Cathy, if I were a lesbian, I would have no problem telling you that I was. And so what if I was? There is nothing wrong with being a lesbian.

CATHY: But you are an atheist, you hate Catholics and I'm Catholic, so that means you hate me, don't you?

MARGIE: I don't hate Catholics, I hate Catholicism, there's a difference, and let me tell you something Missy, you'd be surprised at just how many Catholic boys and girls I find sitting in my office in need of the services OF MY CLINIC!

CATHY: I suppose you're sorry that you didn't have an abortion when you were pregnant with me!

MARGIE: I wasn't sorry then but I'm sure STARTING TO BE NOW!

(Brief pause. CATHY starts to cry.)

CATHY: This is horrible.

MARGIE: Now she cries, of course, she cries.

CATHY: This isn't how I thought this was going to go at all. Oh my Lord.

MARGIE: How did you think it was going to go?

CATHY: Not like this! This is awful. This is horrible.

(CATHY puts her head in her hands and cries even harder. MARGIE looks at her a moment, then reaches into her handbag and pulls out some Kleenex. She hands the Kleenex to CATHY.)

MARGIE: This is not that awful, trust me. There are much more horrible things happening in the world than this.

CATHY: It's just terrible, it's simply just terrible.

MARGIE: What's so terrible? We shouted at each other, so what? People shout at me all the time and I shout right back. It's not the worse thing.

CATHY: I guess I had it in my head that we would talk and get to know one another, get close and find out stuff about each other.

MARGIE: Well, I would say that's definitely what's happening, wouldn't you?

CATHY: I thought it would be happier than this. I thought we would maybe be friends.

MARGIE: I told you, Cathy, I don't make friends very easily. Don't take it personally.

CATHY: I thought maybe you'd be happier to meet me and find out how I turned out.

MARGIE: I wasn't unhappy to meet you. I'm a little displeased with the Catholicism choice, of course, but for the most part, I'm glad you were adopted by a nice couple who love you and took care of you in a way that I was not able to, at that time. I'm ... I'm very happy to know that, to know that I made the right and prudent choice at that time in my life. I really am. Believe me.

CATHY: Yeah?

MARGIE: Yes. *(MARGIE looks at her watch.)* I'm really late. I think we've both scratched our itch more than enough, wouldn't you say? I should be going.

CATHY: But—

(MARGIE stands and gathers her bag.)

MARGIE: It's been ten minutes. I'm glad you've come, but I really—

CATHY: Margie?

MARGIE: Yes?

CATHY: Why didn't you?

MARGIE: Why didn't I what?

CATHY: Why didn't you have an abortion? You could have, right?

MARGIE: I could have, yes. It was harder to do back then, but not impossible. I could have.

CATHY: So why didn't you?

MARGIE: What difference does it make?

CATHY: It might have made a difference to me. Why didn't you?

(MARGIE looks at her a moment, sighs and sits back down.)

MARGIE: Because I was Catholic at the time.

CATHY: You're Catholic?

MARGIE: Was Catholic. I'm not Catholic anymore. I got over it.

CATHY: What happened, why are you not Catholic anymore?

MARGIE: Two primary reasons, one, I got myself educated and learned how to think for myself, educated enough to see through all the malarkey and crap they call the church. As for two … two …

CATHY: What? What's two?

MARGIE: Doesn't matter, forget about two.

CATHY: I'm not gonna forget about two, tell me what the two is.

MARGIE: You don't want to know what two is.

CATHY: I do too want to know what two is.

MARGIE: You can't handle two.

CATHY: I can handle a lot more than you think, I tracked you down, didn't I? I sued a government agency, I hired a private detective, I faced a large shouting black lesbian, I even managed to get you into a conversation without getting shot. I can handle a lot, thank you very much.

MARGIE: *(Short pause.)* Reason number two, the man that impregnated me was my priest.

CATHY: Oh no. Oh my Lord.

MARGIE: The Lord had nothing to do with it, it was a man wearing the collar of a priest. He took advantage of me when I was fifteen, and I'm fairly certain that I wasn't the first nor the last. I wouldn't tell my folks who did it, and because of that they kicked me out of their house. The priest just let them do it and said nothing.

CATHY: But … but you can't blame the church for the actions of one man.

MARGIE: I can blame whomever I choose, Cathy. I can blame the priest, I can blame my parents, I can blame the Pope, I'm a free person to blame or not to blame anybody. For a long time I blamed myself, but I was able to let go of that and now I just blame ignorance, especially organized ignorance, which often comes in the form of a religious or political group.

CATHY: So what happened to him?

MARGIE: He stayed a priest, kept on doing what he was doing for a long time. He died eight years ago, of testicular cancer, which makes you wonder if there is perhaps somebody watching and doling out justice. But I sincerely doubt it.

CATHY: I'm sorry it was so tough for you, back then.

MARGIE: There are a lot of people that have had it worse, believe me. I survived. That's the good thing. So. Well. Has curiosity been honored?

CATHY: So this is it then?

MARGIE: Yes. It's the prudent thing. You have a pair of wonderful and loving, if somewhat misinformed, parents at home. Go back home and honor the work they've done. Get married, be happy and chase your dreams, whatever they are. Just do me the favor of reading some book other than the bible and I will be pleased. Okay?

CATHY: All right. Thank you. I just wanted to know where I came from.

(MARGIE stands.)

MARGIE: Isn't it obvious? You come from Oklahoma.

(MARGIE looks at her for a moment, and then walks away. CATHY picks her card up from the table.)

CATHY: Margie, wait.

(MARGIE stops and looks at CATHY. CATHY holds her card out to her.)

CATHY: Take this. Just in case.

MARGIE: I can't promise that I will ever—

CATHY: I know. Take it anyway. Just in case. You never know when you might need a friend, right?

(MARGIE hesitates, and then takes the card from her.)

MARGIE: Thank you. Just in case.

CATHY: Just in case.

(MARGIE pauses for a moment, steps forward and kisses CATHY on the top of her head. MARGIE exits. CATHY sits quietly.)

CATHY: It's the prudent thing.

End of Play.

PRUDENCE NOTES:

FIRST PRODUCED at Manhattan Theatre Source in 2004, featuring Cindy Keiter and Maggie Bell, directed by Tina Polzin.

IT WAS ALSO PRESENTED in 2005 at Manhattan Theatre Source as part of their five-year anniversary. Ironically enough, no one told me that they were doing it (I was in Los Angeles at the time) and didn't find out until months later.

I ALSO HEARD through a friend who'd been at that anniversary show that I'd gotten some award, too, I think (I'd done a lot of work at that theatre) but whatever it was, no one ever gave it to me or mentioned it later. Heh-heh.

THAT'S THEATRE BIZ, man.

39

Something Situation (3f)

THE EXTENDED ONE ACT PLAY VERSION

CHARACTERS

BERDINE – A grandmother in her 60s.

RITA – a 13 year-old math prodigy.

ARLENE – BERDINE's daughter and RITA's aunt, 40s.

SETTING: A hospital room.

TIME: Present.

(BERDENE, 65, is sitting upright in her bed. She wipes her eyes with a handkerchief.

RITA, 13, enters carrying a book.)

BERDENE: Rita, What are you doing up here by yourself?

RITA: Mom sent me to cheer you up.

BERDENE: Oh. Well. All right. *(Short pause.)* So. Where'd your mother get to?

RITA: She's hiding from Aunt Arlene.

BERDENE: Arlene is here? Oh my Lord, here we go.

RITA: She's on her way. Mom and Aunt Arlene have been fighting.

BERDENE: I'm not surprised, they've fought ever since they were your age, so don't worry about it. Come here and have a seat. What are you reading there?

(RITA sits in a chair next to BERDENE's bed.)

RITA: The Mechanical Theory of Heat by Rudolf Clausius.

BERDENE: Oh. Are you reading that for a class or something?

RITA: No. Just for fun.

BERDENE: Oh. Okay.

(Brief pause.)

RITA: Are you all right, Grandma?

BERDENE: Not really, no.

RITA: Do you want me to get a nurse?

BERDENE: No, don't, it's just … it's nothing. It's just, having to be here, in this situation … going through this, having all this stuff happen to me and all that. Doesn't seem right.

(Brief pause.)

RITA: Look at the bright side. It's not a pickle.

BERDENE: What's not a pickle?

RITA: This is not a pickle.

BERDENE: Where do you get pickle, how do you get PICKLE out of all this?

RITA: I'm just saying—

BERDENE: Where is this PICKLE THING coming out of?

RITA: I'm just saying it's not the pickle that you think it is.

BERDENE: What is?

RITA: The situation.

BERDENE: My situation?

RITA: The situation, it's not the pickle that you think it is.

BERDENE: *(Short pause.)* You know, I know that you're supposed to some sort of genius and all, but would it be TOO much to ask if you could just make a LITTLE bit of sense every now and then instead of throwing pickles at me?

RITA: It's a saying, you know, a folk saying, when something happens to someone and they find themselves in a tight situation, sometimes people say, "She's found herself in a pickle" or "I'm in a heck of a pickle." And all I'm saying is that the something situation that you have currently found yourself in is not the pickle that you think it is.

BERDENE: *(Brief pause.)* You READ entirely TOO much!

RITA: Of course I do. That's all I do.

BERDENE: And the OTHER THING, HOW can you say this situation is not a pickle?! This situation is mostly CERTAINLY a pickle, it's nothing BUT a pickle! This is the biggest Goddamn Dill Pickle that I've ever seen, that's for sure!

RITA: I can see how it may be perceived that way.

BERDENE: What other way can it be perceived?

RITA: The other way it can be perceived is as something that happens. It's just something that happens to everyone. All of us. You. Me. Everyone.

(Brief pause.)

BERDENE: And why is it described as "being in a pickle?" Certain situations, I mean. Why would someone say that, where does that come from anyway?

RITA: Because pickles traditionally taste very sour. To actually being INSIDE of one is thought to be sour beyond all recall.

BERDENE: If that's the case, then this situation is definitely a pickle. In fact, pickle is the nicest thing you can say about it. THIS IS A PICKLE!

RITA: It's not the pickle that you think it is.

BERDENE: Well honey, it sure as hell ain't a TWINKIE, either!

(Brief pause.)

RITA: You're right. It's not a Twinkie situation either.

BERDENE: I thought the reason you were sent in here was to cheer me up?

RITA: It was.

BERDENE: Well honey, you're doing a HELL of a job!

RITA: I'm sorry. My social skills are somewhat stunted. I don't interact with real people very well, especially during something situations.

BERDENE: Don't you interact with other people up there at that school of yours?

RITA: I do, but most of them are more socially handicapped than I am.

BERDENE: You're not handicapped, honey, don't ever say that you're handicapped and don't ever let anyone TELL you you're handicapped.

RITA: It's all right, it's a natural result of my intellectual being growing so much faster than my emotional being. It's just something that happens. I'm only thirteen years old and I'm going to graduate from MIT this spring. That's something, and as a result of that, something else happens. It's how things work. The price of being a prodigy.

(Brief pause.)

BERDENE: I used to know this fella named Pickle. He used to come into my Daddy's bar all the time, almost every day, we'd say "Hey Pickle."

RITA: His name was Pickle?

BERDENE: I don't think his real name was Pickle, it's just what everyone called him. I never knew what his real name was. We all just called him Pickle. Not exactly sure why.

RITA: I imagine that there was some sort of sexual connotation attached.

BERDENE: Someone's not nearly as socially stunted as she's been pretending to be. Yes, I'm pretty sure he got the nickname because of something like that, but he was always real polite and decent to me. I was kind of sweet on him, even though I was nothing but sixteen and he was almost my father's age, I always batted my eyes at him. He always smiled at me. I was always hoping something would happen between us, though it never did. Nothing ever happened. He liked me, though. I could tell. He was always real sweet to me. Real sweet fella.

RITA: So he was more of a Twinkie than a Pickle.

(They look at each other and both giggle.)

BERDENE: Yes, Pickle was definitely a Twinkie. A big sweet Twinkie. I liked him. I was always sad nothing ever happened between us.

RITA: Where is he now?

BERDENE: I imagine he's passed on. Like my father and mother and brother and sister. Like I'm probably going to do.

RITA: Like all of us. Everyone.

(Brief pause as they look at each other. ARLENE, 42, rushes into the room. She goes immediately to BERDENE and hugs her.)

ARLENE: Oh my God, Mom, oh my God! Where's Doctor Amir, he should be in here, where is he? He should be looking after you!

BERDENE: He is, he was here, he'll be back.

ARLENE: What's going on, what have you heard, have you heard anything? Rita honey, maybe you'd better go downstairs and let us adults talk.

BERDENE: She's got two college degrees, Arlene, she's smart enough to participate in our conversation. She's fine where she is.

(ARLENE stands up and paces, taking out a package of cigarettes.)

ARLENE: Oh God, oh my God. Damn it, you can't smoke in here, can you? Why is it people can't smoke in hospitals, it's the one place a person really NEEDS to smoke and you can't!

RITA: It's because smoking is bad for your health.

ARLENE: So is stress and smoking relieves stress!

RITA: Technically it doesn't. In fact, a lot of people are in the hospital because of smoking.

ARLENE: Young lady, it's not polite to contradict your elders. And Rita, I really need to speak to your mother and I can't find her anywhere. Have you seen her?

RITA: Yes.

(Brief pause.)

ARLENE: Well? Where was she when you saw her?

RITA: I saw her in the lobby right before I came up here.

ARLENE: Well she's not there now. Just like her, whenever there's a situation … where is everyone? Everybody should be here!

BERDENE: What for? It's not a funeral, I'm not dead yet.

ARLENE: Don't talk that way, Momma, I can't take it. The family should be here, this is a FAMILY SITUATION. How did you find out, Mom, what happened? Tell me.

BERDENE: *(sighs)* This morning while I was in the bathroom doing my business, I noticed that there was blood in the toilet, a lot of blood.

ARLENE: Oh God, and you called Doctor Amir right away?

BERDENE: No Arlene, I went to the salon and got a pin and curl first! Of course I called him, why do you think I'm here in this bed?

ARLENE: Same thing happened to my friend Janice's mother, same exact thing and … Oh. Damn it, I need a cigarette. Where is everybody?

(ARLENE takes her cell phone out and starts to dial.)

RITA: You can't use your cell phone here.

ARLENE: What? Why not?

RITA: Because the radio waves from a cell phone can potentially disrupt much of the electrical equipment the hospital has in use. It's the same reason you can't use your phone on an airplane.

ARLENE: I don't know where you heard that, Missy, but I've been in a lot of hospitals with my phone and I've never heard that one before.

RITA: I didn't hear it anywhere, it's written on a sign on the wall over there. It's a hospital rule.

(ARLENE briefly glances at the wall and continues dialing her cell phone.)

ARLENE: Well, it's more of a guideline than a rule, honey, they make exceptions for emergencies. *(Into phone)* Gerald! It's me, listen, you have to stop by the apartment before you come to the hospital and make sure the cat is fed. It's very important, if she doesn't get fed on time she tears up the furniture. Gerald, don't bicker with me at a time like this, my mother's in the hospital! She's sick and I have to be here and you have to feed the cat!

RITA: Blood in your stool or blood in your urine?

BERDENE: Both, I'm afraid.

RITA: Mom didn't tell me that. I guess this is a pickle situation, after all.

BERDENE: Told you so.

(ARLENE hangs up the phone and paces.)

ARLENE: What did Doctor Amir say, did he say anything, does he have any idea what it could be, what's going on?

BERDENE: He said what doctors always say, Arlene, they'll run some tests and then we'll see. I don't think there's any question that something's wrong, the question is just how BIG that something is. Right now all we can do is wait for the test results. I should know in an hour or so just how much trouble I'm in.

ARLENE: Oh God. Oh my God.

(ARLENE sits and puts her head in her hands, sobbing.)

BERDENE: Arlene—

ARLENE: Momma …

BERDENE: Arlene please, would you please at least wait until there's news that's worth crying about?

ARLENE: I'm sorry, I just … it's just so horrible, this whole situation is so horrible that—

BERDENE: It's just a pickle, Arlene, that's all that it is.

ARLENE: What's a pickle?

RITA: This situation. This situation is a pickle.

ARLENE: Pickle?

BERDENE: Pickle.

(Brief pause.)

ARLENE: Why are you both talking about pickles? Are you hungry Ma, do you want something to eat, or—

BERDENE: No, Arlene.

ARLENE: Then where do you get pickles from, why are you talking about pickles at a TIME like this?

BERDENE: Arlene, never mind.

ARLENE: Are you all right, Ma, are you thinking straight, maybe I should page a nurse—

BERDENE: I don't need a nurse, they come in here every five minutes as it is, I can't get any peace and quiet. Please, just sit here with me quietly, please.

ARLENE: Maybe this is affecting you upstairs, you DO recognize me, right, do you know who I am?

BERDENE: Arlene, sit your butt down and shush up!

(Brief pause as ARLENE sits.)

ARLENE: Yes Ma'am.

BERDENE: I declare, you keep it up and you're the one that's going to need a doctor. I'm trying not to lose my mind here and you're not helping the situation. Just sit with me, quietly and calmly, until we find out what's going on.

(Pause.)

ARLENE: You know, when I was pregnant, I craved pickles all the time.

RITA: Really?

ARLENE: You bet, I think I lived on pickles for almost three months, some days pickles were the only things I could keep down, the more bitter they were, the better.

BERDENE: I went through the same thing when I was pregnant with you.

ARLENE: You did? I never knew that.

BERDENE: Yes, same thing, only when I was pregnant with you, not your sisters, I don't know why.

ARLENE: I was the pickle baby.

BERDENE: We had the pickle connection.

ARLENE: We did.

(Very brief pause.)

BERDENE: How's your boy doing?

(ARLENE gets up and paces again.)

ARLENE: Luke? Luke is doing great. Almost as big as his dad, eats like a horse, you should see the food he can put away. He is getting held back a grade in school this year and we just can't understand it. He's smart enough, he's a bright boy but his teachers just can't get him to concentrate. He doesn't sit still, I think he gets it from his father. God, I need a cigarette.

BERDENE: You know, Arlene, there is something you can do for me, if you don't mind.

ARLENE: What? Of course. What is it?

BERDENE: I got this sudden craving for Twinkies, I guess my sweet tooth is kicking in. Would it be a bother for you to go down and get me some?

ARLENE: Not a problem. Are you allowed to eat Twinkies?

BERDENE: I'm allowed to eat Twinkies, I'm an old woman, I can eat whatever I want. I just got here, they haven't put me on any diet yet.

ARLENE: I would be happy to, do you want anything else, a soda or juice—

BERDENE: Just the Twinkies, Arlene, I need Twinkies.

ARLENE: I'll take care of it, Mom, I'll go down to the store and be back before you can say Jack Robinson.

(ARLENE kisses BERDENE on the cheek exits quickly, taking out her pack of cigarettes as she goes.)

BERDENE: I declare, she's my daughter and I love her, but I declare that woman was born in a constant state of crisis.

RITA: You don't really need any Twinkies, do you?

BERDENE: What I needed was to give Arlene a chance to go smoke.

RITA: She's very worried about you.

BERDENE: I'm very worried about me. I shouldn't be telling you this, Rita, but I'm pretty scared right now.

RITA: You're scared?

BERDENE: Yes. I'm scared. I'm really scared.

RITA: You haven't gotten the test results back yet. You could be fine.

BERDENE: This time, but what about next time or the time after that? I'm old enough that I'm feeling my mortality. After all, it's only a matter of time, isn't it?

RITA: Time is relative to all things.

BERDENE: That's all I can think about while I'm sitting here.

I'm feeling it down deep in my bones. I'm feeling the crush of time.

RITA: Have you ever heard of Stephan Hawking?

BERDENE: Fella in the wheelchair, right?

RITA: Yes. He has some interesting theories on the perception of time. I've been toying with some of his theorems as of late. Can I give you an example?

BERDENE: Keep it simple, sweetie, remember that I'm a civilian.

RITA: Simple is best anyway. You ever notice a bicycle tire, how when it spins, the spokes of the tire seem to go in the opposite direction of the tire?

BERDENE: Like a wagon wheel.

RITA: Exactly. The tire is going one direction but we perceive it as going the other. Perception is key. Long and short of it, life to us appears as though we are born, we live and then we die.

BERDENE: And that isn't what happens?

RITA: That's what we PERCEIVE happens. The reality, like the spokes of the wagon wheel, could be and probably is the opposite. Instead of birth as the beginning and death as the end of the cycle, birth could be the end and death could be the beginning. That's what it could be and most of us simply aren't in a position to see it.

(Brief pause.)

BERDENE: Are you currently in that position?

RITA: I think I could be.

BERDENE: And you can see ... something?

RITA: I've always seen something. The big difficulty is in describing it.

BERDENE: So it could be?

RITA: It could be. I'll keep working on it.

(Very brief pause.)

BERDENE: I just wish I knew for sure. What happens, I mean, when we ... when I die. I never bought into any of that other jumbo, the bible and all that silliness, it just never seemed right or even fair to women. But the only alternative I can see is that nothing happens, and that doesn't seem right either.

RITA: And that's why you're scared?

BERDENE: Yes. Because I don't know what's going to happen when I die, if anything. That's what I'm frightened of most. Maybe nothing happens. I just hope … I really, really hope … that something …

RITA: Grandma?

BERDENE: Yes dear?

RITA: I don't know everything. I know quite a lot about a lot of things, but I don't know everything. But one thing I definitely do know.

BERDENE: What's that?

RITA: When you die?

BERDENE: Yes?

RITA: Something happens. Something definitely happens.

(BERDENE looks at RITA for a moment, then opens her arms and RITA goes to her. They hug for a long moment.)

THE END.

SOMETHING SITUATION (EXTENDED one act version) NOTES:

FIRST PRODUCED in 2003 at Manhattan Theatre Source, featuring Holland Hamilton, Carla Hayes and Fiona Jones, directed by Laura Walczak.

AS MENTIONED, this is an extended version of the ten-minute play, same title but with Aunt Arlene. I like Aunt Arlene a lot, and I like that she comes around to a pickle connection and that there's something tragic in her, within her anxiety.

BUT I DON'T KNOW if this play is better with Aunt Arlene (and longer) than it is without her. Both work for me. So you can decide, for yourself, which one you like best.

40

Like The Song (2m, 1f)

CHARACTERS:

DANIEL – Handsome, in his late 20s, an actor.

DREW – Wiseass geeky type, 20s or 30s.

KATHY – Drew's sister, no-nonsense, same age.

SETTING – An apartment.

(DANIEL ENTERS FURIOUSLY. He stops in the middle of the room and stands, silent and steaming. Finally he opens his arms and screams at the ceiling.)

DANIEL: FUUUUUUUUUUUUUUUUUUUUUUUUUU-

UUUCCCCCCCCCCCKKKK!!!!! FUCK FUCK FUCK FUUUUUUUUUUUUUUUUUUUUUUUUCCCCCKKK!!!!!!!!!!!

(DANIEL jumps up and down, stamping his feet on the floor.)

DANIEL: SHIT PISS FUCK FUCK FUCK! GODDAMN COCKUCKING SHIT SHIT SHIT!

(DANIEL races around the apartment kicking and hitting things.)

DANIEL: Fuck fuck shit fuck! Pig shit eating motherfucking boil on my ass pain in the BALLS FUCK!

(DREW enters, eating a bowl of cereal. He watches the last bit impassively. DANIEL takes off his shoe and beats it on the floor.)

DANIEL: FUCK FUCK FUCK FUCK FUCK!!!!

(DANIEL flops on the floor, on his back, kicking and screaming.)

DANIEL: MOTHERFUCKING BALL-LICKING COCKSUCKING CUNT!!!!!!!

(DANIEL stops kicking and lies quiet for a moment, breathing heavily.)

DREW: Is there something bothering you, Daniel?

DANIEL: CUUUUUNNNNNTTTTTTT!!!!

(KATHY enters in her pajamas, enraged.)

KATHY: What is all the fucking SCREAMING ABOUT!

DREW: Now you've done it, you woke her up.

KATHY: It's fucking six in the morning! Are you crazy! What's going on?

DREW: Daniel's just a bit upset.

KATHY: Well what did you do to him and can you shut him up?

DREW: I had nothing to do with his present state and neither will I attempt to "shut him up," and besides, he was your friend first. Notice, Daniel, that she remained uninvolved until the word "cunt" was invoked.

DANIEL: CUNT!

KATHY: STOP IT! Both of you, I mean it! You're not allowed to say that word and you KNOW IT! HOUSE RULES!

DREW: Kathy, we really need to address that particular house rule, I mean let's face it, sometimes no other profanity but THAT one will do.

KATHY: It is DEMEANING to women!

DREW: But we don't know if Daniel's referring to a woman, he could be directing it toward a male subject.

KATHY: So?

DREW: So if he is indeed calling a man a cunt, it's a man being demeaned and not a woman.

DANIEL: I AM referring to a man, a MAN who is a fucking CUNT!

DREW: There! See?

KATHY: Stop it! Shut up! It doesn't matter WHO he's calling a … it doesn't matter WHO it is directed at, it's still demeaning to WOMEN!

DREW: But isn't that the whole point of profanity anyway, I mean, what good is a profane word if it doesn't demean somebody somewhere? There's no fun in that.

KATHY: I'm not getting into another rhetorical ping-pong match with you, Drew, that … WORD … is banned from this apartment.

DREW: Violation of our right to free speech. And I noticed that it doesn't stop you from watching Trainspotting whenever it's on cable.

KATHY: So what?!

DREW: So? There is frequent usage of the aforementioned cunt word in Trainspotting.

KATHY: That's different, it's a movie, it's Scottish and so it doesn't count!

DREW: So if I were Scottish and looked like Ewen McGregor, then it would be all right?

KATHY: Drew …

DREW: Kathy …

(Short pause.)

KATHY: Daniel, are you all right?

DANIEL: Kathy, can I borrow your gun?

KATHY: You want to borrow my gun?

DANIEL: I want to borrow your fucking gun.

DREW: You're right, Daniel, a firearm is JUST what you need at this point in your life.

KATHY: Why do you want to borrow my gun, Daniel?

DREW: And Kathy, the bigger question is, why do you even HAVE a gun?

KATHY: Don't start. Daniel—

DREW: Freedom of speech banned, but by all means exercise your right to bear arms, is that it?

KATHY: Drew you'd better … I'm going to … don't start. Daniel, why do you want to borrow my gun?

DANIEL: Because I want to kill someone.

DREW: Here we go.

DANIEL: Give me your gun so I can kill someone.

KATHY: Daniel. No.

DANIEL: Why not?

DREW: Yeah, why not?

KATHY: Why not? What do you mean, why not?! I'm not going to give him my gun so he can KILL someone!

DREW: Why not? It's what a gun is for, right? Why else would you have it lying around? That's what guns are for, killing people.

KATHY: That's not the ONLY reason to have a gun! People keep guns for PROTECTION.

DREW: No, people keep CONDOMS for protection, guns are kept in case you need to shoot someone.

KATHY: There is something wrong with you, DREW. What the hell is wrong with you?

DREW: Nothing wrong with me, I'm not the one with a gun stashed in my garter belt.

KATHY: Are you honestly telling me that you think it's all right that Daniel wants to kill someone?

DREW: As long as it's not me, who cares?

DANIEL: It's not you.

DREW: That's a relief.

DANIEL: It's not Kathy, either.

DREW: I look on that as a mixed blessing.

KATHY: Drew, shut up.

DANIEL: What if it's somebody that really deserves to be killed?

KATHY: Nobody really deserves to be killed.

DREW: Yeah, RIGHT.

KATHY: Drew SHUT UP.

DREW: I can't believe you told me to shut up, and like, you even did it fucking TWICE.

KATHY: I did tell you to shut up twice and I'm saying it again, SHUT UP!

(Brief pause.)

DREW: Talking all tough. Just because you have a gun …

KATHY: You know what Drew? I've had it!

DREW: You've had what?

KATHY: I've had it with you. I want you OUT!

DREW: You're throwing me out?

KATHY: I am THROWING you out, get out!

DREW: You can't throw me out.

KATHY: I can too throw you out, the lease is in my name so get the fuck out!

(Short pause.)

DREW: I'll tell Mom.

KATHY: Go ahead and tell Mom, I don't care.

DREW: Are you sure about that?

KATHY: I'm sure Drew! Get your shit and get out!

DREW: She'll be REAL interested when she hears what we were arguing about—

KATHY: So what, why would she care?

DREW: The argument, you know, concerning you exercising your constitutional right to bear ARMS.

KATHY: You wouldn't DARE—

DREW: Dare me.

KATHY: You KNOW how she feels about guns—

DREW: Dare me, Sundance, dare me.

(Short pause as KATHY glares at DREW.)

KATHY: You know Drew, you haven't changed a bit since you were five, you are the same whiny brat that has to run to Mommy whenever we have a fight.

DREW: Thank you.

KATHY: Prick.

DREW: Cunt.

KATHY: Oh MY GOD I'M GOING TO KILL YOU!

DREW: Well it's a GOOD thing you bought that gun then, isn't it?

(KATHY looks at him a moment, then stamps her foot several times.)

KATHY: Damn it damn it DAMN IT!

DREW: She did the same thing when she was eight.

(KATHY picks up DANIEL's shoe and throws it at DREW. It hits him in the leg.)

DREW: Ow. Hey.

KATHY: You are a very, very bad little brother! Shame on you! Shame on you!

DREW: Hey. You hit me with a shoe.

(Very short pause.)

DANIEL: Kathy, please let me have your gun? I'll bring it right back.

(KATHY glares at DREW a minute, and then kneels on the floor next to DANIEL.)

KATHY: Honey, what's wrong? Why do you feel you need it? Did you get into a fight with someone?

DANIEL: Not yet.

KATHY: Did you and Jen break up? Is someone bothering Jen, stalking her?

DREW: Is Jen stalking someone? Is Jen doing something else with someone? Is Jen doing anything with anybody?

DANIEL: It's not Jen, we're fine, we didn't break up, she's not even around, she's in Ohio visiting her Grandmother in the hospital.

KATHY: Then what is it, what's wrong?

DREW: Does Jen know you're contemplating murder?

DANIEL: No, she doesn't have any … I think … shit, I think I'm going to be sick. I'm gonna be sick!

(DANIEL jumps up and runs off to the bathroom. A retching sound is heard.)

DREW: Very interesting roommate you've discovered for us, Katherine.

KATHY: Don't you dare speak to me.

DREW: Or else what, you'll hit me with another shoe? You threw a shoe at me.

(Brief pause, then KATHY starts to smile a bit.)

DREW: Don't you dare smile, you threw a shoe.

(KATHY begins to giggle a bit.)

DREW: It's not funny, you threw a fucking shoe at me.

KATHY: You deserved it.

DREW: So nobody deserves to be shot, but some people deserve to be SHOED?

KATHY: That's right, bucko, keep it up and I'll bounce another boot off your brain. And you can tattle to Mom all you want, I don't care.

DREW: You're a mean sister.

(They look at each other and at the same time giggle. DANIEL enters from the bathroom, carrying a toilet plunger.)

DANIEL: If you won't let me borrow your gun, can I borrow this?

KATHY: That depends.

DREW: Depends on what you're going to do with it.

DANIEL: I'm going to use it to suck the life out of someone.

(DANIEL sits heavily in a chair.)

DREW: Then I say yes. Borrow it, have fun.

KATHY: Daniel, what's going on?

DANIEL: My father.

KATHY: Your father?

DANIEL: I want to kill my Dad.

DREW: You want to kill your Dad?

DANIEL: Yes. My dad. My Old Man. I wanna drop him like a toilet seat.

KATHY: Why?

DANIEL: To get his attention.

DREW: Well um, that will probably do it. It will also attract the attention of the local authorities, mind you. And then you go to jail, haven't you seen the movies on that, the violence, the rape and the food, the food isn't any good in prison.

DANIEL: Right now I don't care.

KATHY: Why do you want to get his attention anyway, what's so important about it? I mean our father's been gone for years so maybe I can't understand, but I sometimes wish, and Drew don't you dare breathe a word of this to her, but I sometimes wish that Mom would pay LESS attention to us than she does.

DREW: Much as it pains me, I'm going to have to agree with my sister on this, love my mother but my God does the woman need to relax.

KATHY: I mean, nobody has it exactly the way they want it, do they? Do you remember what Grandma used to say?

DREW: She'd say, "It's too bad God let you pick your nose and not your family."

(Short pause.)

DANIEL: Do you know that song, "Cat's In The Cradle"?

DREW: Do I? Who doesn't?

KATHY: Which song is that?

DANIEL: "Cat's In The Cradle." You'd know it if you heard it.

(DREW sings the first few lines. DANIEL picks it up and they end of a verse.)

DREW: That song, man, that song always fucks me up.

DANIEL: I can't even listen when it comes on the radio.

KATHY: I still don't know what song you're talking about.

DREW: It's because you're not a son, if you were a son you'd definitely remember it.

KATHY: Oh well, EXCUSE me for being born a female.

DANIEL: That's not it, it's just … the song is about fathers and sons and there's just something about it that if you were a boy you'd remember, you know? It's a song about a father who doesn't pay attention while his boy is growing up and then when the father is retired, NOW he wants to spend time with his son but he realizes that his son is now ignoring him as much as he was ignored.

(DREW and DANIEL sing more of the song.)

KATHY: Okay, stop, I get it I get it. But what does that have to do with you, your dad and my gun?

DANIEL: My dad is a self-made man, has his own business back in Philly, he runs a textile company, he built it from the ground up almost by himself. I didn't see much of him when I was growing up, when I had a ball game or a school play, he'd say he'd try to come and then he wouldn't be able to.

DREW: Just like the song!

DANIEL: Yeah, just like the song. Yeah. Even when I graduated college, he couldn't make it to the ceremony, there was an emergency at the plant or something, so it was just me and Mom. I understood that he had things he needed to do. He was Dad, he worked a lot and was busy. I never got mad. Never ever got mad at my Dad. Not till today. My father retired last year, had to be dragged kicking and screaming, but he finally retired. And I was thinking, hey, maybe this is where he'll realize that he wants to spend time with me, maybe now he'll get it like the father in the song did, you know? In the song the son ignored the father because it was too late but it's not too late for my dad to pay attention to me. I wouldn't end it like the song. I kept waiting and waiting for him to call me and stuff. And then …

DREW: He didn't.

DANIEL: He didn't. I'd call him, I'd talk to him, but having a conversation with him was just as difficult as it was before he retired. Worse even. He wasn't coming around like the Dad in the song.

KATHY: But that doesn't mean it's too late, he might come around.

DANIEL: That's what I kept telling myself. I didn't want to give up on him. You know what? I think the main subconscious reason that I became an actor is because if I get a job on TV or something, then he'll have to notice me, he can't NOT notice me, because there I will be, on the big screen or TV, he will be forced to notice me. That's all I'm doing. And then it happened. Today, it happened.

DREW: What happened?

DANIEL: Today was the day I found out that I landed the lead role in the new mini-series on HBO.

KATHY: What?

DREW: What?

DANIEL: I had about fifteen callbacks for it over the past two weeks. I didn't even tell Jen about it, or you guys or anybody, because I figured it would be like every other audition, I would come close and it would go to somebody else, so I kept quiet and figured fuck it, I have no chance so fuck it. And my agent called to tell me I got it, a lead in the new HBO mini-series that everybody wants, they gave it to me, an unknown. All of a sudden, I'm a working actor. All of a sudden, I'm on TV.

DREW: Jesus Christ, congratulations!

KATHY: That's wonderful!

DANIEL: And I was so happy. I tried calling Jen, but she's got her phone off while she's at the hospital. So I called home and Pop answered the phone. And I was looking forward to this. This particular speech was one I had practiced a lot, a fucking lot, you know? This is the speech where you tell your folks you've finally done it and it is a lot more important than those wimpy Oscar speeches, this is the big one, this fucking monologue I have fucking worked to death in my head, you know what I'm saying? I got it all mapped out and in particular, Dad is the exact person I want to deliver it to and I want to really fucking enjoy it. So I start my preamble, and before I even get halfway into the first act of my speech, he's like, interrupting me, he says, "Look, I don't have all night, what do you want? Are you calling to borrow money, what is it?" he threw me off my rhythm, really bad. I said I didn't need any money, and he goes, "Then what do you want, what are you calling for?" And I … and I just told him, cut to the end, just blurted it out that I got the job and I'm going to be on TV, no elegance and not like I rehearsed, I just fucking told him. And you know what he said? He said, "When are you going to do something serious with your life?" He said that and I just wanted to KILL him. Kill him dead. I got so fucking homicidal I couldn't even talk, I just hung up the phone. I've never hung up on him before, but I did today. I went "AHHHHHHH" at him and slammed the phone down. If he'd been in the same room I might have strangled him. I hung up on him and went out and got blind stinking drunk instead. *(DANIEL slides down out of his chair onto the floor, still holding the toilet plunger.)* I got so angry. See, I finally realized it. He doesn't get what I'm doing. It doesn't matter how much I'm on TV or how many movies I do, he's doesn't get it and he's never going to get it. He's never going come around like the dad in the song and it … it just kills me.

(KATHY and DREW slowly sit down on the chairs behind DANIEL.)

KATHY: There's still time. He might still get it. Someday.

DANIEL: No. He will never be like the song.

(Short pause.)

DREW: You know what I think?

DANIEL: What?

DREW: I think you just might need a new song.

DANIEL: A new song?

KATHY: You definitely need a new song.

DANIEL: Which song?

DREW: Well. You know, Kathy and I lost our father when we were young, still in school.

KATHY: Oh my God. Of course.

DREW: And it was tough, but there was a song she always used to sing to me that never failed to make me feel better.

DANIEL: What was it?

(Brief pause. DREW and KATHY look at each other. They both begin to sing HEY JUDE. When they get to the chorus, DANIEL joins in.)

Lights fade.

The End.

LIKE THE SONG NOTES:

FIRST PRODUCED in 2003 at Manhattan Theatre Source, featuring Lou Carbonneau, Jenn Shirley and David Gravens.

41

Bodily Functions (2m)

CHARACTERS:

WEASEL – An Italian hit man, small and thin and anal about cleanliness to the point of obsessive compulsiveness.

BEAR – Another Italian hit man, older and much bigger, in size and also in temperament.

SETTING: WEASEL's apartment in New Jersey – very clean and organized. There is a couch in the center of the room, facing the audience, and a small table with a television. There is a door leading outside, stage right, and a door leading to the rest of the house, stage left. On the back wall, in the center, is a closet door. There are little tables and lamps, here and there.

NOTES ON SOUND: Sound is very important to this play, obviously, and my recommendation is, if at all possible, that the sound effects are done live.

GENERAL NOTES: It is my observation that this play works best when played real, in other words, don't play it just for the laughs, play the reality and the drama of the situation and it makes the play all the more absurd and therefore, funnier.

Scene 1

(A very neat, tidy and dark living room. WEASEL, in a black suit and thin black tie, is obsessively dusting with a feather duster. WEASEL is also wearing a flowered apron. Suddenly there is a loud thump on the door and WEASEL jumps. He pulls out a revolver and steps forward, gun in one hand and feather duster in the other.)

WEASEL: Bear? That you?

(Another loud thump.)

WEASEL: Bear? Is that—

(Suddenly the door is flung open as BEAR enters. He is dragging a large trunk.)

BEAR: Of course it's me, you peckerhead, who else is it gonna be? You gonna let me freeze my balls off outside all night?

(The two men eye each other cautiously, then suddenly run into each other's arms in a warm Italian embrace. BEAR looks at the apron WEASEL is wearing and WEASEL quickly takes it off.)

WEASEL: Bear! How the hell have you been? It's been a long time.

BEAR: Fine an' dandy, fine and dandy. How's life been treatin' you Weez?

WEASEL: Life's been good, good. Bear! Bear, it's good to see you, Goddamned good to see you. Now where the FUCK have you been? You're two days late!

BEAR: They had that town sewed up tight as a motherfucker. I hadda stay in your aunt's attic the whole time. They was watching the buses, the trains, they had roadblocks at every intersection, it was a pain in the ass big time. Finally I slipped out.

WEASEL: So where is he? Outside?

BEAR: Nope. He's right here.

(BEAR pats the trunk.)

WEASEL: What! What'd you bring him in here for? Why didn't you leave him in the trunk of the car! This is my house! My clean, clean house!

BEAR: The car is STOLEN, dickhead. Now, if the cops pick up the car now, empty, no big deal, they don't do nothin'. They find a car with a DEAD BODY in it, they're gonna bust their ass tryin' to figger out where it came from so they don't look like morons. Use your head for chrissakes!

WEASEL: Jesus fucking Christ what a pain in the ass job this is. How long's he been dead?

BEAR: Three days.

WEASEL: Three days! Oh man, he's gonna stink, he's gonna stink this place up to high heaven. We gotta sit with him a whole other day yet an' it's gonna smell so bad we won't be able to see straight. My poor clean house.

BEAR: Quit your whinin', you're making me sick. It won't be that bad. I got him all wrapped up in a big plastic bag. An' he spent the first two days in your aunt's freezer in the basement. So shut up, you'll live.

(BEAR goes to WEASEL's refrigerator, gets a beer, opens it, and guzzles it down.)

WEASEL: This is such a pain in the ass. Why do we hafta go through all this crap, why didn't you just dump the guy right away? This is way too risky, this isn't good business. What's the big deal?

BEAR: They didn't tell ya? This one was real personal. Morrie tole this guy, to his face, that he was gonna be a permanent part of his patio, an' he was gonna take personal satisfaction outta barbecuing steaks two feet above his dead ass. That's why we gotta wait so long. They ain't gonna be layin' the cement until the day after tomorrow. Morrie's word is Morrie's word.

WEASEL: Shit, Morrie musta been really pissed.

BEAR: Weez, they don't tell you jack shit, do they? Don't you know who this is? This is RICK THE DICK.

WEASEL: Rick the Dick? But that guy ... I heard he had an outstanding reputation as a hit man.

BEAR: One of the best, he'd drop anybody for a dime, cops, judges, grandmothers, you pay him and he'd shoot it. A MAN among men. The thing was, the FUCKER, the fucker didn't have any FUCKING MORALS! He was gonna rat us all out to the FEDS!

WEASEL: What a piece of shit!

BEAR: If there's one thing I can't stand, it's a squealer!

(BEAR kicks the trunk and swears in Italian.)

WEASEL: Piece of shit squealer!

BEAR: Rat fink fuckin' prick BASTARD!

(WEASEL also kicks the trunk.)

WEASEL: Bastard! Fuckin' immoral bastard!

BEAR: This motherfucker ... Morrie was real particular about it, too, it all had to be done a certain way.

WEASEL: Oh yeah? So how'd you do him?

BEAR: Strangled him.

WEASEL: Strangled him? I hate that. Too much of a mess. Ice pick is much better.

BEAR: Whatta ya talkin' about, the ice pick is just as much of a mess as the garrote.

WEASEL: No, no, when you garrote somebody they usually end up shittin' on themselves an' everything else. I hate that.

BEAR: Well, the boss wanted it done a certain way, he wanted to be starin' in the guy's face as he croaked slow. Took fuckin' forever, it was murder on my blood pressure, let me tell you.

WEASEL: Morrie musta been really pissed. So what now?

BEAR: Stick this stiff in a corner somewhere, have a drink and order Chinese takeout. What else? Give me hand with it, will ya? I've been luggin' it all over an' I think I threw my back out.

(BEAR and WEEZ slide the trunk over to the middle of the room. Bear stands, stretches and sits on the couch.)

BEAR: You got cable in this dump?

WEASEL: Yeah uh, Bear, we can't leave the trunk here. It's in the way, we gotta find the right spot for it.

BEAR: Jesus Christ Weez, what difference does it make, it's only for one fucking day.

WEASEL: It throws the whole balance of the room off, makes it look cluttered. There's Feng Shui to be considered here. We gotta move it, I think, maybe under that end table, that might do it.

BEAR: Weasel, you gotta be fucking kiddin' me, I lug that thing over a whole state an' now you want me to help decorate?

WEASEL: Bear … this is my house, show some fuckin' respect. *(Brief pause)* You take that end and I'll get this one.

(They both stand at each end of the trunk, then begin to bend over at the same time. Suddenly there is a huge farting noise.)

WEASEL: Nice going, Bear.

BEAR: Whatta mean, nice goin' Bear? It wasn't me.

WEASEL: Sure Bear, sure it wasn't you. A guest in my home and the first thing you do is smell it up.

BEAR: I'm tellin' ya, it wasn't me! You wanna break wind, that's your business, just don't try an' blame your stink on me.

WEASEL: Sure Bear, whatever you say. By the way, the bathroom is down the hall and to the left, in case you need to wipe or something.

BEAR: Okay smartass, that's enough fun, let's get on with it. You lyin' smelly bastard.

(They look at each other, then begin to bend down to the trunk again. As they do: Huge farting noise.)

WEASEL: What the fuck Bear!

BEAR: Whatta ya mean, 'What the fuck Bear!'

WEASEL: What'd you have for dinner, burritos and beans?

BEAR: Goddamn it, you little prick, stop blaming your gas on me! I didn't do it!

WEASEL: Hey, when I pass gas I own up to it, I don't shrug the responsibility off on somebody else like some people I know.

BEAR: It was you, you lyin' prick, it was you, stop bustin' my balls!

WEASEL: Did that sound like the kind of explosion that would come outta my ass? That was a Bear fart and you know it you lyin' bastard!

BEAR: You fuck, you're crazy in the head!

(BEAR pulls his gun.)

WEASEL: And you don't have no fuckin' manners!

(WEASEL pulls his gun. Pause as they stare each other down.)

WEASEL: Wait a minute, hold on. Are you serious, you really didn't pass gas?

BEAR: I'm dead serious, I didn't cut no fuckin' cheese.

WEASEL: Well if you didn't do it, and I didn't do it, then who?

(Pause as they look at each other, and then down at the trunk. Another huge FART. They both jump back and point their weapons at the trunk.)

WEASEL: He ain't dead. Oh Jesus, he ain't—

BEAR: He's dead, I saw to it myself.

WEASEL: Dead people don't make farts like that. He ain't dead, I'm telling you!

BEAR: Not only did I garrote him, but he's been in a plastic bag in a freezer for three fuckin' days! He's dead!

(Another large FART from the trunk.)

WEASEL: Jesus Christ, the stench, he may not be dead but he definitely smells like he died.

BEAR: Shut the fuck up, Weez, he's dead!

WEASEL: Maybe he's in one of those whatta-ya-call it, states of suspended animation! That's it! That's it!

BEAR: Weasel, you read too many comic books. That's what it is.

(Another huge farting noise.)

WEASEL: Well, we gotta make sure. We gotta be sure he's dead.

BEAR: I'll make sure.

(BEAR cocks his gun.)

WEASEL: No guns! Somebody might hear! I got neighbors! Use this!

(WEASEL takes a large screwdriver from a toolbox and gives it to BEAR.

WEASEL flings open the lid to the trunk and BEAR lurches forward and stabs the body several times. Every time he stabs, there is a loud farting noise. Finally BEAR stands back.)

BEAR: Well, he's dead now.

WEASEL: We can't leave him here. He might bleed and leak through the trunk onto my carpet.

BEAR: Weasel, I swear to God I'm gonna kill you one of these days. Who gives a SHIT about the carpet?!

WEASEL: Bear ... it's my house, so shut the fuck up. I'll put down a drop cloth and we'll hang him in the closet.

BEAR: In the closet?

WEASEL: In the closet.

BEAR: The fucking closet.

Scene 2

(BEAR and WEASEL sit on the couch, drinking and eating Chinese food while watching TV.)

BEAR: The eighties, the eighties were the best for wiseguys.

WEASEL: The eighties and Reagan.

BEAR: Reagan an' the eighties, that's right, it was a fuckin' paradise for hoods. So much money flyin' around, an' people couldn't wait to be bought, they couldn't wait! They were beggin' for it, everybody wanted on the payroll. Cops, judges, schoolteachers. You could do anything.

WEASEL: Absolutely fucking anything. Sell drugs at an elementary school, beat up a nun, and juggle stocks and bonds. Anything.

BEAR: Anything you could do, you'd do it, and it didn't matter, cause everyone else was doin' whatever they could get away with too. The eighties were heaven on earth.

WEASEL: Heaven on earth.

BEAR: The best thing about it was, if you had a rep, an established rep like we do, all you had to do is look at somebody tough and they were handin' over everything, their wallets, cars, houses, even their old ladies. Remember? Oh yeah, baby! We never had to hardly pop anybody in the eighties at all, maybe what, we put a hit on somebody maybe once every other month?

WEASEL: At the most.

BEAR: Yeah, all we had to do is squint at a guy an' he was rollin' over an' peein' his panties. But not these days.

WEASEL: Oh no, not these days.

BEAR: These days we gotta put the knock on somebody every week. Like that knucklehead in the closet.

WEASEL: Everybody thinks they're tough.

BEAR: Everybody thinks he's Charles Bronson.

WEASEL: Now we gotta work our ass off to keep business goin' good.

BEAR: Yep, it's hard to be a Hit Man.

WEASEL: Yep, we do all the work, take all the risks.

BEAR: Yep, yep. Damn, I miss Reagan and the eighties. The good ole' days.

WEASEL: Yep, the good ole days. I gotta take a squirt. Be right back.

(WEASEL gets up and exits. The room is very dark except for a small light from the TV. BEAR keeps talking to himself.)

BEAR: Yep, the eighties and Reagan, the fucking wonder years. Goddamn Clinton set us back years, the efficient fucker, if we hadn't sent that broad in as an intern, who knows how much worse it woulda got. Lucky for us Clinton has a weakness for broads with big asses. It's gonna take years to undo all the damage the Democrats did to organized crime. What the hell happened to the Republican Party? Usta be a smart operation. Neither of those Bush pinheads is even smart enough to be good crook. It's a sorry situation, bad enough to make a man think about voting.

(From the darkness, a loud sneeze is heard.)

BEAR: Gesundheit.

(WEASEL re-enters.)

WEASEL: What'd you say?

BEAR: I said gesundheit.

WEASEL: What for?

BEAR: What for, whatta think what for? Don't be such a fuckin' moron, Weez.

WEASEL: It's just a fuckin' question Bear, don't get your panties all in a bunch. Jesus Christ. An' would you use a coaster under that beer glass, for cryin' out loud! I don't want no rings on my clean table.

BEAR: Of all the people to be on the lam with, I gotta be stuck with June Cleaver.

(Pause as they stare at the TV. Then, from the darkness, another loud sneeze is heard. BEAR and WEASEL turn to each other.)

BEAR & WEASEL: Gesundheit.

(Short pause. BEAR and WEASEL look at each other, then jump up, drawing their guns. BEAR stumbles against the television. They cautiously look around the room, seeing no one. Then they slowly look toward the closet door. Another loud sneeze is heard.)

BEAR: WHAT THE FUCK!

WEASEL: What the fuck's goin' on here, what's goin' on, you said you killed him, you said!

BEAR: I did kill him you saw it he's dead!

WEASEL: You dumbass, does he sound dead to you?

BEAR: It's a motor reflex, that's all it is, a motor reflex, like twitchin'. Dead people sometimes twitch.

(Another loud sneeze is heard.)

WEASEL: Dead people don't SNEEZE, dead people don't get the sniffles!

BEAR: Fuck you Weasel!

WEASEL: Well, I'm gonna make sure, once and for all, fuck the neighbors. Get the closet door, Bear.

(BEAR goes to the closet door, and WEASEL stands ready with his gun. Another loud sneeze is heard. BEAR flings the door open and WEASEL fires into the closet three times.)

WEASEL: There's a fuckin' gesundheit for ya.

Scene 3

(WEASEL is down on the floor next to the TV, trying to fix it. BEAR is standing next to him, tapping his foot impatiently.)

WEASEL: Did it have to be the TV, did you have to bump the TV when you jumped up?

BEAR: Weasel don't start with me, I mean it, don't fucking start.

WEASEL: Why couldn't you watch what your doin', it's my TV ya big clumsy bastard.

BEAR: Weasel don't fucking start, we had a sneezin' dead guy on our hands, I'm not in the mood.

WEASEL: If you had done the job right we wouldn't be in this mess.

BEAR: I swear to God, any more bitchin', I'm stickin' you in the freezer, I mean it. Just get the fuckin' TV fixed, I ain't spendin' the whole day in here with you and no cable! That's cruel an' unusual punishment! Even in the JOINT you get cable!

WEASEL: I've almost got it, all I've gotta do it plug this in …

(WEASEL plugs in the TV. There is a loud ZAP and most of the lights go out.)

BEAR: Great, just great, Weez, congratulations you're as efficient as Con Ed.

WEASEL: Shit, blew a fuse. Bear, there's a couple of flashlights hangin' on Velcro underneath the couch, will you get 'em for me?

BEAR: Flashlights velcroed under the couch? What the hell are they doin' there?

WEASEL: In case of emergencies, what else?

BEAR: Weasel, you got problems, you know that?

(BEAR turns on a flashlight and tosses the other to WEASEL.)

WEASEL: I'm gonna go get the fuse.

BEAR: No, I'll do it, in your capable hands you're liable to burn the whole house down. You keep workin' on the TV.

(BEAR exits to the kitchen. WEASEL keeps working.)

WEASEL: Bitch, bitch, bitch, like he can do anything right. WHAT? BEAR? DID YOU SAY SOMETHING?

BEAR *(Offstage.)* I SAID I FLIPPED THE FUSE AND NOTHING HAPPENED!

WEASEL: THEN YOU DIDN'T DO IT RIGHT!

BEAR *(O.S.)* #@#@#@@##***!

WEASEL: WHAT?

BEAR: *(O.S.)* I SAID, FUCK YOU ASSHOLE!

WEASEL: Great, great, what a night this has been. Oh shit, now my flashlight's startin' to go out, I knew I shoulda recharged those batteries. Shit.

(WEASEL's light is dimming and we hear footsteps behind him. WEASEL is in deep concentration over the TV set.)

WEASEL: Christ Bear, you're pathetic, you can't even flip a goddamned fuse right? What happened to your flashlight, did it go out on you too? Fuck, I knew I shoulda recharged those batteries, I usually do it every six months.

(There is a loud cough.)

WEASEL: The good news is that I know what's wrong with the TV, the insulation on this wiring came off, but I'll get it fixed in a jiffy, then I'll get the lights on.

(Another deep cough.)

WEASEL: Bear, cover your goddamn mouth, you wanna get me sick too? You know, I tole you, you should watch your health, you're a big guy, you should get more exercise an' shit.

(BEAR enters quietly.)

BEAR: What? Your fuse box is fucked.

WEASEL: Yeah, yeah. Christ, it sounded like you were gonna to hack up a lung.

BEAR: Weasel, what in the hell are you babbling about?

WEASEL: Bear, you know what I'm talkin' about, so next time, cover your mouth and shut up, alright? Shine your light over here Goddamnit.

BEAR: Weasel, I never know what the fuck you're talkin' about, you might as well be another species as far as I'm concerned.

(Another deep cough.)

WEASEL: Cover your mouth Goddamnit!

(Short Pause as WEASEL looks at BEAR. They both draw their guns.)

BEAR: There's somebody in here.

WEASEL: No way, I got the alarm on an' it's powered by an

outside system. Nobody can get in or out without us knowin' about it.

BEAR: Then where'd he come from?

(Pause as they look at each other, then they slowly turn to look at the closet.)

WEASEL: Oh shit.

(They creep toward the closet with their flashlights and guns pointed at it.)

BEAR: Are you ready? One … two … three!

(BEAR flings the door open and they both point their guns inside. The closet is empty except for a tattered bloody plastic bag.)

WEASEL: Oh shit oh shit.

BEAR: Empty. Where'd he go? How'd he go?

WEASEL: Oh shit oh shit oh shit.

BEAR: How the fuck does … something ain't right here, somethin' ain't right at all.

WEASEL: We're in deep shit now, Oh boy, oh boy. Deep doo-doo.

BEAR: You know what this is, Weez? This is WAR. Somebody is fuckin' with us, an' I intend to fuck them right back. I've never met a man I couldn't kill, and I never will.

WEASEL: Oh shit shit shit SHIT on me.

Scene 4

(WEASEL and BEAR have made a fort out of the couch and the other furniture in the middle of the room. The couch is overturned on its back and they look over it like a barricade. They have their guns drawn and are flashing their flashlights all around. The power is still out and the light dim.)

BEAR: It's simple Weez, if he's here for us, he has to come an' get us, and we'll be ready.

WEASEL: I don't get it, I put three slugs in the bastard, how could he be runnin' around?

BEAR: Weasel, stop tryin' to think, it only gets in the way of things.

WEASEL: But Bear—

BEAR: Shaddup!

(Pause as they listen intensely to the darkness.)

WEASEL: Bear, this really pisses me off.

BEAR: Pisses me off two times.

WEASEL: I mean I don't know how this is comin' about, but I am pissed off major.

BEAR: Pissed off big time.

WEASEL: I mean, look at my house! It's a mess!

BEAR: *(Chuckling a little.)* Big mess.

WEASEL: Dead or alive, someone's ass is goin' in a sling for this!

BEAR: Shhh. Didja' hear somethin'?

WEASEL: It's just the goddamn furnace. Shit. I am really upset about this, Bear.

BEAR: Well how do you think I feel, do I look happy to you?

WEASEL: Not only am I upset and angry, I gotta take a leak in the worst way.

BEAR: Don't think about it.

WEASEL: I can't, all I'm thinkin' about is water water water. I gotta piss like a foamin' racehorse. I gotta go Bear.

BEAR: You ain't leavin' knucklehead, that's just what he would want us to do, divide an' conquer, you are stayin' here.

WEASEL: But I gotta go.

BEAR: Tie it in a knot an' shuddap!

WEASEL: But I gotta go bad!

BEAR: Jesus Christ. Okay, here's what you do. Piss in glass or ashtray or somethin'.

WEASEL: Are you kiddin' me?

BEAR: Just do it.

(WEASEL ducks down behind the couch. He finds something to pee in and positions it. He then waits. He looks over at BEAR, who is watching him.)

WEASEL: Could you … turn the other way?

BEAR: What's the matter, now you're shy too?

WEASEL: I can't go if people are lookin' at me, so stop lookin!

BEAR: I don't believe this, Weez, you really got problems, you know that?

(BEAR turns the other way. We can tell that WEASEL is able to relieve

himself by the expression on his face. There is also the sound of someone gurgling, as if choking softly.)

BEAR: Hey Weez, you hear somethin?

WEASEL: Just a second, ahh that feels good.

BEAR: I'm hearin' somethin' strange.

(Bear cocks his gun.)

WEASEL: That's me you blockhead, you're listenin' to my piss action.

BEAR: No, it's somethin' else. Listen, it's getting louder.

(The sound gets louder. It becomes the sound of violent regurgitation.)

WEASEL: Oh my God, someone's blowing chunks on the back of our fort!

BEAR: Quick, get him!

(The flashlights disappear as they dive into the back of the fort. We hear the sound of gunshots and screaming and then footsteps running away. BEAR jumps up with his flashlight. WEASEL jumps up and follows.)

BEAR: Quick, he's gettin' away!

(They both exit through the door to the kitchen, screaming and yelling.)

Scene 5

(BEAR and WEASEL stick their heads through the door. They enter slowly and cautiously. WEASEL is holding the flashlight.)

BEAR: Okay, all right, we been through the whole fucking house, nobody there.

WEASEL: No one, not a soul.

BEAR: So where'd he go? He couldn't get out, could he?

WEASEL: Not without trippin' the alarm, nobody can get in or out without setting it off.

BEAR: So where'd he go? What is he, a ghost or somethin?

(WEASEL is aghast at what he sees on the floor behind the overturned couch.)

WEASEL: Oh man, look at my floor, he yarked all over my carpet!

BEAR: He'd have to be a ghost. I gotta sit and think about this.

WEASEL: Look at this! Look at my rug! Looks like the guy gave birth to a swamp on my rug!

BEAR: Weasel, shut up! Hand me my beer, would ya? All this runnin' around is givin' me a thirst.

(WEASEL picks up a beer bottle from behind the couch and hands it to BEAR. WEASEL begins to pace.)

WEASEL: Fuck fuck fuck. I don't get it, he's got more holes in him than a plate of Swiss cheese, an' yet he's still walkin' around! What gives here?

BEAR: Weasel I said Shut up! I'm tryin' to think! *(BEAR takes a big drink from his beer bottle.)* Christ, my beer's gotten warm an' now it tastes like horse piss.

(WEASEL stops pacing suddenly and looks up.)

BEAR: What is it, what's wrong?

WEASEL: Uh, nothing, nothing.

(BEAR takes another swig of beer, grimaces then belches.)

BEAR: You know what I'm worried about?

WEASEL: What?

BEAR: Morrie. If we don't show up tomorrow with a body, we're gonna become ghosts ourselves.

WEASEL: Morrie, shit. I'm worried about this ghost. You think it's really a ghost?

BEAR: What else could it be?

(There is another loud fart. WEASEL jumps, pointing his weapon around wildly.)

WEASEL: Oh shit!

BEAR: Relax, relax. That was me.

WEASEL: Jesus, ya about gave me a fuckin' heart attack.

BEAR: It's just my colon kickin' up a fuss. All this runnin' around gets it goin'.

WEASEL: Jesus. Jesus Mighty Christ! Bear, you got one bad stink. I can hardly breathe here!

BEAR: Shaddup, smart-ass.

WEASEL: I'm serious, you're rotten. Man, I hope that smell doesn't stick, I can barely see straight.

BEAR: Hey, wait a minute, wait a minute. *(Sniffs the air.)* That's ain't one of mine!

(There is the sound of the toilet flushing. They both jump up and move cautiously toward the bathroom. The toilet flushes again and again and muffled farting noises are heard.)

WEASEL: The smell, the smell is horrible!

BEAR: Shh. He's in there droppin' a log. Gimme the flashlight. You get the door while I go in an' pop him while his pants are down.

WEASEL: Okay, okay, ready? One, two, THREE!

(WEASEL flings the door open and BEAR runs into the bathroom, yelling and firing his weapon, then suddenly runs back into the living room and slams the door shut behind him. Bear is almost sobbing.)

WEASEL: Did'ja get him did'ja get him?

BEAR: I don't know.

WEASEL: You don't know?

BEAR: I shot it, but I don't think it took. Weez, you won't believe this but in there, on the floor, was the biggest pile of shit I ever saw in my life.

WEASEL: Shit as in people shit?

BEAR: I never thought I'd live to see shit stacked that high. It was as big as a MAN! It was a MAN-SIZED SHIT!

WEASEL: You don't mean—

BEAR: Rick the Dick has turned into pile of SHIT!

WEASEL: Whatta we gonna do, Bear, whatta we gonna do?

BEAR: I don't know what we're gonna do, but I know what I'm NOT gonna do. I'm NOT goin' into that bathroom again, that's for damn sure!

(Sirens and flashing lights are seen and heard.)

WEASEL: It's the cops! The neighbors musta called the cops! Hey where are ya goin'?

(BEAR starts to walk toward the door.)

BEAR: Out. I'm turnin' myself in.

WEASEL: You can't do that! We talkin' hard time here!

BEAR: Weez, I just now came face to face with a stack of human shit tall enough to spit in my eye. Hard time in Federal Penitentiary is nothing next to that. I'm outta here.

(WEASEL points his gun at BEAR.)

WEASEL: Can't let you do that Bear. If you go, then there's no chance for me. I'm too young to spend the rest of my life in the pen. You're gonna stay, and we're gonna find a way outta this.

(BEAR points his gun at WEASEL.)

BEAR: You little bastard, who are you to tell me what to do? Who taught you how to use an ice pick? Who showed you how to shake down bookies? Who was there when you made your fuckin' bones? Me. And you stand there pointin' your piece at me and try to order me around? Fuck you, you little prick!

WEASEL: We can still get outta this, I'm tellin' ya. I gotta special room in the basement we can hide in until the cops take off, so put down your piece and lets go. I ain't goin' to jail.

BEAR: No way, no fuckin' way. Weez, listen to me. I don't care where I'm at, as long as I'm not here, in this stinky shitty house. Drop your gun and let me go.

WEASEL: Can't do that, Bear.

BEAR: So whatta gonna do, then? Whatta gonna do, punk?

(Pause. Silence is finally broken by another loud fart, which prompts WEASEL and BEAR to shoot each other many times. They each fall tragically to the floor in slow motion as fine Italian opera music plays.

Lights and music fade. In the darkness, sounds of flatulence suddenly explode.

It sounds almost like someone chuckling. Chuckling evilly.)

End of Play

BODILY FUNCTIONS NOTES:

FIRST PRODUCED in 1995 at Camilla's Theatre Gallery, featuring Chuck Bunting and Jason Howard, directed by Catherine Zambri. Later produced in 2000 at Manhattan Theatre Source with the same cast and director.

OKAY, this is an early, early play (though it has been updated some for the 2000 production) that features a lot of what I found funny when I was in my early twenties.

IT STILL MAKES ME LAUGH, and it was during this play that my good friend Chuck discovered that props hate and will sometimes run away from him.

42

Quitting (2 m)

CHARACTERS:

TODD – A 32 year-old man.

BEAU – His father, age 59.

SETTING: A park.

(TODD, 32, sits on a bench in the park. BEAU, 55, slowly enters and sits next to him.

TODD pretends not to notice BEAU at first. Finally, after a moment, TODD gives in.)

TODD: What are you doing here?

BEAU: I stopped by your house, your wife said you would be

here in the park. She said you come here just about every day, rain or shine, to think about things.

TODD: I'm not talking about the fucking park, Beau, I meant, what are you doing here, in this city, hundreds of miles away from where you live, why are you here in the area where I live?

BEAU: I came to see you.

TODD: Why?

BEAU: Why? Do I have to have a reason?

TODD: Yes, you do.

BEAU: *(beat)* Your wife is very nice. Sweet, loving, very pretty too. Seems like a very wonderful woman.

TODD: She is. That's why I married her.

BEAU: Very pleasant woman, your wife. Good choice, always avoid marrying an unpleasant woman, I've unfortunately made that mistake a couple times late in my life.

TODD: I'm assuming, for your sake and mine, that you are not referring to my mother.

BEAU: No, hell no, I'm talking about the two wives after her, your mom was fine, a good ... great ... lady.

TODD: She was.

(Brief pause.)

BEAU: So how long have you been married?

TODD: Three years.

BEAU: Right, three years, now I remember. I remember when your Aunt Helen called, said you'd gone to Vegas and got yourself hitched. I always thought it was interesting because I'd gotten married myself just a few weeks earlier at city hall. Kind of ironic, don't you think?

TODD: To you, maybe. What do you want, what are you doing here?

BEAU: I'm here to see you.

TODD: Why?

BEAU: Why? Because you're my son.

TODD: Since when has that ever been important?

BEAU: It's always been important.

TODD: Bullshit. When was the last time we've seen each other?

BEAU: It's been awhile, I know …

TODD: When was the last time we've even spoken?

BEAU: Todd …

TODD: It's been five years, five fucking years since we've seen each other or said anything other than hello.

BEAU: I know. You're right.

TODD: I got a card from you after I got married, and another one each Christmas, but that's it and not only that, it wasn't even your handwriting on the cards anyway, it was your wife, what's her name, Chrissie, I think she's the one that sent the fucking cards.

BEAU: Cassie, not Chrissie, Cassie was the last one. Yeah, you're right about that, cards on important occasions were very important to Cassandra, she'd buy holiday cards by the carton, had them all organized months in advance, write 'em all out, that kind of thing she lived for. Cassie was a demon for organization, she was. You can only imagine how much fun it was for her to have to live with a disaster like me, I can barely remember where I parked the car. That's why the marriage only lasted a couple of years. Actually, we're still technically married, can't afford to pay for a divorce yet. I hear she's taken up with this fella that sells satellite dishes, don't know him, but she's probably going to send the papers on to me eventually. She's a good woman, though.

(BEAU reaches into his shirt pocket and takes out a packet of cigarettes. He shakes one loose and puts it into his mouth.)

TODD: Don't you dare light that thing up …

BEAU: I'm not gonna light it up …

TODD: I fucking mean it, I can't stand the smell of those fucking things, and not only that …

BEAU: It's okay, it's all right, I quit smoking, I quit smoking.

TODD: You quit smoking again?

BEAU: Yes. Didn't Helen tell you? I quit smoking.

TODD: If you quit smoking, then what hell is that cigarette doing in your mouth?

BEAU: It's there for comfort.

TODD: Comfort?

BEAU: Comfort. I find it comforting. When I first quit, at least this last time, the hardest thing was trying to find something to do with my hands and mouth, I went through toothpicks, chewing gum, none of it worked so this is what I do, I have a pack, play with it like a smoker usually does, I put the cigarette in my mouth but I don't light the damn thing, I just let it sit there comfortable-like and so far, it seems to do the trick.

TODD: When did you quit? This time.

BEAU: I officially quit at your Grandpa Maynard's funeral, three weeks ago.

TODD: Quit 'cause of Grandpa Maynard?

BEAU: Well, yeah, he did have throat and lung cancer as I think you know, and I guess it did something to me. I smoked as much as he did, so I decided to quit.

TODD: You tried to quit smoking a bunch of times before.

BEAU: You're right, I have tried many times to toss the habit, but I'm thinking this time will be different. Made up my mind out at the cemetery when they put him ground. I decided that it was time to be a man. That was the last time I had a cigarette and, God willing, that will be the last cigarette I ever smoke in my life.

(Brief pause.)

TODD: I don't believe in God.

BEAU: Since when don't you believe in God?

TODD: Beau, I haven't believed in God since I was nineteen years old.

BEAU: What? Son, are you sure about this, I mean, this is God were talking about here. I remember that you used to go to church all the time when were a boy.

TODD: I did, but I got over it. I can't believe you're surprised that you don't know this, I mean, how would you know? You don't know anything about me. And where is all this newfound respect for God and the Church coming from? It never seemed important to you when I was growing up.

BEAU: It wasn't, back then. I guess it's easier to think about the older you get. Are you sure you've thought this through, what about your wife, what about when you have kids—

TODD: What the fuck do you care, anyway?

BEAU: Son—

TODD: What the fuck does it matter to you, Beau? What do you care what I do or don't believe? Did you really come all this way just to tell me about God?

BEAU: No, I guess not.

TODD: So for the last time, what the hell do you want from me?

BEAU: I just want to talk.

TODD: I've got a phone, you could have just called. You could have called me at any time during the past ten, fifteen years.

BEAU: You're right, I could have. I should have. I was hoping to talk to you at the funeral, but you weren't there.

TODD: You weren't even able to call and tell me Grandpa Maynard was in the hospital. I had to hear it from Aunt Helen. Aunt Helen. Beau, I can't stand Aunt Helen.

BEAU: Not a lot of people can, even those that love her.

TODD: I can't stand Aunt Helen but if it wasn't for her, I wouldn't know what was happening about anything. If it wasn't for her, I might not have been able to see him in the hospital, I would have missed my chance to say good-bye.

BEAU: You visited your Grandpa when he was in the hospital?

TODD: Yes, I did, no thanks to you. Helen was also the one that called when he died. Why didn't you fucking call and tell me about him?

BEAU: Well I knew Helen would, it's what she does, she calls everybody whenever somebody dies or something happens, so I figured you knew and I didn't have to. Tell you, I mean. I didn't know what else there was to say.

TODD: And now you DO have something to say?

BEAU: You're right. I should have called. I'm sorry. So you visited your Grandpa Maynard in the hospital?

TODD: Yes.

BEAU: Did he … how was he … when you were there? Was he well when you were there?

TODD: He was dying, Beau, he wasn't well at all. I don't … I don't think he even knew I was there. It was a couple days before he passed away. I'm pretty sure he didn't know who I was. I sat with him for a while, a few hours or so, then I said my good-bye to him and I left. I said my good-bye as best as I could.

BEAU: It was rough, watching him go through that. Really, really rough. You holdin' up all right with it?

TODD: Nobody enjoys watching someone die of cancer, Beau, but if you want me to be brutally, brutally honest, I didn't know Grandpa Maynard all that well at all. I do remember him drinking a lot. I do remember him NOT being there for things, events, birthdays and graduations. I haven't talked to or seen him in years and years. I knew him even less than I know you.

BEAU: Yep, that was him. He was a hard man to get close to. I'd agree on that. Pretty set in his ways. I used to admire that about him.

(Brief pause. TODD stands.)

TODD: Look, I gotta go. I appreciate you driving all the way up here to see me …

BEAU: I was hoping to see you at the funeral.

TODD: Why?

BEAU: I wanted to talk to you.

TODD: Well, now we've talked. Take it easy, Beau.

BEAU: Todd, wait …

TODD: What for?

BEAU: Damn it, what's your rush to get away? Can't you just sit and have a quiet word with your Dad? I really need to talk to you!

TODD: I DON'T WANT TO FUCKING TALK TO YOU! Why SHOULD I want to talk to you? Why now? You know, there were times in my life when I needed to talk to you and you weren't there. You weren't there for me most of the time, so why should I be anywhere for you? The hard truth is I got used to life without you, it wasn't my choice, it was something I had to do and I did it and now I'm pretty used to it. I'll tell you something else, Beau, I WAS at Grandpa Maynard's funeral, I wasn't going to go but then I did anyway, by myself, I didn't go inside for the service, I sat outside in my car. I followed you all out to the cemetery and watched them lower Grandpa into the ground, I watched it all from a distance where nobody could see me. Most of all I watched you, Beau, and when I did I was glad I stayed away. Now, I'm sorry about Grandpa dying and I'm sorry that you probably feel bad but that's the most I can offer you today. As far as you or I are concerned, I am all fucking TALKED out!

(Brief pause. TODD begins to walk away.)

BEAU: I quit drinking, too.

(TODD stops.)

TODD: Quit?

BEAU: Quit.

TODD: Really?

BEAU: Yeah. Really. I've given it up for good, I hope. I'm tryin', anyway. No drinking.

TODD: You're not holding Budweiser in your mouth for comfort, are you?

BEAU: No, I wish, but no, they don't let you do that, my sponsor, I mean. I don't go near the stuff, don't go to bars, don't keep it in the house, no Budweiser, no Johnnie Walker, nothing at all.

TODD: Quit after the funeral?

BEAU: Not till the week after. I was drunk as a skunk during the funeral as I'm sure you observed. I was drunk the whole week after the funeral. Hell, I was drunk years and years before Dad's funeral, I just didn't realize it. Funny, I didn't realize how much I really, actually drank until I decided to stop. Man, I drank a lot. Every night. Never considered myself an alcoholic because I always got to work, did my job good and drank on my own time. But I am. I am an alcoholic. Decided to go sober and quit, been sober now fifteen days. Guess that's also why I've been thinking about God and stuff these days, now that I don't go to the bar every night, church is the only other place I can go and see other people.

TODD: *(beat)* You could go to the mall.

BEAU *(chuckles)* I could, I guess. Ain't really into shopping, though, and church has been doin' all right for me.

TODD: You drove all this way just to tell me you quit drinking and smoking?

BEAU: Don't quite believe me, quitting it, I mean, don't quite buy it yet, do you?

TODD: I guess I'm going to wait and see. Okay?

BEAU: Okay. That's fair.

(Brief pause.)

TODD: All right then. Thanks for coming up to see me.

(TODD turns to leave. BEAU stands up.)

BEAU: Todd … I'd really like to talk with you more often.

(TODD stops and looks at BEAU.)

TODD: All right. Call me sometime.

BEAU: It's just … I ain't so good at it, talking. At least, talking to family and all. I was a hell of a conversationalist when I was drunk in the bar, at least I thought I was, but talking to sober people about sober things, I ain't good at it. I want to be. I look at you, my son, and there's so much I wanna say but when I open my mouth everything just dies. So what happens is that I end up not saying anything. But I want to tell you … I gotta say that … I came to say that I know that I wasn't a real good father to you, I know that I wasn't there for you, I recognize that and I am very, very sorry that I didn't do a better job at being your Dad.

TODD: You're apologizing to me for being a bad dad?

BEAU: Yeah. I wasn't a good dad, I wasn't good husband to your mother, bless her soul, and I wasn't even a good man, I drank, I fought, I whored around, I acted pretty selfishly most of my life. And I want to apologize for it.

(Brief pause.)

TODD: Okay.

BEAU: You know, your grandpa treated me pretty much the same way I treated you, the only time he ever talked to me was when we went fishing or hunting or drinking, especially when we were drinking, that's the only time he talked and he never talked about important stuff, it was always about who he was pissed at this week or local gossip or what have you, he never spoke about me and him in any way. I never knew his feelings toward me or anything. He never called me unless I called him, all that. And I don't want you to think bad about him, he was of a different time and generation, before men spoke about what they felt and before there was any such thing as a twelve step program, that's where he came from and he just didn't know any better. When he went to the hospital, I went in to visit him and there he was, lying there small and shrunken, the cancer was working fast on him, and a funny thing happened, the day before he died, how he looked at me, it was strange. His eyes were so bright and big and he looked right at me, right at me. At first I thought it was because he was sick. Then I thought it was because he was sober, I didn't see him sober a whole lot, but then it hit me. He's really, really looking at me, he's really trying to reach out to me like a dad for the first time. I could tell. He wanted to talk to me like a son, I could tell he did, but he'd already lost his voice box to the cancer, so he couldn't speak, couldn't say anything. I couldn't either, I couldn't talk I couldn't do anything except sit there and hold his hand. I held his hand like I used to do when I was little and he just looked at me. All night. Then he died. It stayed with me, his eyes looking at me, all through the funeral and the week after, no matter how drunk I got I couldn't get away from them. I got so scared, scared I was gonna end up lying down on my back somewhere, wanting to say something to you and not be able to. I got really scared. I don't want to end up that way, Todd, and most of all I don't want to end up that way with you. So I decided a couple of weeks ago just to quit. Not just smoking or drinking, but quit everything like that, all that stuff, all that selfishness, I decided to quit while I still can. Quit being quiet and absent when I should be present and accounted for. Quit while I still got a chance. I don't expect it to be easy and I don't expect you to welcome me with open arms after all these years, but I'm here to tell you, man to man, that I ain't gonna kick without giving it my very best shot. That's what I really wanted to say to you.

(Short but full pause.)

TODD: I appreciate you telling me that.

BEAU: I appreciate you listening to me, son.

TODD: *(beat)* Quit drinking and smoking all in the same week, huh?

BEAU: Oh yeah.

TODD: Been drinking a lot of coffee?

BEAU: You have no idea. I don't drink coffee, I breathe it in. And eating, my God, I inhale food, I'm eating like every meal is my last.

TODD: You know who is an excellent cook?

BEAU: Who?

TODD: My wife. My wife is a great cook.

BEAU: Really?

TODD: Yeah, really. Dad?

BEAU: Yeah?

TODD: Would you … like to have dinner with us tonight? She'd love to … we'd love to have you over dinner.

BEAU: *(beat)* I'd love to, son.

TODD: All right. Let's go then.

(Brief pause, then TODD slowly goes to BEAU and carefully hugs him.)

The End

QUITTING NOTES:

First produced in 2003 by The Defiant Ones at Manhattan Theatre Source, featuring R. Paul Hamilton and Taylor Ruckel, directed by Anita Hollander. A fantastic production.

Personal note: My father's nickname was Beau, and this play was very much a fantasy of an accord that I hoped (at the time this play written) to have with him. But while it reflected real life emotions on my part, it didn't reflect real life. It's fiction, inspired by real life, but not the reality of my life, nor my father's.

As Stephen King has said, none of it happened, but all of it was true.

My father, except for a fondness for Budweiser, wasn't like the character in this play, nor was I able to attend my grandfather's funeral (whose name was Maynard) it's all fiction in that regard. And my father only married two women in his lifetime and was married to each (at different times in his life, of course) for over twenty years.

He and I never had a conversation like the one featured in the play, nor did my father ever give up his taste for Budweiser. Plus, I got married in Japan, not Vegas.

He and I went quite some time without speaking for various, stupid reasons (for which I take equal responsibility) and this play was written during one such time.

Years later, we had a re-approachment, for which I'm very thankful.

My father was an Iowa country boy of a specific generation and some things just were never talked about. But we did make our peace.

We never talked about intimate stuff, but he eventually got to know me as an adult, my wife, our children (his grandchildren) and spend time with us, and we spoke regularly on the phone even since I became a father myself.

Sadly, just as I was putting together this edition of plays (and wondering how the hell I was going to explain QUITTING to my dad) my father took ill and passed away on September 8th, 2013.

I was with him when he passed.

This play is dedicated to him.

Last Words

In putting this collection together, I discovered (I hadn't ever stopped to count before this) that I had fifty short plays (these forty-four and the six that were published previously by Original Works Online), which was astounding to me.

I didn't remember writing fifty short plays (this doesn't include the ten full-length plays I've written) but it seems that I did (and this doesn't even count the short plays and sketches that went missing over time and were never recovered as I switched computers, lost floppy disks, remember those, when I moved around, etc.)

This collection does, however, cover a very specific time and place in my life, when I packed my bags, hopped into a truck and drove from Iowa to New York City.

Reading through this now, in the present, it seems all a dream, and maybe that's what it was. I was living a dream, that of a renegade penniless playwright, sleeping on a mattress on a floor and writing theatre for no reason other than to follow my creative jones.

Much of the work we did was usually in a theatre that held less than fifty, even full, and a short run that maybe two hundred people at the most saw and enjoyed. We would do that, with different shows, again and again, and we'd make those who attended, and ourselves, very happy.

Interestingly enough, nearly none of the theatres where these plays were first seen even exist any longer. The Riant burned down. Surf Reality, Nada,

Times have changed.

And just like the city of New York itself has changed, so have I.

I don't really do theatre these days, I have two sons and a ton of responsibilities and write a lot of other things, books, screenplays, pilots, and try to be a responsible citizen.

In other words, make a living, pay the bills.

Which means I don't do theatre.

Because unless you teach, you can't, in the words of Sam Shepard, "make a living at theatre, you can just barely scrape by." And that was fine when I was single.

Now that I'm a dad, not so much.

But I am proud of the work. For better or worse, the plays in this collection cover the breadth and arc of my days as a playwright.

One reason I put this collection together and offered it, royalty-free, was to share the work that was done during that specific place and time and give people a glimpse into that window of time. I suspect there are many other artists out there who are just like me, who offered up great work that was done and briefly enjoyed by those lucky enough to witness it then it was gone like a breath in the wind.

I offer my thanks to you, the reader, for reading this collection and, if you feel it worthy, please pass the word along to others.

So we're near the end, and I'm going to leave you with one more piece of work, which is the very first real play I'd written and had produced in New York City.

LOVE, LUST & LIFE is actually three ten-minute plays that can work together or separately, and have been produced countless times.

I started the first section of it (A BOY, A GIRL AND A DOG) while still in grad school at Iowa and nursing a broken heart from a failed relationship. I got stuck because I had no way of ending the piece and finally got the ending a year later while on my own in New York City. But I couldn't leave it with Boy as he was, and had to continue the story until I found the right place to end it. You'll see.

The first production was put up in the fall of 1994 by Developmental Stages in New York City. That show was directed by the wonderful Nick Corley, but sadly I don't have a cast list for that first production.

It's since been done at The Riant Theatre, Manhattan Theatre Source, and many, many other places, even including China, no lie.

There was a great production in 1997 at the Loft in Soho, featuring Chuck McKinney, Abigail Lopez, Jim McCauley, Michele Ammon, Debbie Jones and Clyde Kelly.

The third movement, GRANDMA, GRANDPA AND THE CAR has been performed more than any other and was also a finalist in the Louisville ten-minute play contest. If you want to do that one separately, you of course have permission to do so.

The singer / songwriter Dan Fogelberg once said that he'd written a lot of songs, but if he had to choose to only write ONE song to write, it'd be THE LEADER OF THE BAND.

He'd be fine if that's the only song he'd ever written in his entire life.

I kind of feel the same way about the following play.

I have my favorites, but if I had written only ONE short play, it'd be the following.

43

Love, Lust & Life

Three very short plays

1. **A Boy, A Girl and A Dog**
2. **A Man, A Woman and A Cat**
3. **Grandma, Grandpa and The Car**

SPECIAL NOTES ON STAGING:

IT IS VERY important that *the individual actors do NOT look at or acknowledge each till the very end of the last play*. In other words, only Grandma and Grandpa ever look at each other and even then, ONLY when it's stated that they do in the script. This is very, VERY important. *Each actor only talks to the audience, NOT to each other at anytime.* Also, whenever possible, it is best to cast age-appropriate actors when you are able.

VERY SIMPLE SET, just two stools. The Dog and Cat noises can be supplied offstage by one of the other actors. The sound effects in the first play (Angels, Thunder, etc.) are great when possible, but the play works just as well without them and therefore they are optional. These three plays can be staged together or separately, but I have found that they work best when performed in sequence.

A BOY, A Girl and A Dog

(Spotlight comes up upon the BOY.)

BOY: For a long time it was just me and my dog, Skippy. Just the two of us. Me and man's best friend. We were each other's best friend, best buddies, best PALS, inseparable together, soul brothers to the end. Ain't that right Skip?

(Offstage sound of a dog, SKIPPY, barking joyfully.)

BOY: That's right, Skippy my buddy, Skippy my PAL! Skippy, the best dog a guy could ever know! You, know what? Whenever I needed someone to talk to, I could go and talk to Skip! Whenever I had a problem that needed to be ironed out, I could tell Skippy, and, let me tell you, he'd understand!

(SKIPPY barks.)

BOY: Skippy understands cause we share something', something' special between us, a friendship that happens maybe once every hundred years. That's what we have. A friendship based on TRUST. We TRUST each other. I know that when it seemed as though the world was ganging' up on me, I could look to my side and there he would be, Skippy my buddy, my friend, my PAL!

SKIPPY barks again.

BOY: And Skippy trusts me. He knows I'll be there for him. He knows I look out for him, take him for walks in the park, feed him every day, care for him when he was sick. Skippy knows that I would never, under any circumstances, play fetch with him and PRETEND to throw the stick and then hide it behind my back to fake him out and make him look stupid. I respect him too much as a friend to do that. And he respects me. He never pees in the apartment, never chews on any of my shoes, nothing. It's an ideal relationship. I know if I were in an accident or a fire or something', and I was trapped, I know Skippy would go and get help and save my life, just like the dogs on TV. Ain't' that right Skip?

(SKIPPY once again barks joyfully.)

BOY: So, life was pretty fine for me and Skip, a boy and his dog. Then, my life changed. Then, I met HER.

(Spotlight downstage right comes up upon the GIRL. They never acknowledge one another.)

GIRL: He met me.

BOY: I met her and she met me, and I heard music playing. Which may have been because we met in an elevator, I'm not sure. Regardless, our eyes met and it was truly an event of epic proportions. I saw her, and she saw me, and somewhere inside our souls touched together. I asked her out right away, which is unusual for me.

GIRL: And I said no, which is usual for me.

BOY: But I kept after her! I didn't give up! I felt certain that somehow we were meant for each other, destined to be together. I was persistent, until finally …

GIRL: I said yes.

BOY: She said yes. And I heard angels sing a heavenly choir with that single word. Yes.

(Offstage sound of angels singing the word "YES".)

GIRL: He was kinda cute in an unusual sort of way. Why not?

BOY: I took her to dinner, and then to a concert. Afterwards, we went for a walk by the lake under the moonlight. It was great. Her eyes sparkled like the stars in the sky. I thought she was beautiful, and I told her so.

GIRL: He made me feel pretty, and I liked that. And he was cute.

BOY: But I didn't try nothin, no sir, I respected her too much.

GIRL: Cute, but kinda timid.

BOY: But we went out again.

GIRL: And again.

BOY: And again.

GIRL: And again.

BOY: To movies, plays, picnics, you name it, we were there together, inseparable. Then, one night over wine and cheese out on the riverbank …

GIRL: Finally.

BOY: I asked her if I could kiss her, and she said …

GIRL: I said yes.

BOY: She said yes. And I again heard angels sing a heavenly choir with that single word. Yes.

(Offstage sound of angels singing the word "YES".)

GIRL: About time he made his move. Worth the wait, though. I don't know if it was the wine or what, but that was one hell of a kiss.

BOY: Then we started seeing more of each other.

GIRL: We certainly did.

BOY: And we started talking a lot about ourselves. Sharing things. I even met her family.

GIRL: Well, they were in town, so why not?

BOY: It got to the point where not a day went by without us seeing or talking to each other.

GIRL: He kinda grows on you after awhile, you know?

BOY: Until one night, when we were alone in my apartment, under candlelight …

GIRL: It was very romantic.

BOY: I asked her if I could make love to her. And she said …

GIRL: I said yes.

BOY: She said yes. And I heard angels sing a heavenly choir with that single word. Yes.

(Offstage, once again the angels sing the word YES".)

GIRL: The timing was right, and I was curious. Besides, it's been six months since we started seeing each other. Why not?

BOY: Then I knew what love was. Then I knew. We became inseparable together. We went everywhere together, we did everything together. We were in love. I told her I loved her. She said she loved me.

GIRL: Well, I did, in my own way, I did love him. I cared for him quite a bit.

BOY: But now I knew. Now I knew what love meant. If you've never been in love, then you don't really know. It was just like it was in the movies, when two people that love see each other and music plays and the sky thunders. That was us. That was love. It was just like in those books, when the touch of the person you love would send jolts up and down your spine. That was us. That was love.

GIRL: There was definitely some chemistry happening there. We made love just about every night, and it was wonderful.

BOY: Then, there was a slight problem.

(Offstage, SKIPPY barks angrily.)

BOY: Skippy didn't like the love of my life, I don't know why.

GIRL: And I didn't like him. Bastard tried to bite me.

(SKIPPY growls.)

BOY: Easy Skip. I tried to work it out, but it turned out she's allergic to dogs.

GIRL: Especially that dog.

BOY: So it came down to a choice.

GIRL: The Mutt or me.

BOY: Sorry Skip.

(SKIPPY whines.)

BOY: I was sad for a while, but I figured Skip would understand that this was love, love that happens only once in lifetime. We were in love, and together almost every night. I'd send her flowers and write her poetry, and she'd reward me with a kiss.

GIRL: He was very cute when he did that.

BOY: Most of all, I shared with her everything, everything about me, my childhood, my past, my hopes, my fears, and my dreams. I held nothing back. We had love. We had trust. Till finally, one night in an Italian restaurant over champagne, I gave her a ring and got down on one knee and asked her to marry me. And she said …

GIRL: I said no.

BOY: She said no. And the walls of the world surrounding me crumbled.

(Sound of distant low thunder.)

GIRL: I couldn't see spending the rest of my life with this guy. I had already heard all his stories and stuff at least twice. I mean, he was nice and all that, but I wanted more.

BOY: I thought she loved me.

GIRL: I loved him but I wasn't IN love with him, you know what I'm saying?

BOY: I didn't get it.

GIRL: I didn't think he would understand.

BOY: So, because I had asked her to marry me and she didn't want to, she left me.

GIRL: The heat in that kitchen was definitely too hot for me, so I got out.

BOY: And she was gone.

GIRL: And I was gone.

(Spotlight on GIRL goes out.)

BOY: I walked around in a daze for awhile, like a zombie. It was like the year of my life that I had spent with her had been stolen, sucked out of me by a giant bat that flapped away in the dark of night, never to be seen again, and all that I was left with was cold, empty dreams.

(Brief pause.)

BOY: Then I started thinking, wouldn't it be great, if I could do absolutely anything I wanted to. What if I could just snap my fingers, and BOOM!

(Loud Thunder.)

BOY: Thunder at my fingertips. A wave of my hand and …

(Loud Rain.)

BOY: Raindrops for all. I could raise both arms and all the dogs in the world would howl!

(Howling of all dogs.)

BOY: I was thinking wouldn't it be great if I could control the tides, make the sun rise and set, stop all fighting and wars, abolish all the hunger in the world and maybe, just maybe get my dog Skippy back!

(SKIPPY barks).

BOY: I was thinking wouldn't it be great if I were all-powerful, a supreme being, lord and master of the universe and maybe, just maybe she would like me again and come back!

(Loud thud of something heavy falling.)

BOY: But then I thought some more. And I realized that maybe there is a limit to even what God could do. So I went out and bought a puppy instead! I'm staying with what I know. Now maybe, just maybe I'll be happy again.

(Lights down.)

A MAN, A Woman and A Cat

(Spotlight comes up upon the WOMAN.)

WOMAN: For a long time I didn't do much of anything except stay at home, watch TV, and pet my cat.

(Sound of CAT purring.)

WOMAN: I love my cat, and my cat loves me.

(Purring gets louder.)

WOMAN: Katherine is her name, and she has been my best friend for the past two years. She likes to play games with me, like hiding my socks under the bed, and jumping at my feet when I'm not looking. When I'm typing at my computer, she likes to jump up and stick her face right in there to see what I'm doing.

(KATHERINE meows.)

WOMAN: And she talks to me, too. If I'm in a really bad mood and I'm pounding around the apartment and feeling sorry for myself, she'll look at me and go …

(KATHERINE meows again.)

WOMAN: As if to say "Hey, lighten up, it can't be that bad." And she's right. So life has been fine for me and my little kitty, Katherine. Then, my life changed. Then I ran into him.

(Spotlight comes up on the MAN. They never acknowledge each other.)

MAN: She ran right into me.

WOMAN: Literally.

MAN: I was backing my Chrysler out of my parking place at the office and she plowed right into me.

WOMAN: I was so embarrassed. I didn't have any insurance.

MAN: She dented the shit out of my fender. But she looked so woebegone I couldn't help but laugh. She looked pretty hot too. I told her to forget about it.

WOMAN: He seemed very understanding.

MAN: What the hell, it's only money. And she was pretty.

WOMAN: But then I figured him out.

MAN: I asked her to have dinner with me.

WOMAN: I suppose he thought I should sleep with him just because I smashed his car.

MAN: I assured her it was nothing like that. Although the thought did cross my mind.

WOMAN: I took his number and told him I'd think about it.

MAN: And think about it she did.

WOMAN: In the end, I thought, "why not?" It's been two years since I broke up with that ape of a boyfriend I had before. They can't all be animals. Maybe he was different. He wore a tie, he looked liked he bathed regularly and he used words with more than three syllables. All plusses in his favor. I decided to take a chance. So I called him.

MAN: Finally.

WOMAN: And I said, let's go out.

MAN: It'd been three fucking weeks, I almost forgot who she was.

WOMAN: The next thing you know, I had a date.

MAN: So we went out for dinner. I love to eat out, but I hate first dates.

WOMAN: It was a lovely restaurant, and so expensive.

MAN: It's always a question of, what do we talk about?

WOMAN: He insisted on paying.

MAN: I mean I really suck at small talk.

WOMAN: I kept wondering, does he think I have to sleep with him now, since he paid for dinner?

MAN: So I'm fumbling around, trying not to talk with my mouth full and look like a moron

WOMAN: If he thought that, he had another thing coming.

MAN: I went through the usual routine, you know, what do ya do, where are you from and so on.

WOMAN: But I kept worrying about it. So I thought I should just tell him straight out.

MAN: I thought I was doin' pretty well, when all of a sudden …

WOMAN: So I said … No SEX!

MAN: BANG! I was shot right out of the saddle.

WOMAN: I just wanted to be clear.

MAN: As if I didn't suspect it already, I mean, she'd ordered CRAB, for crying out loud!

WOMAN: It's just that I value myself as a person. I didn't want to be deluded or deceived by physical desire. I wanted purity.

MAN: My older brother, who taught me everything I know, said if you wanna get any dick action with a woman, then there are three things you should never talk about on a first date. Politics, religion and … SEX. But she brought it up. I didn't know what to do.

WOMAN: I considered myself a woman of principle.

MAN: I panicked.

WOMAN: He seemed to understand.

MAN: I just started agreeing with everything she said.

WOMAN: In fact, he was really sweet about the whole thing.

MAN: I probably should've dumped her and forgot about her, but you know, she was really cute.

WOMAN: I just believe that you should be in love to make love to somebody.

MAN: Cute, but with crazy ideas.

WOMAN: I thought he would be disappointed and not call me again, but he did.

MAN: Hell, I wasn't seeing anyone else at the time. Why not?

WOMAN: So we went out again.

MAN: And again.

WOMAN: And again. Went out and talked and laughed and shared stories together and it was wonderful.

MAN: It was kinda fun.

WOMAN: Best of all, there was no sex flapping around to confuse everything.

MAN: Fun, but the sexual tension in the air was so thick I was choking on it.

WOMAN: I really started to care about him, and I think he cared about me.

MAN: The anticipation was making me cross-eyed. I woulda done anything to get in her pants.

WOMAN: And I thought, maybe this is it, maybe this is love.

MAN: If I didn't find some sort of release soon I was gonna explode.

WOMAN: So one night when we were having a romantic dinner by candlelight at my place, I decided to ask him directly how he felt.

MAN: Finally it looked like she was gonna come across.

WOMAN: Then there was a slight problem.

(KATHERINE the cat snarls and hisses.)

MAN: That fucking cat.

WOMAN: Katherine Kitty didn't like the new man in my life. And he didn't like her.

MAN: The little fucker snagged my good pair of slacks.

WOMAN: So it came down to a choice.

MAN: The cat or me.

WOMAN: What was I going do? The two I cared about most and they didn't like each other.

MAN: I wasn't gonna get anywhere with that little monster distracting her all the time.

WOMAN: So we came to a compromise. Whenever he came over I would lock Katherine Kitty in the closet.

(Kitty wails.)

WOMAN: Oh, and she hated it. But I knew that she would understand that could be love, true love that happens maybe once in a lifetime.

MAN: Finally the little beast was gone and I had room to maneuver.

WOMAN: So finally we got it all worked out and I told him how I felt and I asked him, point blank, if he loved me, and he said …

MAN: I said yes.

WOMAN: He said yes! I was so happy! Finally a man who felt with his heart and not his sex organ. A man who loved me!

MAN: Well I did. At the time.

WOMAN: So we made love and it was wonderful. It was so wonderful to be loved again.

MAN: Finally I got her into bed.

WOMAN: It was so wonderful to have a lover again.

MAN: So we did it, and at the time I'm thinking, all this waiting, all that time, just for this?

WOMAN: Best of all, we were completely honest and clear with each other.

MAN: I mean, it was all right, but it wasn't the Fourth of July.

WOMAN: We took steps so we wouldn't hurt each other.

MAN: And after awhile, listening to her chirp on and on, it started to get kinda dull.

WOMAN: It was just a matter of time till he got me a ring and we set the date.

MAN: And that cat, it always looked at me like I was a piece of shit.

(KATHERINE hisses.)

WOMAN: In fact, I decided to talk to him about it that very night.

MAN: All in all, I was feeling kinda crowded. So I got out.

WOMAN: But when I got home from work, he wasn't there.

MAN: But hey, I'm no barbarian, I left her a letter.

WOMAN: There was a note taped to the refrigerator.

MAN: And on my way out, I gave that fucking cat a swift kick in the ass.

(KATHERINE wails in anger and pain.)

WOMAN: It said he couldn't do this any longer.

MAN: And I was gone.

WOMAN: And he was gone.

(Spotlight on MAN goes out.)

WOMAN: Suicide came to mind, but it seemed like too much work. I just sat around, watching TV, and wondering just where did

I go wrong? Was I such a repulsive person? Was I stupid, naive? What did I miss about this whole thing?

(KATHERINE the cat starts purring.)

WOMAN: Then I remembered that I was loved. And I resolved that in the future, I was going to listen closer to the one I trusted and loved the most.

(Purring gets louder and spotlight fades.)

GRANDMA, Grandpa and The Car

(Two separate spotlights come up on a dark stage, revealing GRANDMA and GRANDPA, sitting in chairs. They speak to the audience without looking at or acknowledging one another.)

GRANDPA: You know you're old when, instead of thinkin' about all the stuff you're gonna do, you sit an' think about all the stuff that you did.

GRANDMA: You've heard this one, everyone has, 'you can't teach an old dog new tricks', everyone in America has probably heard that one ten times.

GRANDPA: I spend my days on the porch, sippin' iced tea with lemon and dreaming' about the life I've led on up to this point. If I had any ambition at all, I would write it all down an' make a pile of money. But I don't have no ambition for that kinda thing. Not at all. I'm a simple man with simple tastes an' simple pleasures.

GRANDMA: What do think of when you hear the word old? You think of somethin' rotted, and decayed, and useless, that's what you think. I don't like to think of myself as old. I prefer to think of myself as accomplished.

GRANDPA: I used to be ambitious. Very ambitious. Not for money or land or ed-u-ca-tion, none of that bullshit. This was nine-teen fifty we're talkin' about here, only sissies went to school, what was important in nineteen-fifty was that you be a man, a proud man who worked hard an' kept his word. A man.

GRANDMA: For I am accomplished. I've done more in the last ten years than many people do their entire lives.

GRANDPA: A man had to have a home, a good car to take you to work, a good steady job, and a family. An you had to take care of all of 'em. Those were a man's responsibilities.

GRANDMA: Only two years ago did I receive my college degree, and I am the first in the history of my family to have done that. And I owe it all to my husband.

GRANDPA: I'll never forget the day it hit me, the day I knew my place in the scheme of things, it was the day I first saw her. I was walking down to the corner of Wiltshire Blvd an' almost ran right smack dab into her. I'd have to say it was love at first sight. She was beautiful.

GRANDMA: Girls at that time, while you were in high school, you looked for a possible husband, one that wouldn't be too mean, you got him interested in you, teased him along but you weren't fast, boys wouldn't marry fast girls, you got him so worked up till he'd almost bust, then he'd ask you to marry him. You got married, then you had kids and took care of the house.

GRANDPA: I had never seen anything in my life as beautiful as her. I knew the moment I laid eyes on her that I had to have her. I had a good job as a welder down at the foundry, good benefits, respectable. I set my jaw and went after her.

GRANDMA: Now when I was in high school, I had a boyfriend, just like everyone else, because that's what you did, you had to have someone to take you to dances and drive-inns and ice-cream socials. He was nice, he was older and he never got too fresh. He liked me and my parents liked him. The word love just never came up.

GRANDPA: The next thing you know, she was mine. I called her Priscilla. My little Priss. She was a cherry-red 1947 convertible Chevy with white sidewall tires. The first car I owned all by myself. Gawd, I loved that car. That was the day I knew I was a man.

GRANDMA: So I had this boyfriend, and eventually, because we didn't know what else to do, we got married.

GRANDPA: After that I got married an' bought a house. A house with a big garage.

GRANDMA: Then we had kids.

GRANDPA: I bought a Buick, a four door, for family drivin', couldn't have the kids spillin' their ice-cream on Priss's leather seats, now could I? The Buick was for drivin', the Chevy was for show.

GRANDMA: So I was a housewife, which was all I was trained to do, since I was a little girl. Do the laundry, make dinner, iron the clothes. Girls are trained to be task-orientated, thinking only of the job in front of them. That way they can be good housewives. It's only natural that they would start to think of their lives in the same way. Get a boyfriend, get him to marry you, have children, raise a family and keep the house clean in case company drops by unexpectedly.

GRANDPA: Nobody but me drove Priscilla, and every Saturday that it wasn't raining I would wash an' wax her out in the front drive where everybody could see, then I would take her for a spin down around the town square. The kids and the missus would sometimes come along.

GRANDMA: It's not until later, when all the tasks are done, the kids grown up and are married themselves, that you sit and wonder.

GRANDPA: I babied Priss like no one else, an' after the kids growed up an' left home, the missus and I would drive her to car shows an' so on, it was a hell of a time. Every fourth of July we would drive her in the big parade. She was a by-gum classic.

GRANDMA: You wonder, just what the hell have I been doing these past twenty odd years? I've done something, I've got a good home, raised good children, but these were all unconscious acts, in a way, do you know what I mean? I wanted to do something conscious, for a change. To do something, anything, for myself. I tried to explain to my husband, but he just didn't understand.

GRANDPA: The wife, now with the kids gone, she was startin' to get itchy britches. She was jealous, I had Priscilla and she didn't have nothing.

GRANDMA: He was a good man, but like all good men he had his blind spots. His was that damn car.

GRANDPA: She started actin' by-God crazy.

GRANDMA: I just could not believe, that after all these years of marriage he did not trust me enough to drive his stupid car.

GRANDPA: She started makin' crazy demands.

GRANDMA: What it came down to is that he had our golden years all mapped out, and it was a cavalcade of car shows and parades. I rebelled.

GRANDPA: She flipped her lid.

GRANDMA: I told him, "It's the car or me!"

GRANDPA: An' I said, "Get the hell out!"

GRANDMA: And I was gone.

GRANDPA: And she was gone.

GRANDMA: That was ten years ago today.

GRANDPA: I found out that I wasn't too old for divorce. She got the furniture and the Buick. I got the house and the Chevy.

GRANDMA: I really owe it to him, though, if he'd humored me, if he hadn't of thrown me out, the most I probably would have done is served on a school board or headed some church group. Instead, I went to college, got my degree in women's studies, wrote articles for magazines and became a part-time professor. I discovered my own individual worth. Him and his damn car galvanized me into action.

GRANDPA: My father, he was the one who taught me the value of things, and I'll always remember his lessons. Work was equal to worth, the harder you worked, the more you was worth. I felt I had worked hard, and I was worth somethin'. I don't know why the wife didn't understand that. I had my house and my classic car, but now I didn't have my wife.

GRANDMA: Still, there were times when I'd remember him driving his red convertible with the top down and the proud look on his face, and how it would tickle me. He was like a boy with a favorite toy. But I didn't have any room for boys in my life anymore.

GRANDPA: I'd always thought that she'd get scared an' come back to me, cause that's what girls did.

GRANDMA: When I had those thoughts I just pushed him from my mind.

GRANDPA: I waited for her to come back, and she didn't. So you know what I did? I went back to her.

GRANDMA: He came courting, just like the old days.

GRANDPA: I sent her flowers.

GRANDMA: I sent them back.

GRANDPA: I sent her candy.

GRANDMA: I asked, "Did he want me to get fat?"

GRANDPA: The woman was so dad-gum stubborn!

GRANDMA: I never thought he was serious.

GRANDPA: I couldn't get her to listen.

GRANDMA: Then, he did something extraordinary.

(Very brief pause.)

GRANDPA: I sold the car.

GRANDMA: He sold the car. I couldn't believe it.

GRANDPA: My father he taught me a lot of valuable things about bein' a man, but there was a couple of things he left out. I guess he figured I'd learn 'em on my own. One of these things was the art of compromise.

GRANDMA: You don't understand how many years of his life he sacrificed by selling that car. I thought, maybe he does love me.

GRANDPA: She cried when I told her what I had done. Maybe she does love me.

GRANDMA: I do.

(She reaches out and takes her husband's hand. They look at each other for the very first time during the course of this play and smile.)

GRANDPA: So now I'm a simple man with simple pleasures, sippin' iced tea with lemon with my wife an' discussin' what we're gonna do today. I'm happy, I have a home and a car and most of all, my beautiful wife.

GRANDMA: And I have my life and a husband who loves me.

GRANDPA: And when we go out, the wife drives.

GRANDMA: Who says you can't teach an old dog new tricks?

(They look at each other and smile.)

Lights down.

The End

Oh, And... by the way...

Thank you so much for reading my work, I greatly appreciate it.

In addition to what's collected in this book, I have more than a few others available... including three free ebooks (links to follow) and the majority of that and the rest of my published work is also royalty-free (where noted) for amateurs and educators... just follow the guidelines.

I simply and humbly ask two things... pass the words along to others (**refer the books** to those fellow travelers in theatre) and please **leave reviews** online wherever the books are available.

The reviews help, all of them.

Thank you so much and keep scrolling for information on my other plays.

Also by Joshua James

Playwright and screenwriter Joshua James has collected nearly fifty monologues for men from his plays THE MEN'S ROOM, TALLBOY WALKIN', THE PLEASURE PRINCIPLE and many more... for auditions, class study, solo performances and more...

The ebook is **FREE**, get it HERE:

BUILT FOR ABUSE: ACTING MONOLOGUES FOR MEN

Also by Joshua James

Playwright and screenwriter Joshua James has gathered thirty monologues for women, collected from his plays 2 VERY DANGEROUS PEOPLE SHARING 1 SMALL SPACE, RUNNING IN PLACE, OLD DOG and many more... for actors for auditions, students for class study and for solo performances.The ebook is **FREE**, get it at the link below:

Built For Abuse II: Acting Monologues for Women

Also by Joshua James

"Joshua James' work is bold, intelligent and subversive.
Read it.
Then find a way to make it happen on stage."
Obie-winning playwright Naomi Wallace

An up-close comic examination
of what it means to grow up with Penis,
the first time you touch it,
the first time someone else touches it,
the first time it touches you.
Everything you really need to know
in order to own and operate a penis.

An up-close comic theatrical examination of what it means to grow up with penis.

The first time you touch it...

The first time someone else touches it...

The first time it touches you...

Everything one really needs to know in order to own and operate a **penis**.

- **THE PENIS PAPERS**: a play by Joshua James

ROYALTY-FREE for educational and amateur production!

The ebook is **FREE**, link here: **THE PENIS PAPERS**

Also by Joshua James

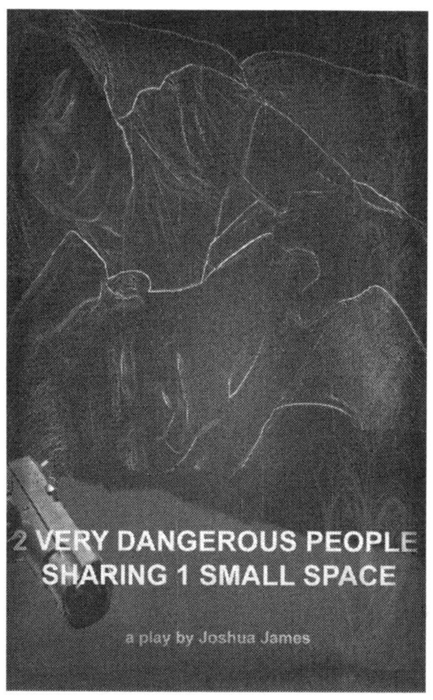

She's a chemical analyst.

He's a poet.

She has issues.

He has scars.

Separate they're unstable.

Together they're combustible.

2 Damaged people

1 Loaded Gun.

A savage, witty drama about two people who don't want to die alone but find staying alive around other people intolerable. A battle of will, wit and emotion, **2 Very Dangerous People Sharing 1 Small Space** is what happens when two suicidal people meet and fall in love.

Also by Joshua James

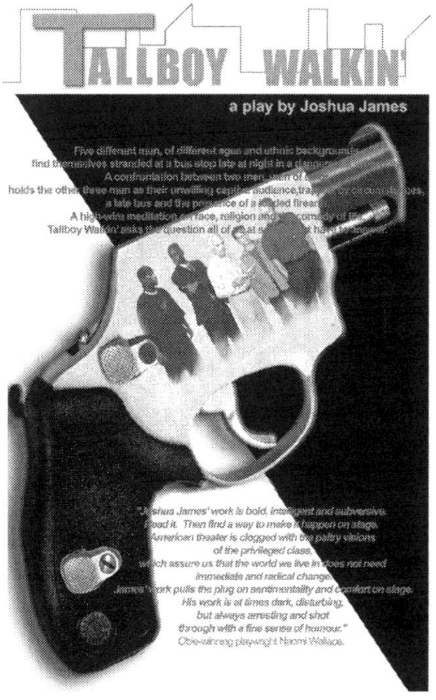

Five different men, of different ages and ethnic backgrounds, find themselves stranded at a bus stop late at night in a dangerous urban city. A confrontation between two men of color holds the other three as their unwilling captive audience, trapped by circumstances, a late bus and the presence of a loaded firearm. A high-wire meditation on race, religion and the comedy of life, **Tallboy Walkin'** asks the question all of us at some point have to answer in our lives.

"Joshua James explosive, scathingly funny play Tallboy Walkin' now at the Trilogy Theatre ... James' characters, brought to life by Essandoh and Rashed, thoroughly engaged the audience

from the beginning to the end ... Tallboy Walkin' is a thought-provoking and trenchant work."

-New York Amsterdam News

Also by Joshua James

A disgruntled elf and an understudy reindeer are determined to blow up Christmas. Only Wendi, a nine- year old girl, and her friend the Easter Bunny can stop their diabolical plan as they travel down to the South Pole in pursuit in this wildly comic adventure that's NOT FOR CHILDREN.

ROYALTY-FREE for amateur and educational production!

Available here: THE ELF, THE BUNNY AND THE BIG XMAS BLOWUP

Also by Joshua James

Chicago.

Friday night.

Seth's getting married.

Ray's pissed off.

George is on the hard stuff.

Todd's worried about a funny vibe he's getting from another guy.

Bill and Bob just want to get laid.

The Men's Room ...

Where real men live for Wrestle-Mania and discovering a sensitive side can be a difficult business. Through hangovers and heartaches, **THE MEN'S ROOM** explores how six very different guys stay friends through thick and thin and everything else in-between.

"There's a scene in The Men's Room, written and directed by Joshua James, where a gaggle of male buddies, having a drunken night on the town, visit a peep show, only to be grossed out when they realize that the girl in the act is, in fact, a guy. This one scene demonstrates more wit and insight into men's attitudes toward women and their own sexuality than the full 90 minutes of (Off-B'way's)'Peep Show' ... (THE MEN'S ROOM is) a hilarious poke-fun at my sex. I laughed and laughed and laughed."

--D.L. Lepidus - THE WESTSIDER, NYC - April '98.

"This is a gritty, fast and funny play . . . a side-splitting cocktail of laddish banter."

--Christine van Emst, THE CROYDON GUARDIAN, London, UK - Feb 28th 2002.

"In turn funny and touching."

--Liz Arratoon - THE STAGE, London, UK - March 7, 2002.

"Each scene draws you in to their lives and although littered with expletives and some coarse talking, you really begin to care about these individuals. They are totally believable, and as events strip away their tough guy exteriors, vulnerabilities,

emotions and prejudices are all laid bare . . . One moment I was laughing, the next minute agonizing over the anguish of a character."

--Christine van Emst - THE CROYDON GUARDIAN, London, UK - March 7, 2002.

ROYALTY-FREE for educational and amateur productions!

Available here: **THE MEN'S ROOM**

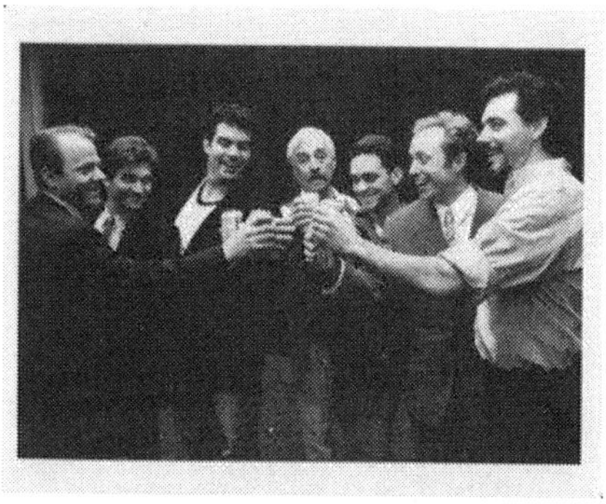

About the Author

JOSHUA JAMES is a screenwriter, novelist and playwright based in New York City, he's written two movies you may have seen but he was not credited for, but happily he was paid for that, which is always nice, and a film starring Jean Claude Van Damme named **POUND OF FLESH**. He also has some very cool credited work currently in development.

As a playwright, Joshua made his London debut when **The Men's Room** was produced at the Croydon Warehouse Theatre. He made his Off-Broadway debut in **The Fear Project** at The Barrow Group with his piece **Extreme Eugene**.

His play **Spooge – The Sex & Love Monologues** was published by Original Works Publishing, as was his collection of short works titled **The THE Plays**. His plays have been produced throughout New York City, Los Angeles, Chicago, all across the United States and various other parts of the world.

Joshua loves ice-cold tea, cool summer breezes and hot Brazilian Jiujitsu, though not necessarily in that order. www.writerjoshuajames.com

VAN DAMME
POUND OF FLESH
THE BLACK MARKET
ODYSSEY

31632361R00236

Made in the USA
San Bernardino, CA
06 April 2019